THE JOURNAL OF A GEORGIAN GENTLEMAN

THE JOURNAL OF A GEORGIAN GENTLEMAN

The Life and Times of Richard Hall, 1729–1801

By his own Hand,
and as edited by his descendant
Mike Rendell

Book Guild Publishing
Sussex, England

First published in Great Britain in 2011 by
The Book Guild Ltd
Pavilion View
19 New Road
Brighton, BN1 1UF

Typesetting in Georgia by
Keyboard Services, Luton, Bedfordshire

Printed and bound in Great Britain by
CPI Antony Rowe

A catalogue record for this book is available from
The British Library

ISBN 978 1 84624 523 7

Contents

Preface

On 11 January 1780 the sexton at the church of St Magnus the Martyr by London Bridge rang his bell six times, paused, and then rang off another 46 peals, thereby informing the parish of the death of a 46-year-old female. That woman was Eleanor Hall, first wife of Richard Hall, and her death marked a watershed in Richard's life. Up until her death, Richard had been based in London – a successful businessman with a City lifestyle – but the events following her death were to cause a breach within the family and lead him to desert the City (and his family) for a farming life in the Cotswolds.

A silhouette of Richard Hall, made by his daughter Martha.

In his lifetime Richard kept copious notebooks, diaries and journals as well as everyday ephemera of the time – newspaper cuttings, admission tickets, catalogues and so on. Apart from a dozen contemporaneously written diaries which are still extant, Richard completed numerous retrospective accounts of events which had influenced his life. These were often interspersed with details about the weather, the price of bread, recipes for making wine, inventories of his assets, and so forth. Separately he also maintained little notebooks on favoured topics – 'Observables' (referring to what he had seen and noted, e.g. eclipses, earthquakes, violent storms and other natural phenomena), 'Fossils' (which he took to mean anything dug out of the ground) and 'Receipts' (i.e. recipes, which included medicines rather than just meals). He left behind his collection of coins, shells and fossils. He was also, from the 1750s onwards, an avid collector of books, many of them bought from local booksellers.

Frontispiece label from one of Richard's books, bought from 'John Barbor, stationer, at the Golden Lion in ye Borough of Southwark'.

Richard often wrote his thoughts and ideas – as well as copied out sermons – in manuscript books, which were then bound up. Many remain. A fastidious record-keeper, at the end of each year he would set out a list of the books which he had read – and most of these lists survive, too. Together these collections give a fascinating insight into the man and his times. Many of the items were stored in Richard's horse-hair trunk.

One of the retrospective journals is entitled 'Family and Personal Recollections'. It begins:

I have frequently thought of writing a little history of my life interspersed with as much information as I could collect from letters and memorandum in my possession, of my family connexions. No very striking incidents, I am fully aware, will be presented. Still I trust it may be attended with benefit in awakening feelings of deep humility and a lively gratitude in my own mind whilst it will afford an outline of a family history to my children they could not otherwise obtain. This then is my story. Read it, dear reader, and reflect: we are born innocent, we die corrupt, and then the things we found important when we were alive no longer matter at all.

What follows is a story of the life of Richard Hall – my great-great-great-great grandfather. It is based on what Richard himself wrote and collected – with some additional material from his

FAMILY, AND

PERSONAL, RECOLLECTIONS.

I have frequently thought of writing a little history of my life, interspersed with as much information as I could collect from letters, and memorandum, in my possession, of my family connexions. [illegible] incidents I am

Family, and Personal, Recollections

son, Benjamin, who maintained the family tradition of retrospective musing and diary-keeping, and from his brother-in-law William, whose three surviving diaries give a fascinating counterpart to what was happening in the Hall family in the middle part of the eighteenth century. To this family source material has been added background information – to give a fuller picture of Richard's life and times.

1

Ancestry

Writing in the mid-1700s Richard states:

> My ancestors were very respectable – originally of Berkshire which is evident from the description of the family coat-of-arms I have in my possession and from some of my Father's letters from distant relations in that county. I believe that the family worshipped at the Church at Inglesham, as is apparent from the records held there and relating to forbears baptised in the latter years of the last century.

Inglesham Parish Church

Inglesham Parish Church

Inglesham Church is a delightful building in what is now Wiltshire, but which was then in a Berkshire enclave, close to the border with Oxfordshire. It has remained substantially unaltered for five hundred years, and is therefore exactly as it would have been when the Hall family worshipped there in the seventeenth century. The church was declared redundant in 1979 but its significance was recognised a century earlier by the designer and artist William Morris, who lived nearby and who founded the Society for the Protection of Ancient Buildings.

The interior is laid out like a series of 'cattle stalls' – presumably with each family reserving its own section in which to sit. Inglesham as a village had disappeared centuries earlier – a medieval community based upon the wool trade. The trade dried up and the village died with it, leaving little more than the church. Parish records were originally held by the vicar – they would now be with the county archivist were it not for the fact that the records were destroyed in a bombing raid in the Second World War. But fortunately a hundred years ago Richard's great-granddaughter had made enquiries of the then incumbent as to what records were held in the name of the Hall family. She noted the results:

Thomas Hall baptised 1 February 1673 – buried 22 December 1711;
William Hall baptised 16 May 1676
and Sarah Hall, buried 5 August 1681 shortly after being born.

The parents were shown as Thomas Hall, whose first wife was Mary. When Mary died Thomas married Rebecca and had a child, Francis (born 25 August 1699). Francis was to become

Richard's father, and Richard's own diaries go on to mention the death of his grandmother Rebecca on 23 November 1745 at the age of 77. The family tree at this stage therefore looked like this:

Family Tree 1 – The Halls

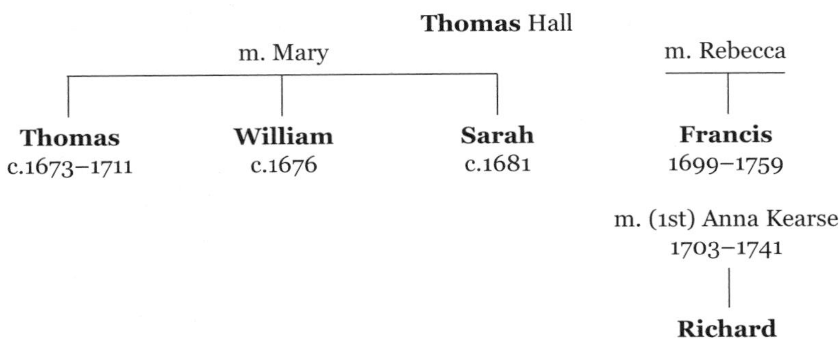

Earlier records of the family are hard to trace. At least one of the family appears to have been a farmer in the Cotswolds – as evidenced by the earliest diary still held by the family, from around 1640, detailing a trip to Burford 'to buy one cowe – seven shillings and sixpence'. Another diary, apparently from 1687, details the purchase of some nineteen cows – mostly at Burford – during the months of March and April at an average cost of £2 10s. They would presumably have been fattened up before being sold in the late autumn, since feedstuffs did not exist to keep livestock alive all the year round, and meat would be salted down or smoked for use during the winter months.

The 1687 diary contains a (printed) 'compendious chronology' –

'Years since the invention of guns by a monk 312,
of printing by a souldier 232,
the first use of coaches in England 186,
tobacco first brought to England 107...'

It also contained a curious guide to telling the time of day, using a piece of straw as a gnomen – casting its shadow on different, numbered, sections of the index finger. It would have been of dubious value on a fine day, even with a compass, but if Thomas was using it to decide when to come in for his evening meal after a wet day inspecting his stock, it would have been useless. But it is a reminder of how imprecise time-keeping was in the days before accurate pocket watches.

It looks as though grandfather Thomas would have been born around 1650, and died around the mid-1720s. He presumably lived the early part of his life in or around Inglesham, which is near Swindon, but the records show that he also owned land at Cassington (halfway between Witney and Oxford) some twenty or thirty miles away. His lifetime spanned the tumultuous years following the end of the English Civil War – the execution of Charles I, Oliver Cromwell's Protectorate, the Restoration of Charles II, the upheavals of the reign of James II, the accession of William of Orange and the start of the Hanoverian dynasty. It was an eventful time to have been living through!

But his own life was to save the greatest upheavals until the end: he appears to have fallen victim in his old age to one of the most notorious scams of the period – the South Sea Bubble. This was the 'Enron' of the early eighteenth century. It had started out innocently enough: burgeoning trade encouraged investors to put money into new ventures. Fuelled by rumours of exclusive trade arrangements with Spain, the stock soared. Some of the rumours were true – Spain had no access of its own to the lucrative slave market, and it allowed one ship a year to trade with its colonies in South America. There is evidence that the English cheated regularly and had numerous back-up ships to re-stock the one vessel permitted by the Spaniards, and in some years the trade was suspended. The public seemed immune to the idea that 'what goes up comes down' and gambled on what for many years was a sure-fire bet. More and more schemes were brought out to entice investors, all of them now lumped together under the heading of the South Sea Company. Some schemes were semi-legitimate (prospecting for gold in the New World, trading in silk or tobacco etc.) but others were wonderfully absurd with absolutely no chance of financial reward. The list included projects such as:

For supplying the town of Deal with fresh water.
For importing a large number of jackasses from Spain in order to propagate a larger breed of Mule.
For wrecks to be fished off the Irish coast.

For improving the art of making soap.
For improving of gardens.
For insuring and increasing children's fortunes.
For a wheel for perpetual motion.
For importing walnut-trees from Virginia.
For paying pensions to widows and others, at a small discount.
For making iron with pit coal.

Maybe, just maybe, the prudent punter should have smelled a rat when he saw the ultimate money-making scam: 'For carrying on an undertaking of great advantage; but nobody to know what it is.'

Despite the dubious (or even non-existent) prospects for growth the stocks still rocketed upwards, making fortunes along the way for the ones lucky enough to get out at the right time. Just as the staple topic of conversation around the table at twentieth-century dinner parties often appeared to be the rise in house prices, so early eighteenth-century conversation must have been dominated by the relentless rise in South Sea stock. People borrowed in order to invest – and unfortunately the ageing Thomas was one of them.

For ten years the gambling craze continued until one day in 1720 when the stock ceased to rise. No one was willing to buy, the perpetrators of the scheme were exposed as fraudsters and fled the country, and Thomas lost heavily. Of course, there were others afflicted to a greater degree – Sir Isaac Newton lost twenty thousand pounds of his fortune and was said to have remarked as a consequence: 'I can calculate the movement of heavenly bodies, but not the madness of people.' There were predictably a few winners (apart from the directors who promoted these scams). Thomas Guy got out just in time – with a tidy profit approaching twenty thousand pounds – and was able to found Guy's Hospital in London out of his huge wealth.

The crash was to have devastating effects upon thousands of what would now be termed the middle class. And an immediate effect on Thomas's son Francis, then twenty-one years old, was that he had to go out and work. Like many before and since, Francis set out for London. The City was a magnet, drawing in a labour force of migrants as never before. Francis was fortunate to gain an apprenticeship – as a hosier, that is, a maker of stockings. He was old to start his training – fifteen was more usual, and conditions would have been hard. If you were a hosier you found yourself towards the lower end of the class of 'tradesmen' – quite a step down for a young man brought up as the son of a 'gentleman farmer'.

It appears that his father, Thomas, died shortly after Francis's departure – leaving his land at Cassington and Kelmscott to Francis. His lands near Inglesham had gone to meet his debts, but Thomas left enough money for his widow Rebecca to live on. The remainder of what was left of his fortune passed to Francis.

Richard recalled in his later retrospective jottings that his father had told him that, when *his* father, Thomas, was a young man and required a bride, he had had no choice but to go out on horseback and ride to the various villages within a journey of one day, visiting the homes of suitable persons and introducing himself to those with daughters of marriageable age. His whole world consisted of those parts of Berkshire, Oxford and Wiltshire as extended for a distance of perhaps thirty miles from his home. 'Amazing then,' Richard wrote, 'to consider that in my lifetime we have seen horizons extend so markedly that a man may catch the Express Stage from Oxford and be in London later that same day!'

For the young Francis, then, making his way to London and learning a trade must have been an enormous eye-opener. No trappings of comfort and privilege here, no servants at his beck and call – and all around him the examples of poverty and illness. No wonder he determined that his son should do better…

2

The 1720s

Richard was born in Red Lion Street, in the Borough of Southwark, on 4 March 1728. By the modern calendar this would now be 1729. His mother, Anna (née Kearse), was twenty-five years old, having married Francis two years earlier. They had no other children, presumably by accident rather than design, and he grew up much loved – and possibly spoiled.

It seems highly unlikely that the decision to have only one child was a matter of choice; a third of all children born at this time were likely to die before they were two years old, and a further third would not expect to see their thirteenth birthday. Child mortality was so high that parents really needed to aim for a family of at least three if they were to have any hope of seeing their grandchildren – the life expectancy for those who reached adulthood was really quite good, but the death rate among the young was catastrophic. Towards the end of his life Richard bought an almanac which listed, among other statistics, the fact that in December 1729, the year of his birth, more than one thousand people died in London in a single week, many of them children.

There are no family records to show whether Anna became pregnant and miscarried, and the likelihood is that the delivery of Richard as a baby in itself led to Anna becoming incapable of having any other children. Primitive midwifery could easily lead to a botched delivery and a damaged uterus. Poor diet may also have contributed, because a lack of vegetables in the diet frequently led to rickets. This did not just mean a population with bandy legs – it also meant pelvic problems for women, leading to considerable difficulties in childbirth.

The one cause for having such a small family which we can perhaps dismiss is contraception. Yes, there were 'French letters' (though the French preferred to call them *capotes anglaises*) – animal intestines bound up with ribbon – but these were expensive and not in general use. The condom was made from part of the gut of a sheep, turned inside out, soaked in alkaline solution, pounded, scraped, washed, inflated, dried, cut to size and tied with a ribbon. All the user had to do was soak it for some time to make it supple for use! Small wonder they were not regarded as effective instruments to prevent unwanted pregnancy. One writer in France (Madame de Sévigné no less) described them as 'an armour against enjoyment and a spider-web against danger'. Besides, they were not seen as being designed to help limit the size of families – they were intended to reduce the risk of catching venereal disease. Why would Francis use a condom unless he had reason to believe that his own wife had the pox? It would have been a humiliation for her. It is far more likely that, having had one child, Anna was incapable of having another – so Richard would have been brought up as a rather over-protected and probably over-indulged young child.

Red Lion Street in Southwark was certainly not a fashionable area – not for Richard a childhood in the newly developed West End, which was the playground of the rich and famous. Not for him one of the grand houses built around an elegant square, laid out at the behest of the Cadogans or the Sloanes. Instead, a modest house south of the river. The splendid series of maps by Richard Horwood in his *Plan of the Cities of London and Westminster, 1792–1799* shows the actual street leading off Borough High Street (highlighted on p. 9).

The area seems to have been well served by inns and hostelries – opposite the entrance into Red Lion Street was The White Hart, first mentioned in 1406, The Talbot Inn, The George, The Queen's Head, The Three Tuns Tavern, The Spur Inn, The Nag's Head and The Ship. All were within a hundred yards of each other. The George was famous as a coaching terminus – and it is almost inevitable that Richard would have started and finished his journeys to Kent, Sussex and so on via this inn. Of the inns mentioned, The George still survives, the only remaining example of a galleried inn in London. Owned by the National Trust, it still operates as a public house, making it a rare link of a business local to Richard's which is still going after nearly three hundred years.

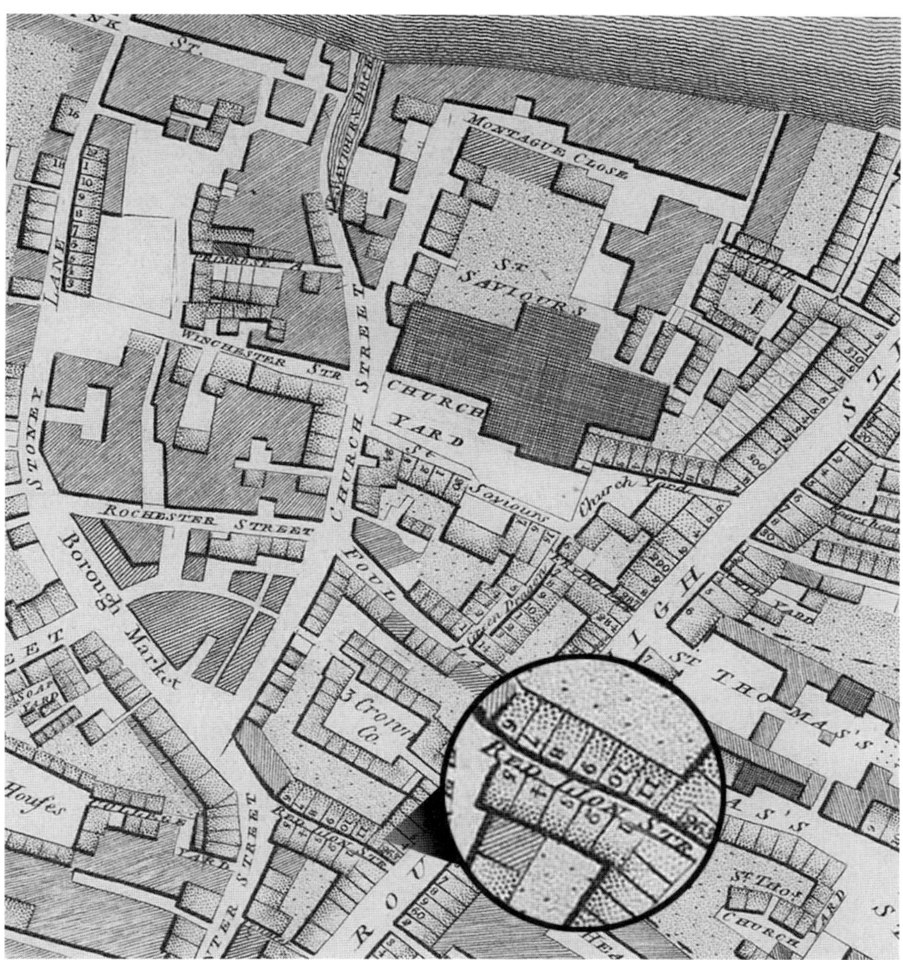

Horwood's 'Plan of the Cities of London and Westminster'.
Courtesy of Motco Enterprises Ltd (www.motco.com)

The area immediately leading to the London Bridge was called Bridge-foot – home of The Bear Inn, one of the most popular public houses in London. It was finally pulled down in 1761, but at the time of Richard's birth would have been a noisy, crowded meeting place. Much of the area had been rebuilt following a fire which swept through the area in May 1676. Coming a decade after the Great Fire which had engulfed the city on the north side of the river, the Southwark Fire was no less devastating to the old timber and thatched dwellings of the

Paper cut-out from the time showing a stagecoach arriving at an inn.

district. The Southwark Fire started in the immediate vicinity of The George, within yards of Red Lion Street

Red Lion Street was just off the Borough High Street, which in turn led straight through to London Bridge. Indeed, so crowded were the shops and tenements both on and off the bridge that pedestrians would not originally have noticed where the bridge ended and where Southwark began. That changed in 1725 when another fire destroyed all the houses and shops at the Southwark end of the Bridge, including the first two arches and the Great Stone Gate. The remaining premises on the bridge became increasingly derelict until Parliament authorised the clearance of all houses from the bridge in 1756. But by the time Richard was born the chaos and congestion had already led to the introduction (in 1722) of two measures – a toll for all bridge users and a 'traffic must keep to the left' rule (the latter establishing a highways precedent that we keep to this day).

Red Lion Street was one of those rare things in a busy noisy part of town – a group of perhaps a dozen houses constructed either side of a pedestrian walkway, reached by passing through an archway off the main street. The engraving by J C Buckler, drawn exactly a century after Richard's birth, shows that carts were blocked from using the access – bollards at both ends of the street saw to that.

Within a stone's throw of the Halls' home was: to the north-west, the Borough Market, which had been in existence since 1276; to the north, the Water Company (responsible for pumping water at

Red Lion Street, Southwark, by J C Buckler. The original is in the Guildhall Library. Courtesy of City of London, London Metropolitan Archives.

certain times of the day to the wealthier homes in the neighbourhood, via a series of ducts made of elm wood); and to the east both Guy's Hospital (founded by Thomas Guy in 1721) and the much older St Thomas' Hospital. The hospital of St Thomas is nowadays situated opposite the Houses of Parliament, but in Richard's time was sited in Southwark because it was founded by the local Augustinian priory. After the Reformation, the priory had become the parish church of St Saviour, and remained in that guise until 1905 when it was consecrated as a cathedral. Back in 1729 it was already an ancient building, with its origins leading back to 1106.

Perhaps the young Richard witnessed the burial in the church in 1736 of 'Mahomet, Chief of the Mohegan Tribe', who had come to Britain the previous year from Connecticut. Sachem (i.e. Chief) Mahomet Weyonomon, to give him his proper title, had come here in 1735 to petition the new king (George II) for justice; his tribe had been allies of the Crown during the struggles against the French (and other Native American tribes); they had been promised that the Mohegan lands would be safe from confiscation. However, by the time Mahomat had come to power the settlers had largely gone back on their word and the Chief made the long and hazardous journey to London to seek an audience with the King. Sadly, he contracted smallpox and died. There was no question of any of the City churches allowing the burial of this painted foreigner, so his remains were interred at St Saviour's church, where they had a tradition of being rather more welcoming to visitors and migrants alike. Mind you, it was in an unmarked grave and it was left to our present Queen to give a belated recognition to his efforts when she visited the burial site some 270 years later.

The nearby street names of Foul Lane and Dirty Street suggest the district's squalid past and Clink Street (to the north, running parallel to the Thames) was named after the local prison. The phrase 'to be in the clink' (meaning 'to be in prison') comes from this street name. Founded in the thirteenth century, the notorious Clink probably got its name from the sound of the clanking chains and leg-irons used to manacle the prisoners. A modern exhibition near the site of the old prison shows the whipping post, torture chair and foot crusher used on the unfortunate inmates. By the 1720s the prison was in poor repair and generally used only for a handful of debtors. The prison was finally burnt down at the outset of the Gordon Riots in 1780 and was never rebuilt. Even at the time Richard was growing up it would have been a dilapidated and depressing place.

At the time of the 1725 fire Southwark would have been a separate village, surrounded by fields. Roads leading south to villages of Newington and Walworth would have passed through open country but the explosion of building in the early part of the eighteenth century meant that these areas had merged. Writing in 1728 Daniel Defoe in his *A Journey through England and Wales* mentions 'Newington, called Newington-Butts, in Surrey, reaches out her hand north, and is so near joining to Southwark, that it cannot now be properly called a town by itself, but a suburb to the burrough, and if, as they now tell us is undertaken, St George's Fields should be built into squares and streets, a very little time will shew us Newington, Lambeth, and the Burrough, all making but one Southwark'.

The early part of the eighteenth century saw a considerable amount of infilling – with backstreets and alleyways leading off either side of the High Street. In the early part of the century the buildings of Southwark extended along the riverside as far as Lambeth; and in the opposite direction Rotherhithe Street was continued to a point where the river turns sharply to the south. It was a busy, bustling area, with numerous factories, shops and so on – what would later be termed a 'working class area'. So the Hall family, living 'over the shop', would not have had any pretensions to grandeur. The wealthy did their shopping in the more fashionable areas north of the river. However, trade was obviously not too precarious, and the family were in due course able to provide young Master Richard with a good schooling.

The river Thames must have been a fascinating sight for the young Richard – so crowded with ships that it would have appeared that you could walk across the river. Describing the maritime scene at that time, Defoe states that there were 'about two thousand sail of all sorts, not reckoning barges, lighters or pleasure boats or yachts' using the wharves and quays which lined the river. Trade, particularly with the English colonies, was booming in the 1720s, and imports of sugar from the West Indian plantations ensured that the docks were never idle. Southwark had long been the home of an annual fair. Pepys mentions visiting it in 1668 ('To Southwark Fair, very dirty, and there saw the puppet show of Whittington, which was pretty to see'). In fact, the fair had a long tradition of attracting what would now be called 'the fringe' – actors performing parodies of popular plays, as well as reruns of old favourites. The actors would have had to compete for the crowd's attention with dancing bears, magicians, freak shows and often puppet shows. It was an unruly occasion, and the fair was eventually suppressed in 1763, but not before William Hogarth had recorded the tumult in his 1733 painting *Southwark Fair*.

For young Richard, life must have been noisy – maybe not indoors, with no siblings to compete with, but outdoors. The babble of the market, the street traders on the doorstep, the constant clattering of iron-hooped cartwheels bouncing along the granite setts of the street day and night – this was a busy thoroughfare through which all traffic heading to and from the Channel ports had to pass, in addition to the constant stream of wheat, barley, fruit and vegetables coming in from the Kent countryside to feed the metropolis. Then there were the constant cries of the vendors offering their services – the knife grinders, the rag-and-bone men, the chair repairers, the water carriers and the milkmaids. Not that buying milk from an open pail traipsed around town all day would have been very appetising – unless taken straight from the cow, milk was invariably sour by the time it was sold. There were cries of 'pease pudding and a suck of bacon' from the food vendors. There were fights between drunks and there were the obscene calls from the ferrymen plying their trade from the banks of the river. And then there was the din of livestock being driven towards London Bridge en route to Smithfield Market – hundreds upon hundreds of beasts lowing and being cussed by the drovers. Thomas Carlyle, born in 1795 and writing a few years after Richard's death, describes it vividly:

> What a scene! Innumerable herds of fat oxen, tied in long rows, or passing at a trot to their several shambles, and thousands of graziers, drovers, butchers, cattle brokers with their quilted frocks and long goads pushing on the hapless beasts hurrying them to and fro in confused parties, shouting, jostling, cursing in the midst of rain and shairn [the dung of oxen or cows] and braying discord such as the imagination cannot figure.

We tend to think of traffic congestion as a modern phenomenon, but the traffic in London was then, as now, limited to the speed of the slowest. London Bridge was an inevitable bottleneck, and it is easy to imagine cattle massing along the Borough High Street, waiting for their turn to pass over the bridge, and ambling off through the side alleys such as Red Lion Street. The volume of traffic was staggering – even a century later, when there were other bridges available to take pedestrians and livestock across the Thames, there were some 90,000 people a day crossing on foot. Patricia Pearce, in her book *Old London Bridge* gives a daily figure for 1811 of 2,000 carts and drays, 1,300 coaches, 500 gigs and tax carts and 800 riders on horseback. The volume would not have been significantly less at the time of Richard's birth. The commotion must have been amazing, enhanced by the noise of the river itself.

If Richard's sense of hearing was assaulted every time he opened the front door it would have been nothing compared to the full-scale attack on his sense of smell. It must have been gut-wrenchingly appalling. Not just the smell of rotting vegetation – there were no weekly rubbish collections – but the dung of all the horses and animals that passed by. The Thames was little more than an open sewer and, although the houses would have had cesspits built underneath, alongside the cellars, these brick-built structures often gave way and the effluent would spill into the street and into the houses themselves. Emptying the cesspits

A detail from Hogarth's *The Enraged Musician* (1741) showing the infernal din coming from the street – the ballad singer (complete with baby in swaddling clothes), the milkmaid crying out her wares, the knife grinder, the horn blower and oboe player, the bell ringer, the dog barking and the cats fighting on the roof opposite. Meanwhile, a small boy urinates against the railings ... © The Trustees of the British Museum.

was done manually, usually at night, and the waste was then carted off in barrels to fertilise the fields and market gardens of the local countryside – hence the euphemism 'night soil'.

If an animal was run over in the street, its rotten corpse remained. Down the centre of the street was a channel, called a kennel, and in theory this took the rainwater and rubbish away to the river. But these channels were often blocked and the streets would have been strewn with decaying matter. Writing in the decade before Richard was born, the satirist Jonathan Swift describes the Fleet Ditch, which flowed into the Thames just above the bridge with the words:

Now from all parts the swelling kennels flow,
And bear their trophies with them as they go:
Filth of all hues and colours seem to tell
What street they sail'd from, by their sight and smell...
Sweepings from butchers' stalls, dung, guts and blood,
Drown'd puppies, stinking sprats, all drenched in mud,
Dead cats, and turnip tops, come tumbling down the flood.

Crossing the streets, especially for women wearing dresses down to the ground, must have been revolting in any weather but particularly when wet, since clothes coming into contact with the ground would act as blotting paper for all the waste and excrement of the city.

Another environmental hazard was pollution. Imagine tens of thousands of homes all belching out smoke from coal-burning fires. No Smoke Control Orders then, so imagine the fogs in winter. Add to this smog the belching workshop chimneys and the emissions of sulphur and other dangerous chemicals and you appreciate what an appalling atmosphere it was to bring up a young child. There were tanneries for the treatment of leather and tallow works where candles and soap were made from rendered-down animal products. Both caused huge pollution and a foul stench. There were no planning controls so that, for instance, workshops making sulphuric acid could be built next door to a residential street. Why sulphuric acid? Originally because it was used in the hat-making process. For two centuries the Hudson Bay Company had been bringing back furs – particularly beaver – from North America. Broad-brimmed beaver hats were popular but needed to be softened and shaped using dilute sulphuric acid. In addition, a solution of mercury was brushed on to the fur to make the fibres coarse and mat more readily. Workers in poorly ventilated conditions inhaled the mercury compounds along with the acid fumes – causing symptoms such as trembling, dizziness and loss of memory. 'Mad as a hatter' (meaning 'crazy') was a phrase coined by Lewis Carroll in the next century, but the conditions and harmful effects would have been fully apparent to Richard and his contemporaries.

Historical sources refer to bone-crushing works in Fore Street, where 'the smell complained of as a great nuisance; the bone bugs creep through the wall into the next house'.

London was a hive of industry and consequently attracted increasing numbers of migrants. The city was pre-eminent in a way that it has never been, before or since. It is hard to be specific as to population numbers when there were so many migrants and when the first census was not carried out until 1801. True, an attempt had been made to count the population back in 1753 but the House of Lords had thrown out the proposal. ('Totally subversive of the last remains of English liberty...' 'An abominable and foolish measure' – shades of the current opposition to identity cards!) What is apparent is that when Richard was born the entire population of England and Wales was some six million. By 1760 it had increased to around seven million, and by the date of Richard's death in 1801 it stood at just over nine million. Richard himself, writing in an unspecified year, announces as if it was an assured fact that 'London & Westminster – one million & forty five thousand & seventy five people'. Even if the figure were nearer three-quarters of a million it still represented a very significant proportion of the total, particularly when it is remembered that the next most populous city in 1720 was Bristol at a minuscule fifty thousand persons. At least 10 per cent of the entire population of England and Wales lived in the capital. Even in 1760 London and Bristol were the only cities with more than 50,000 inhabitants.

This phenomenon of vast urban growth was without precedent and created huge housing, health and transport problems, but back in 1729 no one could have foreseen the problems – or the associated drift of agricultural workers away from the land and into the towns and cities. What was apparent was that, while London recorded significantly more deaths than live births, the actual population of the capital was soaring because the magnet of London drew in migrant workers by the tens of thousands every year. By way of comparison, whereas the population of London topped one million, perhaps only half that number lived in the French capital, and Paris was generally regarded as the nearest rival in terms of influence and power.

What drew people to London? Perhaps it was the same as had drawn Richard Whittington to the city some centuries before, with tales of pavements paved with gold. There certainly was vast wealth – great ostentatious shows of it, with magnificent and richly decorated houses, fine squares, ornate gardens and impressive public buildings. But it was also a city of great contrasts – if the wealthy were rich, the poor were destitute. Never has the divide between the 'haves' and the 'have-nots' been greater. Trade was king. There was trade in goods and there was trade in human beings and in the fruits of human misery. Violence and crime were commonplace and 'justice' was rudimentary and often harsh. The death penalty existed for many hundreds of crimes which would now pass as misdemeanours. Richard later cut out an extract from the *General Evening Post* giving a comparison, over a 25-year period, of the number of Old Bailey prisoners sentenced to death. In 1750 there were only 39 sitting days – but 84 people were condemned. There was the odd blip – in 1760 there were only 23 sitting days at the Old Bailey and a mere 14 unfortunates were despatched – but over the quarter of a century in total 1,311 people were condemned to die in London alone. It was an era when crimes against property (e.g. theft, arson and malicious damage) were considered as heinous as rape or murder.

This then was the atmosphere in which Richard grew up. It was a world when it was either light or it was dark – there were no municipal street lights in the 1720s. In the winter he would have gone to bed when it got dark because there would have been barely sufficient light from candles to read by. In the summer, when it got light early, he would have risen early. And at night he would have seen from his bedroom window myriads of stars now usually hidden from view in our light-polluted skies. He and his contemporaries would have been far more aware of astronomical occurrences than we are today – which is why his later diaries often mention comets, meteors, the aurora borealis and so on. Man had not tamed darkness any more than he had tamed extreme cold – homes were draughty and reliant entirely upon open fires for any form of heating. Quite simply, you never got undressed if you could help it. Clothes were worn for weeks and weeks at a time. Personal hygiene was simply not an issue.

Why did Richard's father choose Southwark to settle in? Probably because it was unfashionable and hence cheaper than housing north of the river. But, more importantly, it was just beyond the reach of the London Livery Companies – and in particular the Worshipful Company of Haberdashers, who controlled all those working in the textile and clothing manufacturing businesses throughout the City. These medieval guilds (from the Saxon *gildan*, meaning 'to pay') were originally designed to protect craftsmen, maintain standards, arrange training and so on. They had huge powers over the free movement of trade. They could lay down maximum and minimum ages for apprenticeships (remember, Francis was twenty-one when he was apprenticed, which was above the permitted age for entry into the hosiery business). Francis would have found it far easier to start his business south of the River, where the guilds had virtually no influence. The guilds had their chances, but chose to disregard the growing suburbs. Maybe they had had enough of being plundered by successive Tudor and Stuart monarchs, who repeatedly seized their funds to pay for wars and political intrigues, and decided to concentrate on their 'core business' of helping their own people within the City boundaries. Whatever the reason, traders in Southwark enjoyed a considerable freedom from being pestered by rules and regulations.

Being outside the guild had both advantages and disadvantages. Whereas Francis would have been unfettered by the rules of the Haberdashers' Guild, and spared the expenses of paying an annual membership fee, he equally would have been denied access to City premises and left without a voice as to how his chosen profession was governed – and indeed without the right to vote in parliamentary elections which was automatic for full guild members. He also would not have enjoyed immunity from being 'impressed' (that is, seized by press gangs for service in the army or navy) or from having to pay tolls at fairs and markets up and down the country, because these privileges went with membership.

Hosiers came in different groups. The woollen stocking makers were at the lowest end of the scale. They were appallingly paid, and theirs was largely still a cottage industry operating in rural areas. The wealthy would not have been seen dead in woollen stockings. Silk stockings were knitted on a machine and then joined with a seam. The development of the stocking was linked with the decline in the wearing of boots throughout the latter half of the seventeenth century. Shoes became fashionable – and this afforded the opportunity to show off a well-turned ankle. A small triangle of silk would be woven either side of the heel. This was known as a gore, and it became popular for the gore to be richly coloured and often decorated with patterns – 'gore clocks' as they were known. In time, developments to the knitting frames meant that wider silk cloths could be fabricated. This in turn led to a fashion for wearing matching silk waistcoats and stockings. The stockings would either have been held up by garters, or brought up above the knee and worn over the breeches. By the 1730s it became less fashionable to wear black or coloured stockings – white was more usual – but they were nonetheless a vital fashion accessory. For Francis, then, business presumably flourished.

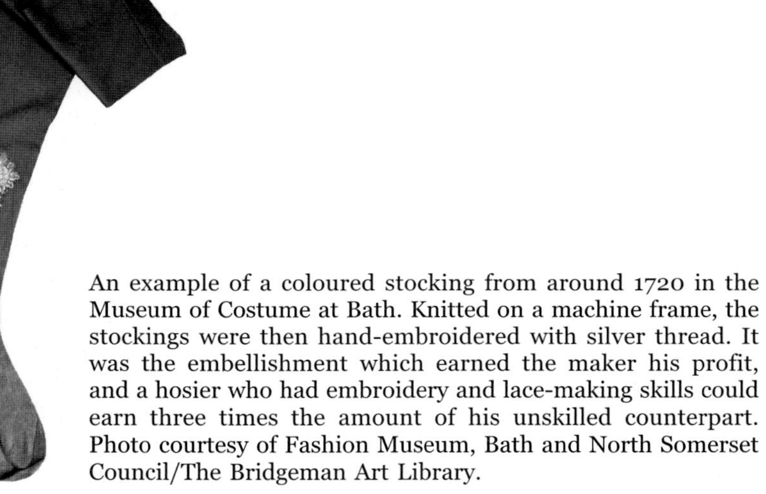

An example of a coloured stocking from around 1720 in the Museum of Costume at Bath. Knitted on a machine frame, the stockings were then hand-embroidered with silver thread. It was the embellishment which earned the maker his profit, and a hosier who had embroidery and lace-making skills could earn three times the amount of his unskilled counterpart. Photo courtesy of Fashion Museum, Bath and North Somerset Council/The Bridgeman Art Library.

3

The 1730s

As Richard's parents kept no diary, there are few clues to his upbringing and early years. As a baby was he sent out to one of the farms in Newington, and wet-nursed by a labourer's wife who would be paid more for breast feeding other people's children than her husband could earn from toiling in the fields? Or did Anna manage to feed him herself? It was sometimes believed that maternal kissing could cause rickets – was he therefore farmed out so that he would have a healthier start in life? If so, he was lucky to have survived at all – the mortality rate for the children sent away for wet-nursing was incredibly high.

Nowadays, within the space of just a couple of generations, wet-nursing seems to have become socially unacceptable, but in the eighteenth and nineteenth centuries it was absolutely commonplace, and children might be sent away for weeks or even months at a time. There was a popular belief that being breast-fed by a woman of the right sort (i.e. morally sound) in the fresh air of the country would be beneficial to the child. Mothers who had fed their own baby for perhaps a year would take on three or more other infants to feed. Cross-infection must have been rife. Babies were swaddled (i.e. wrapped tightly in swaddling bands) – sometimes with a hook sewn into the bandage so that the child could be hung up. Imagine a row of three or four babies, tightly bandaged, hung on pegs from the wall, so that they could view their surroundings and cry incessantly. Prevailing views were that this could not harm the child – and the tighter the bandage the less the chance of bones bowing and becoming rickety. Just imagine the sores and skin diseases, and the unsanitary conditions where soiled bands were re-used on different babies.

In all probability Richard would have been swaddled until he was three months old. As for potty training – forget it! In an era when grown-ups thought nothing of defecating in the fireplace (à la Pepys) or in a corner of the room, or in a chamber pot kept in a section of the sideboard designed for just that purpose, it was left for the child to choose for itself how and when it wished to emulate its elders.

There were an amazing number of superstitions associated with birth, childhood and illness. Did not eating strawberries in pregnancy cause birthmarks? And were not claw hands caused by eating lobster? And was it not the case that you must feed the newborn baby roast pork on its first day, to 'cure it of all its mother's longings' (William Cadogan, *Essay upon the Nursing and Management of Children*, 1748). In general, it was felt that the newborn babe should be fed a glass of ... lightly warmed wine. Some felt that cuddling a young baby was wrong – too much affection was not a good thing. Bouncing a child up and down on the knee was thought to cause water on the brain. And if a youngster was thirsty, it was quite in order to give him or her small beer. Mind you, that may not have been so daft – the water from the river Thames was heavily polluted whereas the beer may well have been made from water drawn from a far more healthy tributary upstream.

There was a tendency for babies to be weaned and put onto solids at far too early an age – parents were 'apt to think their children ... in danger to be starved if they have not eaten flesh at least twice a day,' wrote John Locke. And, of course, if a baby was teething, then sticking a dirty piece of coral (albeit on a lovely silver handle) in his or her mouth was thought beneficial. My family still retains one such 'soother' used by Richard's cousins. Cutting the gums with the edge of a coin 'to help the tooth come through' was another favourite treatment. Not exactly hygienic! Indeed 'teething' was one of the most popular causes of infant deaths listed in the Bills of Mortality.

So much for Richard's infancy – but what did the lonely boy growing up in a sock shop have for his playthings? None of Richard's toys remain, but it is likely that he would have been familiar with spinning tops, hoops and rattles, as well as toy soldiers, marbles and pennywhistles. He may well have 'ridden' round the room with a horse on a stick. Children's toys – and particularly dolls called 'poppets' – were often sold at Bartholomew

Detail from Hogarth's 'Evening'. © The Trustees of the British Museum.

Fair, just round the corner from the Hall household. Presumably as a child Richard would have been dressed as a man in miniature – as shown in the extract from Hogarth's *Evening* showing the tired small boy crying because his elder sister demands his ginger-bread man.

Richard makes no direct mention of his education – but it is likely that between the age of seven and fifteen he attended the local grammar school. There is little clue as to the range of subjects taught – he never uses Greek or Latin in his diaries, although he does occasionally refer to the works of Pliny, but these may well have been familiar to him through English translations. On the other hand, several of the oldest books owned by Richard were written in Latin – *De sensum rerum* from 1637 among them – though maybe such books were bought to impress rather than be read! Also, we know from his later diaries that he expected his own children to learn Latin. Clearly, however, Richard was widely read, even if the subject matter seems somewhat solid by today's standards. Bunyan's *Pilgrim's Progress*, the works of Milton and Fox's somewhat gory *Book of Martyrs* are among his well-thumbed favourites. Religious treatises figure large in his library from a fairly early age. If there were 'children's books' none have survived. But, whatever can be said about his choice of reading matter, schooling obviously taught Richard a love of the written word.

Richard's handwriting can be divided into three types –

excellent; good; and an indecipherable semi-shorthand. The 'Sunday best' he reserved for things like his signature in the front of his books – florid, richly embellished and beautifully written. The everyday writing in his diaries was often tiny but is generally easy to read except where the writing has faded. Richard's shorthand was reserved for copying down the spoken word – sermons, speeches and the like, but also, on occasions, recipes. John Byrom's 'Universal English Short-hand' was patented in 1742, though he had been teaching his system since 1716 (albeit in far-away Manchester). However, since the method was not actually published until 1767 – after the death of Byrom four years earlier – Richard is likely to have picked it up second-hand – that is, from another stenographer.

And what of Richard's spoken voice? London throughout the eighteenth century was a magnet for migrants from the countryside. At an early age Richard would have encountered accents from all over the country – and no doubt would have realised that if you were not to be dismissed as a yokel you had to learn to 'speak properly'. Pronunciation of the spoken word was as important as grammar, spelling and punctuation were to the written word. And so he faithfully wrote down those 'difficult' words – the ones which were not always as they seemed:

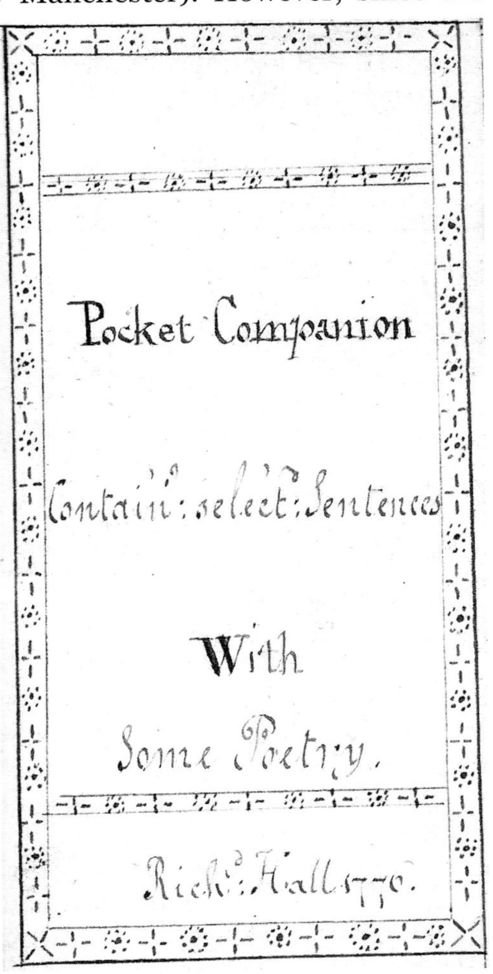
Pocket Companion

Contain: select: Sentences

With

Some Poetry.

Richd: Hall 1770.

Pocket Companion with selected sentences.

Words written very different from their Pronounciation:

Adieu – Adu
Almond – Amun
Apprentice – Prentis
Artichoke – Hartichoke
Apron – Apurn
Autumn – Awtum
Ballad – Ballet
Beau – Bo
Beauty – Buty
Bosom – Boozum
Business – Biznus
Chaise – Shaze
Cucumber – Cowcumber
Diamond – Dimun
Dictionary – Dixnary
Farthing – Fardun
Hiccough – Hiccup
Medicine – Meds'n
Nurse – Nus
Sheriff – Shreeve
Stomach – Stummuk
Toilet – Twaylet or twilit
Yacht – Yot
Birmingham – Brummijum
Cirencester – Sissota
Deptford – Dodfurd
Guernsey – Garnzee

So, while others around him were dropping their 'haitches', Richard was adding them to his artichokes! To modern ears he would have sounded somewhat affected: 'Nus, pass me my meds'n I am going to Sissota for a cowcumber.'

Richard was obviously given a thorough grounding in grammar and punctuation and on several occasions in his later journals he set out the rules for writing correctly. He wrote out the correct use of each punctuation mark, giving relevant examples. In every case, his example is taken from the Bible – an indication that in Richard's time there was an indivisible link between education and religion. You never got one without the other! Richard also wrote out various rules of grammar and it is safe to assume that these rules would have been drummed into Richard at school – wherever that was.

The other marks used in reading are these twelve:

1 Apostrophe '
2 Hyphen - or =
3 Parenthesis ( )
4 Brackets []
5 Paragraph ¶
6 Quotation "
7 Section §
8 Ellipsis - - or —
9 Index ☞
10 Asterisk *
11 Obelisk †
12 Caret ‸

Punctuation marks.

While Richard was no artist he clearly practised his drawing and in his old age amused his grandchildren by drawing his three favourite compositions – goats, owls and squirrels. Richard also carried with him an ivory aide-memoire – made of thin sheets of ivory, bound in a silver clasp, with its own pencil – so that he could jot down lists etc. as well as drawing items of interest.

It can be assumed that it was at school that Richard developed an interest in the world about him. The miscellaneous jottings

A goat, owl and squirrel, as drawn by Richard.

Richard Hall's ivory aide memoire.

which Richard recorded throughout his life show that he loved history and geography – even if the dates and places which he mentions are of doubtful accuracy! One of the books in his library was Sir Walter Raleigh's *History of the World*, published in 1614, but by far the most interesting book in his collection is *A Description of Beasts*, listing animals and insects from the known world, and published in the middle of the eighteenth century.

Among the animals illustrated is a camelopardal. It is now known as a giraffe – but pre-Darwin it was believed that many animals were simply created by crossing different creatures (in this case, by combining a camel and a leopard). And what are we to make of the 'Fox Ape'?

> the fore part like a fox, and in the hinder part like an ape. Under the common belly it has a skin like a Bag wherein it keeps lodges and carries its young, till they are able to provide for themselves. Neither do they come out of the Receptacle except it be to suck the Dam or sport themselves.

Well, how else was the world to imagine a kangaroo when the only clue was the vague and fanciful description of early explorers? So, we can take it that Richard knew exactly what a rhinoceros looked like, as well as 'an unicorn'!

43 *A Defcription of* BEASTS.

59 The CAMELOPARDAL is bred in *Ethiopia*, *India*, *Georgia*, &c. The Head of it is like a Camel's; its Colour, for the moft Part, red and white, beautifully mixed together, and the Skin full of Spots. It has two little Horns upon its Head, of the Colour of Iron; has a fmall Mouth, like an Hart's; a Tongue near three Feet long, and a Neck of divers Colours, of a very great Length, which he holds higher than a Camel's, and is far above the Proportion of his other Parts. His fore Feet are much longer than his hinder. His Pace is different from all other Beafts; for he moves right and left Feet together. This Creature is like both a Camel and a Panther. The Skin of this Beaft is very valuable. It is a folitary Beaft, and keepeth in the Woods, if it be not taken when it is young. It is very tractable, and eafy to be governed, fo that a Child may lead it, with a fmall Line or Cord about its Head. The Flefh of this Creature is good Meat.

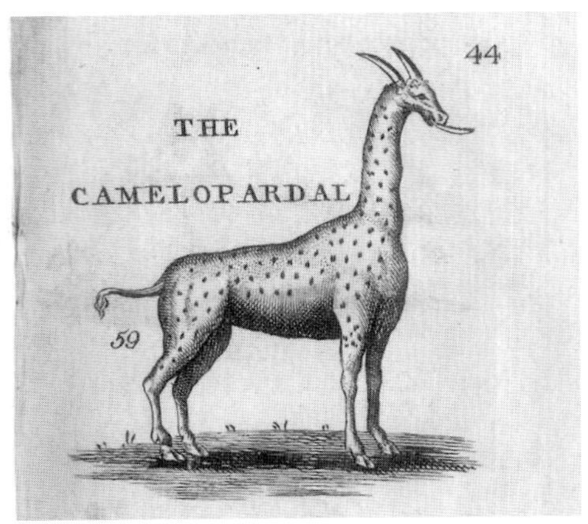

Camelopardal

Richard's knowledge of geography included knowing that the world was divided into four main 'quarters' – Europe, Asia, Africa and America, and he dutifully recorded features of each quarter. He knew the difference between latitude and longitude, and set out the difference in a lengthy explanation.

Rhinoceros & Unicorn

It is clear that, unlike his modern counterparts, Richard was taught French as a central part of the curriculum, and not as some sort of additional subject to be toyed with and then dropped at an early opportunity. Not for Richard the attitude that the French should jolly well learn English – or that speaking slowly or shouting loudly would aid communication! He was fluent in French and wrote

Elle vous a ecrit ce matin
votre mère vous parle et non pas a votre soeur: c'est
pourquoi repondez lui. Je crois qu'elle parle à ma soeur
aussi bien qu'à moi: qu'elle reponde la première et Je
parlerai apres elle: ne savez vous pas que ma soeur est
toujours plus promt a trouver des raisons que moi.
ne lui repondez donc pas, et vous la facherez:
croyez moi allez lui parler mais montrez moi ce livre
auparavant.
laissez lui aller et le pardonnez pour cette fois s'il
jamais Il fait la moindre faute. Je ne prierai plus
pour lui. Parlez lui raison et ne le grondez pas. allez
le voir ou lui ecrivez.

French exercises

pages and pages between neat lines – English on the left, French translation on the right. Presumably because paper was expensive he kept these exercise books – and in later years pasted in articles of interest over his earlier translations.

Richard's arithmetic exercise book is almost entirely made up of trade-specific examples – suggesting perhaps that he had individual coaching. The examples relate to the price of silk, to quantities of stockings, to wages per capita per year and so on. Certainly, he was adept at multiplication and division, ratios and fractions, and no doubt had occasion to be grateful for this in later years when he was serving behind the counter.

Richard himself points to the influence of his mother on his religious education: 'From a child I have small conscience of secret prayer and remember to have been extended thereto by

Required the Price of 9 Yards of Lace
at 18"9½ ℔r Yard

S D
18" 9½
9

£8" 9" 1½

What will 12 Yards of Silk cost at
£1" 11" 11¾ ℔r Yard.

£ S D
1" 11" 11¾
12

Ans 19" 3" 9 —

Mathematics – the cost of lace.

my dear mother when very young, perhaps not more than that six or seven years old.' He would have been taught the Catechism – a series of questions-and-answers which would have been learned parrot-fashion from an early age. Richard's Catechism, published in 1735 when he was six or seven years old, contains the earliest version of his signature on the front page.

Richard would certainly have attended Sunday worship. His parents were devout Baptists and worshipped using the old family bible. This was the Geneva Bible – published in 1560. There had been some 140 editions of this particular bible published between 1560 and 1640, and the one used by Richard appears to have been one of the earliest, as it contains a preface dated 1578. Interestingly, after Richard died the bible eventually passed to his grandson, and he was so impressed by its antiquity that he pencilled in the then current year and subtracted the original date of 1578 – and came up with the conclusion that it was 276 years old! Another 150 years have passed since then, and it is now showing its age – battered, dog-eared, foxed and no longer the focal point of family reading. After 425 years it is perhaps time it was rebound.

The creation of the worlde. 1

THE FIRST BOKE OF

Moses, called * Genesis.

* This worde signifieth the beginning and generacion of the creatures.

THE ARGUMENT.

MOSES in effect declareth the things, which are here chiefly to be considered: First, that the worlde & all things therein were created by God, & that man being placed in this great tabernacle of the worlde to beholde Gods wonderful workes, & to praise his Name for the infinite graces, wherewith he had endued him, fel willingly from God through disobedience: who yet for his owne mercies sake restored him to life, & confirmed him in the same by his promes of Christ to come, by whome he shulde overcome Satan, death and hel. Secondely, that the wicked, unmindeful of Gods moste excellent benefites, remained stil in their wickednes, & so falling moste horribly from sinne to sinne provoked God (who by his preachers called them continually to repentance) at length to destroye the whole world. Thirdly, he assureth us by the examples of Abraham, Izhak, Iaakob & the rest of the Patriarkes, that his mercies never faile them, whome he chuseth to be his Church, and to professe his Name in earth, but in all their afflictions and persecutions he ever assisteth them, sendeth comforte, & delivereth them. And because the beginning, increase, preservacion and successe thereof might be onely attributed to God, Moses sheweth by the examples of Kain, Ishmael, Esau and others, which were noble in mans iudgement, that the Church dependeth not on the estimacion and nobilitie of the worlde: and also by the fewenes of them, which have at all times worshiped him purely according to his worde, that it standeth not in the multitude, but in the poore and despised, in the smale flocke and litle nomber, that man in his wisdome might be confounded, & the Name of God ever more praised.

CHAP. I.

1 God created the heaven & the earth, 3 The light & the darkenes, 8 The firmamét. 9 He separateth the water from the earth 16 He createth the sunne, the moone, & the starres 21 He createth the fish, birdes, beastes 26 He createth man and giveth him rule over all creatures, 29 And provideth nourriture for man and beast.

1 IN THE a beginning
* God created ỹ heaven and the earth.
2 And the earth was b
without forme & voyde, and c darkenes was
upon the depe, & the
Spirit of God d moued
upon the waters.
3 Then God said, * Let there be light: and
there was e light.
4 And God sawe ỹ light that it was good,
and God separated the light from the
darkenes.
5 And God called the light, Day, and the
darkenes, he called Night. ‖ So the evenig
and the morning were the first day.
6 ¶ Againe God said, * Let there be a f firmament in the middes of the waters: and
let it separate the waters from the waters.
7 Then God made the firmament, & parted the waters, which were f under the
firmament, from the waters which were
* above the firmament, and it was so.
8 And God called the firmament, g Heaven. ‖ So the evening and the morning
were the seconde day.
9 ¶ God said againe, * Let the waters under the heavẽ be gathered into one place,
& let the drye land appeare, and it was so.
10 And God called the drye land, Earth, &
he called ỹ gathering together of the waters, Seas: & God sawe that it was good.
11 Then God said, h Let the earth budde
forthe the budde of the herbe, that sedeth
sede, the fruteful tre, ŵ beareth frute according to his kinde, which maie have his
sede in it self upon the earth. & it was so.
12 And the earth broght forthe the budde
of the herbe, that sedeth sede accordig to
his kinde, also the tre that yeldeth frute, ŵ
hathe his sede in it selfe according to his
kinde: & God i sawe that it was good.
13 ‖ So the evening and the morning were
the third daie.
14 ¶ And God said, * Let there be k lightes
in the firmament of the heaven, to l separate the daie from the night, & let them be
for m signes, and for seasons, and for daies
and yeres.
15 And let them be for lightes in the firmament of the heaven to give light upõ the
earth, and it was so.
16 God then made two n great lightes: the
greater light o to rule the daie, & the lesse
light to rule ỹ night: he made also ỹ starres.
17 And God set them in the firmament of
the heaven, to shine upon the earth,
18 And to * rule in the daie, & in the night,
and to separate the light from the darkenes: and God sawe that it was good.
19 ‖ So the evening and the morning were
the fourth daie.
20 Afterwarde God said, Let the waters
bring forthe in abundãce everie p creping
thing that hathe life: & let the foule flie
upon the earth in the open firmament of
the heaven.
21 Then God created the great whales, &
everie thing living & moving, ŵ the q waters broght forthe in abundance, accordig
to their kinde, & everie fethered foule according to his kinde: & God sawe that it
was good.

a.i.

Geneva Bible.

The strongly Protestant Geneva Bible was the first to be printed in roman type, and the first in which chapters were divided into verses. For nearly two centuries it had been the bible in general use in England. Because of its handy size it was suitable for home reading –it measures eight and a half inches by seven inches – not exactly pocket sized, but far more manageable than the massive bibles which gained popularity with later generations. Richard owned a number of bibles – his favourite being Pasham's Bible, which he mentions specifically in his will. What is clear is that his strong religious beliefs were not something peripheral to his everyday life in London – his faith was absolutely central to him.

By the standards of his day, then, Richard was a well-educated man. Above all, he was a product of his time – there was a thirst for knowledge all around Richard as he grew up. There were new ideas in religion, in philosophy, in art and in architecture. This was the age of the grand tour, of trade developments with the Far East, and a new awareness of the planets and astronomy as well as an interest in chemistry and physics. It was a time when the landed gentry were experimenting with new farming methods – inspired by 'Turnip' Townsend and Jethro Tull – and where a nascent industrial revolution was making its faltering first steps. If nothing else, Richard's education taught him his hunger for new ideas, and his diaries are full of facts (and often half-facts!) which caught his interest. (Some of these are listed in Appendix I.)

It may be wondered why did Richard not go to university. Probably there were two reasons. The most pressing was that the business needed an extra pair of hands and could ill afford to support Richard for any prolonged period of study. The second was that Richard's family, being Baptist, were considered Nonconformist. Oxford and Cambridge both closed their doors to Nonconformists – or more accurately, they could attend lectures but were barred from matriculating (getting a degree). The only viable alternative for Richard would have been to study in Holland, where there was a reputation for admitting Nonconformist English students e.g. at Leyden and Amsterdam. The opportunity, if opportunity there was, passed Richard by, and a sock-smith he became.

The clear impression from his writings is that from an early age it had been instilled into Richard that there were only three things which could help stop the fall into the abyss of poverty, sickness and death. The first was a strong belief in the Lord, and that without faith you got nowhere. The second was the importance of education. The third was that you got nothing without working hard for it. These were the cornerstones of his upbringing – and of the whole of his subsequent life.

Throughout the 1730s Richard was living with his father 'over the shop' in Red Lion Street. It seems that at some stage during the decade the paths of Richard and his father crossed with those of the Seward family, particularly the head of the family, Benjamin. The latter had been schooled at Winchester and St John's College, Cambridge and had apparently been expected to enter the Church. Like Francis Hall, Benjamin Seward was in his early thirties. Like Francis, Benjamin was from a well-off family but had gone to London where he too was apprenticed as a hosier. He had married Eleanor Knapp and they had two daughters: Frances who was born in 1732 when Richard was about four years old and Eleanor who arrived in 1733.

We can perhaps visualise the scene the following year. It was the end of December 1734. Mrs Seward was in labour. Mary Glisson, the local midwife, was hurrying to the Seward house at eight in the morning having been up half the night helping the delivery of a boy two streets away. Barely having time to wipe her hands on her apron, which so proudly displayed the stains of her trade for all the world to see, she would quickly have realised that all was not well with Eleanor Seward. Upstairs the two little daughters would have spent the day in fear, listening to the screams of agony from the room below. In vain the midwife tried to ease the birth, first with lotions, then with more vigorous intervention. The shrieking of Eleanor would have reverberated round the house, while the gossips (a term meaning female friends invited to be present at the birth) would have sat around talking and offering advice. But the baby was stillborn, strangled in its umbilical cord. There was to be no let-up for Eleanor in her pain and anguish – the birth produced massive bleeding which Mary Glisson was helpless to prevent. At length the screams stopped, and in that ghastly silence Benjamin Seward would have realised the horrible truth – his wife was dead, and he had two infant daughters to bring up. A day which had promised so much had robbed him of almost everything.

It is entirely possible that one of the gossips was Richard's mother, and it is equally possible that, in those painful days and nights which followed, the Seward daughters were billeted in the Hall household while Benjamin made plans for his future. Eleanor's brother, the barrister George Knapp of the Inner Temple, had recently died without issue. Benjamin therefore found himself in the fortunate position of moving to Kings Bench Walk, though with no means of raising his daughters unaided.

Later, Benjamin was to send his daughters back to Badsey (near Evesham in Worcestershire). This enabled Benjamin to have his children brought up by his own parents, with the assistance of his other relatives, he being one of seven brothers. Again, there is no record of this but it is highly likely that the young Richard would have accompanied his father on a trip to see the Seward family at Badsey – or perhaps to inspect the Mansion House at Bengeworth which Benjamin had purchased (for cash) in 1735. Benjamin presumably chose Bengeworth because of its proximity to Badsey, where his father, John Seward, was steward for Lord Windsor's estates in Wales.

If the young Richard did visit Evesham it would certainly explain his later fondness for the area – it must have been a revelation for the young boy to breathe fresh air and see cherry orchards and farmland in place of the smoke and grime and stench of overcrowded London. Two things point towards the fact that Richard spent time in the country with the Sewards – the first is that later diaries show that both Richard's children and grandchildren were sent off to the Cotswolds for months at a time (i.e. it seems to have become a family tradition) and secondly there is the friendship which developed between the young Richard and Eleanor. As an only child it may have been the first time that Richard ever got to play with other children, albeit younger than him. What else explains the fact that Richard and Eleanor were to become childhood sweethearts? Where else could they have met – unless it was via their respective fathers?

In a letter written by Edward Seward to his father John in about 1738 there is an interesting insight not only into the petty rivalries and jealousies between the two Seward girls but also the everyday culinary affairs of a middling household at this time:

> You shall hear [a story] of pretty Cousin Fannys [Frances]. She was with me by ye little Parlour Fire yesterday I was going to give her a Rosted apple She desir'd me to clean it I desir'd Her to take it in ye Kitchen and give it one of the Servants to clean. No, Says She, I will fetch you a Knife to

Clean It for If I take it there, Miss Nelly [Eleanor] will Cry for It and then Susan will give it Her.

So, what was life like from the perspective of Sue, the cook? At this stage there was still a tradition of killing off livestock before the winter – meat would be salted down and there were many recipes for preserving items. But as the century progressed improved winter feeding methods enabled farmers to keep their livestock alive all year round. There was a move away from farmers on small units growing enough for the immediate needs of their family and local community towards growing larger amounts of one crop specifically for sale at market. New seed varieties – particularly from Holland – led to better yields and new varieties of fruit and vegetables. Potatoes, introduced two centuries earlier, had not at first really caught on, but now became increasingly popular. Vegetables such as sprouts started to appear, and were recognised by Captain Cook and other sailors as a way of avoiding scurvy.

Increased trade between England and Africa and the West Indies brought more people into contact with fruits from those areas, all funnelled through ports such as London and offered for sale on groaning market stalls. There was a passion for anything exotic. Attempts were even made to grow pineapples in Scotland! It had not yet reached the stage where no self-respecting landowner would dream of constructing his new stately pile without an orangery – and even perhaps an ice house, but that was to follow as the century unfolded.

In the kitchen, cooking styles changed as new technical developments influenced food preparation – rolled sheet-iron led to better fire grates and changed chimney designs. Indeed, cooking moved out of the main room, with its inglenook fireplace, and into a separate kitchen. Improved metalworking techniques produced better utensils and the development of the clockwork spit led to more reliable roasting methods. Meanwhile, the use of muslin, invented a century earlier, had led to a huge popularity for steamed puddings, both sweet and savoury. The more that the French – at least the wealthy among them – developed elaborate sauces and the idea of haute cuisine, the more the English clung to their traditional 'Roast Beef of Old England'. Indeed, there was a popular song of that name, sung lustily by the mob whenever they encountered anything 'foreign' which was not to their liking.

Not surprisingly the changes in the kitchen led to an explosion in the popularity of cookery books and recipes. Many of them were highly derivative of existing works – then, as now, recipes were recycled. What is apparent from Richard's writings is that the tittle-tattle of exchanging recipes was by no means a female preoccupation. Richard loved nothing better than to jot down Lady So-and-So's recipe for this or that, and kept a separate notebook for just that purpose. (Lady Dorset and her recipe for cakes appear in Appendix I.) To modern tastes some of these dishes seem incredibly sweet. Sugar, nutmeg and other spices were in great demand.

The mistress of what we would now term a middle-class household like the Halls' would have eagerly handed the job of cooking to her cook, instructing her to follow the recipes of, say, T. Hall (probably no relative) in his best-selling book *The Queen's Royal Cookery*. So, in the scenario of Cousin Fanny roasting her apple on the fire, we have to remember that, just as Fanny's world was changing, so was the world of Susan, the family cook.

4

The 1740s

The decade had started on an icy note – the winter of 1739–40 was so severe that temperatures failed to rise above freezing point for the whole of December through February. The river Thames, prior to the embankment works carried out in the next century, flowed at a more leisurely pace and therefore froze over more readily. It was an opportunity to hold a frost fair on the ice – complete with booths selling trinkets and souvenirs. There was even a printing press. Jugglers, tumblers and musicians would have been out in force – along with the inevitable pickpockets. Bear baiting and ox roasting were popular at such fairs, and as Richard lived within a few hundred yards of the river it is inconceivable that he did not see the fair and share in the excitement.

By 1740 the twelve-year-old Richard would have been aware of one enormous social change in the capital – the widespread consumption of gin. Gin drinking had become an epidemic of catastrophic proportions, particularly among the poor, and at its height (1740–42) London burials outnumbered baptisms by two to one, gin consumption being one of the reasons for this (indeed, it has been estimated that it accounted for one in eight of all deaths at the time). The phenomenon had started innocently enough in the 1720s when Parliament decided not to discourage gin manufacture because it provided a use for surplus grain. The writer Daniel Defoe had commented that the distilling process consumed surplus corn and therefore was in the interests of landowners. Shops selling gin mushroomed in London to an astonishing 7,000 and consumption nearly doubled in the twenty years between 1730 and 1750. As the young Richard walked through the streets in the parish of St Giles he can hardly have failed to notice that no less than one in four of all houses was selling the stuff or have missed the drunken antics of its victims, young and old alike. Tens of thousands of children died – 9,000 in 1751 alone. In the same year Hogarth published his famous prints *Gin Lane* and *Beer Street* – contrasting the horrors of gin drinking with the more socially acceptable effects of drinking beer. Efforts by Parliament to control the situation were half-hearted and misdirected, and it was only in 1751 that an effective Gin Act was passed.

In Hogarth's *Gin Lane* the only person prospering is the pawnbroker. The rest are shown in stages of starvation and death. Corpses are being trundled away in a wheelbarrow. Buildings are left to fall down and there is a pervading atmosphere of poverty and death. © The Trustees of the British Museum.

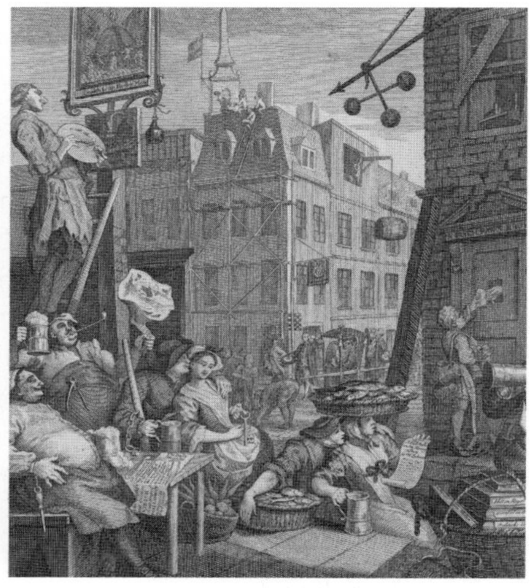

Contrast this with *Beer Street* – where everyone is shown as jolly and well fed and knocking back quart mugs of foaming ale. Except for the poor pawnbroker, who can only afford a pint and whose premises are falling down from neglect. In the background scaffolding is being used to repair the roof of one of the houses, and there is a general air of prosperity and healthiness. © The Trustees of the British Museum.

The later diaries of Richard itemise the considerable amounts of alcohol made or consumed in the Hall household – wine, port, cognac, beer (even, in 1774, Guinness) but never gin. He would have learned that lesson first hand on the streets of London in his formative years. His country cousins on the other hand had no such inhibitions, and his brother-in-law William later records: '1774 13th October paid Mr Syms 2 gallons Geneva 19 shillings, and for best coniac brandy £1.4.0.'

The decade saw other, more positive developments, especially in industry. In 1733 John Kay of Bury patented the Flying Shuttle. Up until then weaving has been a slow, laborious process and the width of a piece of cloth had been limited to how far the weaver could reach between outstretched arms. Now, cloth could be made wider and faster. The weavers needed a better way of spinning, such was the demand for thread. In 1738 Lewis Paul and John Wyatt took out a patent for drafting rollers and their flyer-and-bobbin system led to a move away from spinning and weaving as a cottage industry. Finer, more even, yarns could now be produced. In the silk industry the change was ongoing. The influx of Huguenot refugees to London, from the reign of William and Mary onwards, had brought thousands of skilled silk workers to the City, particularly in the area around Spitalfields. Development of the silk industry was hampered by the shortage of raw silk and by competition, particularly from the Italians, the French and the Chinese. In 1718 Thomas Lombe had obtained a patent for a 'new invention of three sorts of engines never before made or used in Great Britain, one to wind the finest raw silk, another to spin, and the other to twist.' Arguably his invention was simply copied from a silk-weaving machine which had been used in Italy for nearly a hundred years, and the Italians were outraged. Thomas and his brother John built a silk mill in Derby and by the 1730s this was employing over 300 workers. Others imitated their success and silk factories were established in London as well as in Manchester, Norwich, Macclesfield, Chesterfield and Stockport.

Change was the one constant in Richard's life, and few changes would have been more significant than the one which occurred in 1741. Richard was no diary-keeper in his youth, and it is left to his son, writing nearly a century later, to supply some of the data relating to the death of Richard's mother:

> When about 13 on the 17th April 1741 Divine Providence saw fit to remove this honoured and valued parent at the age of 38. The first of those important changes he [i.e. Richard] experienced by the visitation of Death in his family connections. My father was the only child she left behind – the removal of this parent was in a great degree supplied by another of whom he thus speaks: 'January 6th 1742 my father married a second wife – the widow Turner without

> children. A good woman – a valuable example to me, with whom I lived until I entered the marriage state. We lived in more love than mother and Sons in law generally do. [The expression 'sons-in-law' was used to include stepsons.]

The death of his mother Anna must have been a devastating blow to a young and rather sensitive only child.

As we have seen, his father remarried just ten months later, in keeping with general practice (his grandfather Thomas had done the same when his first wife, Mary, died). An only parent bringing up a 'teenager' (the word was not even coined for another two centuries) – particularly a male who had to go out and earn a living – simply could not cope with running a household. Whether Francis found true love the second time around with the widow Turner, aged forty (ten years his junior), or whether this was a marriage born out of necessity is not known. But it was to last another twenty-three years and provided the youthful Richard with the love and stability within a family relationship which he clearly valued.

The death of Anna would have been recorded in the Bills of Mortality. These records date back to the early sixteenth century in London, and the areas covered by the Bills had expanded as London grew. Until 1603 the Bills covered only the City within the Walls and its 'Liberties', that is the area governed by the Lord Mayor of London. The 'out-parishes' (i.e. suburbs) were included in 1604, and in 1636 the 'distant' parishes in Westminster, Stepney and South London were included. The area referred to the London conurbation of the time, and the phrase 'within the Bills' came to mean what might otherwise be termed 'Greater London'.

When the sexton rang his bell to announce the death of a citizen, he was summoning a searcher – usually an old woman of the parish who would otherwise be on Poor Relief – who had the job of visiting the house of the deceased and of establishing the cause of death. She would have had no medical training for this task, and some of the causes of death were unrecognisable to modern eyes.

Some of the more bizarre-sounding and interesting causes of death listed in the Bills were: ague (recurring fever and chills); apoplexy (stroke); barrel fever (debilitation caused by recurrent drinking); bloody flux (dysentery – a major killer, given the lack of personal hygiene); Black Death (also known as camp fever);

typhus; chin cough (whooping cough); chrisom (the 'illness' suffered by an infant who died before or shortly after baptism); consumption (tuberculosis); cramp colic (appendicitis); croup (cough); membranous croup (diphtheria); dock fever (the dreaded yellow fever that could be introduced into London via inbound ships); the Evil (scrofula, otherwise known as 'The King's Evil'); falling sickness (epilepsy) and French pox (also called Great Pox, to distinguish it from smallpox).

Apparently the system of employing searchers was not foolproof since unscrupulous undertakers were known to 'do a deal' with the sexton to keep quiet about a death until the undertaker had secured the body and arranged the funeral. An interesting letter to the editor published in the *Weekly Journal or British Gazeteer* in February 1727 made the following complaint:

> There is a certain parish within the sphere of the Bills of Mortality, wherein it hath been usual for the sexton, to let an undertaker employ whom he pleased, to ring the knell, giving him an opportunity thereby to secure his private interest in the burials, by cutting off the most common method of intelligence in such cases from all others. This practice of engrossing a trade of this kind I conceive to be very unjust... Tho' we hear a knell, yet we shall not know by it who is dead at that time, lest another undertaker by that means should step in to perform the funeral. The very searchers shall be kept in ignorance, for fear they may have a friend to serve by conveying him notice of the job. It is usual with those old women to walk about from one undertaker to another, to be inform'd for whom coffins are made or making. They have been observed to come for their fees, when the corps had been secured in its coffin, sometimes at the burying-house, and sometimes at the church-yard. What report can they make of what they never saw? What security can friends or relations, or even the publick have, that persons come fairly by their deaths, where such clandestine doings are in fashion?

By the time of his mother's death, Richard had already started a scrapbook of printed ephemera, prefaced with his name in

Richard Hall.

Printed at the THEATRE in OXFORD,
July 21. *An. Dom.* 1743.

No, not an indication that the fifteen year-old Richard was writing plays for the Oxford Theatre, but that he cut out and kept a souvenir of his namesake!

print. Years later Richard's son wrote (with the benefit of having diaries and papers which are no longer in existence): 'In noticing the events of 1745 my father mentions my grandfather being convinced of biblical baptism and of his being baptised by Dr Gill at the Barbican. He also records the death of his grandmother Mrs Rebecca Hall who died 23rd November, 1745 aged 77.' It is apparent that Richard, too, was attracted, not to the Church of England, but to the invigorating climate of the Baptist movement. By 1745 he was attending sermons given by Dr John Gill – although it was another twenty years before he 'gave in his experience' and was himself baptised. Meanwhile, he collected the printed versions of many of the good doctor's sermons, and then had them bound up into his own book entitled 'Miscellaneous Sermons'. Dr Gill was a charismatic figure who was either loved or despised by his listeners. A man of huge intellect and learning, he dominated the Baptist movement of his time in the same way as Wesley is associated with the Methodist movement.

Gill's sermons did not make easy listening in the sense that he offered no easy options – he was a High Calvinist, vigorously orthodox on Christian basics, and he demanded the highest standard of commitment from his followers. He wrote extensively and Richard was to purchase and keep many of his works. Dr Gill staunchly defended the orthodox faith, in an age when people were increasingly 'putting God on trial' and devaluing God while elevating the importance of Man. It may have been another two decades before Richard followed his father into full baptism, but there is no doubt that Dr Gill was a most influential figure throughout Richard's formative years – and indeed for the rest of his entire life. His was the teaching by which all other ministers would be judged.

Meanwhile there was a living to be made. Richard was content to follow in his father's footsteps. It was later noted: 'On February 3rd 1743 I was bound an apprentice to my father as a Hosier at Red Lion St in the Borough of Southwark.' He was just short of fifteen years old, and his formal schooling had come to an end.

One event which unfortunately does not make it into Richard's diaries was the famous April Fool's joke which was played on the London populace in 1746. The papers announced, on the last day in March, that there was to be an exhibition of donkeys in Islington the following day. Crowds turned up and spent hours wandering around looking for the donkeys before realising that they themselves were in fact the asses. It is easy to imagine that Richard, with his love of the bizarre and the unusual, would have been there pacing up and down, definitely not seeing the joke!

Another event which would surely have captured Richard's imagination would have been the return of Admiral Anson after his courageous circumnavigation of the world between 1740 and 1744. He had departed with a squadron of six warships with the express aim of attacking Spanish possessions in South America. Successive misfortunes meant that this ill-equipped and much delayed squadron was reduced over a three-year period to just the flagship *Centurion*. But with that one ship Admiral Anson was to return home with a most astonishing amount of treasure. This followed the sacking of the small Peruvian town of Paita (13–15 November 1741) when much booty was captured. However, this paled into insignificance when the *Centurion* captured the *Nuestra Señora de Covadonga* on 20 June 1743. This was the annual treasure ship which sailed from Acapulco, heading for Manila, with the entire output of the Spanish American mines. The cargo included 1,313,843 pieces of eight (Spanish dollars). Anson returned in triumph and was accorded the privilege of transporting his booty from Liverpool to the capital.

His share of the prize money made him an immensely wealthy man whereas the most lowly crewman was paid a paltry few pounds. Anson went on to defeat the French in the First Battle of Cape Finisterre in 1747 and was made First Lord of the Admiralty in 1757. His indomitable perseverance was plain for all to see, since the bullion was melted down and re-minted in both 1745 and 1746 – with the distinctive word 'LIMA' appearing below the monarch's head as an indication of the origin of the metal. Mind you, until Richard read *A Voyage round the World* – written by Anson's chaplain Richard Walter and published in 1748 – LIMA may well have confused Richard (and others) since none of the gold or silver actually came from Lima! But read it he eventually did – his diary for 5 May 1773 reads: 'Returned to Mr Snooke Anson's Voyage'.

It is still unclear why the wrong Peruvian city was used to commemorate the epic voyage, but 'LIMA' was to appear on gold (five guineas and guineas) as well as silver coins (crowns, half-crowns, shillings and sixpences) and would have been in general circulation throughout the remainder of Richard's lifetime. One of the 'LIMA' shillings was in Richard's purse at his death.

The middle years of the decade were marked by the uncertainty linked to the 1745 uprising by 'Bonnie Prince Charlie'. The Scottish Jacobite army marched south led by the Young Pretender, collecting supporters in Manchester and reaching Derby before retreating north again. The following year his followers clashed at Culloden with the army led by the Duke of Cumberland. The Pretender's army was beaten and he fled to the Isle of Skye. This was one of the earliest national events mentioned by Richard – now an eighteen-year-old, and one, moreover, with a Calvinist background, he would have been only too aware of the consequences of a return of a Catholic monarch to the throne of England. King James II had left the shores only sixty years before. Tradesmen had only to think back to the horrors of the Civil War a mere hundred years earlier to remember the dangers – to say nothing of the cost – of religious upheaval. Definitely bad for business. The population was weary of strife and uncertainty – what was needed was a period of consolidation,

1746. The Rebels defeated at Culloden, by the D. of Cumberland Apr:16.

16 April 1746 – The rebels defeated at Culloden by the Duke of Cumberland.

Paper cut-out of soldiers on horseback.

which is presumably why the country put up with 'German George' and his descendants.

By the time of Culloden, Richard's parents had moved house to an area of Southwark known as Newington Butts (not to be confused with Stoke Newington to the north of the city, which was altogether more prosperous). Newington Butts was a farming village with a low level of population until the second half of the eighteenth century. There was a little industry – for example, the manufacture of clay pipes for tobacco smoking. Many businessmen from the City had moved away from the centre after the Great Fire, preferring the fresh air of the country in which to bring up their families, and yet being able to ride to their warehouses or shops in the City. Up until 1666 London had been a city built of wood and thatch but the Great Fire led directly to new building controls and fire regulations. Within a few decades London turned into a brick city – no timber or thatch was allowed and brick and tiles took their place. Newington would have reflected these innovations– though the exact site of the Halls' new residence is not recorded.

The Seward connection has already been mentioned and at some stage during the 1740s Richard and Eleanor became teenage sweethearts. Eleanor was five years younger than Richard.

William Snooke in his Sunday best.

Her elder sister, Frances, had met and fallen for a certain William Snooke – a far more wealthy 'catch' than Richard though that was not to stop the quartet becoming close friends in the years ahead, and the two couples were to marry within a short space of time, apparently with the full blessing of their respective families.

William had been born in 1730 and was orphaned while still in his teens, leaving him to look after his very much younger sisters, Elizabeth (born 1743) and Mary (known to all as Polly, born in 1745). For a while they had continued to live at Compton Abdale Abbey. He was later to sell the abbey to Lord Chedworth (in 1768), but by then had long removed to the Manor House at Bourton-on-the-Water in Gloucester, taking up residence with his new bride on 27 January 1752. He apparently brought his younger siblings to live with him – so that his bride Frances in effect inherited a ready-made family consisting of two children aged seven and nine. The Seward family tree at that time looked like this:

Family Tree 2 – The Sewards

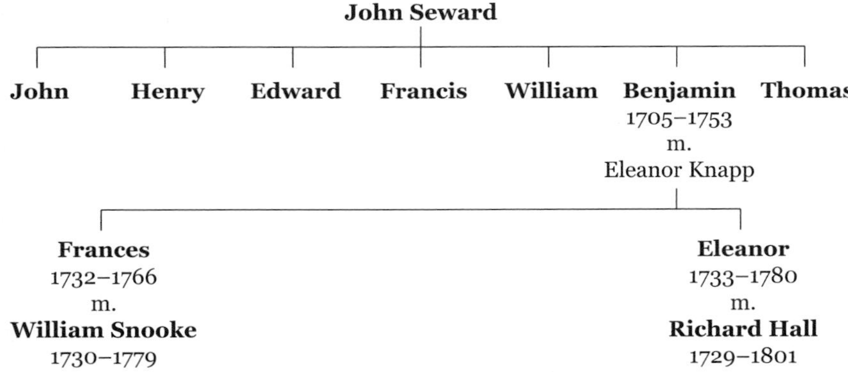

The Manor House at Bourton-on-the-Water.

The Seward family had in the past used the stockbroking services of William Seward, the fifth of the seven sons in that family, described as 'a broker in Exchange Alley'. Unlike his brothers, William Seward had a grammar school education and had not, like most of the others, gone to Westminster School and St John's College, Cambridge. As an adult he chose none of the traditional professions, preferring to live by his wits. In modern parlance he was a 'wheeler-dealer' and at first was seen as something of a black sheep in the family. Subsequently William became churchwarden in the parish of St Thomas the Apostle, and, later, following his conversion by Charles Wesley, he became an ardent disciple of George Whitefield and devoted himself to the new Methodist movement. He took up preaching to large open-air congregations, though apparently not all his listeners were admirers. He died after being hit by a stone on the back of the head while preaching to a crowd at Hay-on-Wye, on 22 October 1740 – one of the first Methodist martyrs. There was also a strong connection between Benjamin Seward and the Wesley brothers – the Methodist society at Evesham was one of the very first to be formed. When Charles Wesley visited the town in August 1739 the embryonic society was already in existence and his brother, John Wesley, actually preached from the Mansion House at Bengeworth in October of that year when he paid Benjamin a visit. He returned on many occasions, preaching under the yew tree in the grounds of Benjamin's property.

Many of the letters from the Seward brothers to each other, and to their father, remain. A helpful article on the letters was written for the Vale of Evesham Historical Society by the Revd. Peter Braby, a former vicar of Badsey. Rather than using a separate envelope, each letter would be folded in three, ends tucked in, sealed, and the address written directly onto the back of the letter. They are now known to collectors as 'entires' and are valued for their postmarks. The cost of receiving the letter was met by the recipient – typically four pence for a letter delivered from London to Evesham. The price varied according both to the number of sheets of paper and the distance a letter travelled. But the Sewards were fortunate. Members of both Houses of Parliament were entitled to free post, as long as they placed their signatures on the envelope, and it was customary for large numbers of blank envelopes to be signed and handed out to friends and political supporters. The Seward family did well out of this because, besides working for Lord Windsor, who would have allowed his steward the use of franks, there was a son and a brother who were Members of Parliament. But privileged franks were limited and son Thomas Seward writes

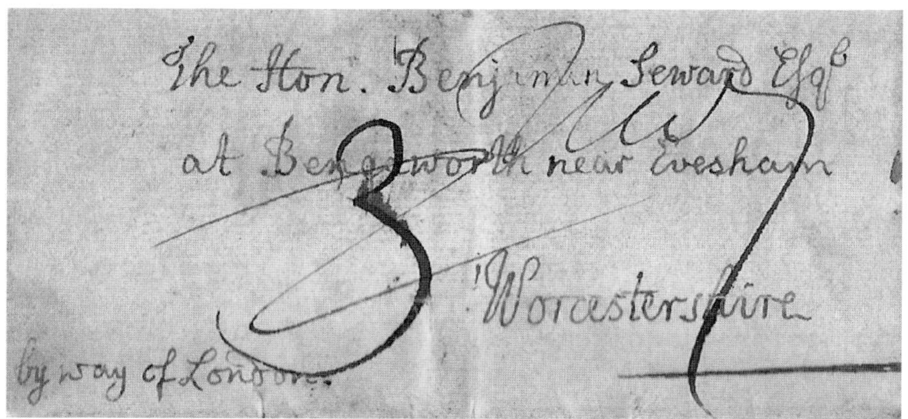
The Hon. Benjamin Seward Esqr
at Bengeworth near Evesham
3
Worcestershire
by way of London

The 'envelope' shown here includes the words 'by way of London' – a reminder that, whereas postal services in the early part of the century were fairly speedy and reliable between the capital and main cities, intercity services were slow and unreliable. A letter from Bristol to Worcester might take far longer to go direct than it would if it were sent via London.

to his father: 'I beg you'd never let me have the pleasure of a letter for want of a Frank; I pay no money with so much pleasure as for letters.'

The haphazard nature of Britain's early postal system can largely be put down to the poor road system in England in the first half of the century – surfaces were appalling. Drive hundreds of cattle along a muddy cart track after heavy rain and the average road becomes totally impassable. People 'lived with it' and it was not until after the 1745 rebellion, and the difficulties faced in trying to move troops north to meet the rebel army of Prince Charles and his supporters, that there was any serious attempt to deal with the underlying problem. Up until this time roads had been the responsibility of each individual parish through which the road passed. There was no incentive to have repairs carried out properly, and there was no Highway Authority having overall control. The solution lay in a series of Turnpike Acts, setting up individual companies charged with raising tolls from passing travellers to pay for improvements to the surface. Some 1,600 separate Acts of Parliament were passed in the last half of the century, each one authorising a particular company to erect gates or other barriers across the highway in a particular area. Improvements were gradual and piecemeal throughout the second half of Richard's life.

Ironically the solution was to lie with a trio of Scottish road builders – 'Blind Jack' Metcalfe, Thomas Telford and John McAdam. Blind Jack, born in 1717, constructed some 180 miles of highway in Yorkshire – despite his blindness – using a three-layered system of large stones, covered with excavated road material, topped with a layer of gravel. Thomas Telford, born in 1757, raised the foundation at the centre of the road to ensure proper drainage – that is, away from the road surface so that water could run off to the sides. McAdam was born the year before Telford and he went on to develop a system of road construction which became known as 'water-bound macadam'. Again, there were three layers: the first two comprised an eight-inch bed of angular broken stones (crushed by manual labour), while the top layer was some two inches thick with a maximum crushed stone size of 1 inch. The layers would be watered before being compressed with a heavy roller, locking the angular stones together. The method required a great deal of manual labour, but it resulted in a strong and free-draining surface. (Roads constructed in this manner were described as 'macadamised' and for that reason when bitumen was added in the nineteenth century roads were described as 'tar-macadamised'. The word 'tarmacadam' was shortened to the now familiar 'tarmac'.)

The stagecoach of the 1750s was lighter than the 'glass coach' prevalent when Richard was first born, which would often need six horses to pull it along at little more than walking pace. By the middle of the century the four-horse stage was far more rapid, but it still had no springs and had heavy wagon wheels. Typically it could carry six people inside, but the journey was no picnic – coaches often turned over, or broke an axle in the rutted surface of the track. In addition, a guard was needed, armed with his blunderbuss, since the audacious highwayman knew that he was always going to be able to outrun a stagecoach. The fate in store for the highwayman who was caught would have been well known to everyone, as is apparent from a cut-out of a hanging scene made by one of Richard's children (probably Anna) in the 1790s:

A four-horse coach.

The gallows. Note the indifference on the part of the gossiping horse riders!

5

The 1750s

The decade started with the phenomena of not just one but two earthquakes felt in the capital. Richard notes: 'An earthquake felt in London February 8th 1750 about Twelve o'Clock at noon. Another shook Thursday March 8th 1750 about half after Five o'Clock in the morning.' It did not take long for the clergy to blame the tremors on divine displeasure at the sinfulness of their flocks – the Bishop of London proclaimed that it was as a direct result of lewd and pornographic behaviour. So one month later the 'end of the world is nigh' brigade led a mass exodus out of town, convinced that the eighth of each month was blighted and that the eighth day of April would see a major earthquake. The city was totally gridlocked, as huge numbers of people tried to leave for the security of the open country.

Observables.
An Earthquake, felt in London
Thursday February 8th 1749/50, about
½ after 12 Clo. at noon.
Another Shock, Thursday March
8th 1749/50. about ½ after 5 o'Clo
in the morning.

Observables: two earthquakes.

Presumably, having driven their carts out of town, they all waited until sunset before sheepishly coming home in the evening, but not before they had given London a taste of traffic chaos of a kind which today would be familiar to us all. Richard, who had little time for bishops, appears to have stayed put, and did not consider the scare worthy of note, but no doubt was miffed that business was down that day!

Travel at that time would invariably have been on horseback – hence Richard's interest in equine matters:

> In the beginning of November 1750 Horses in General seized with a Violent Cold – this extended all over England and I think, several places abroad. Lasted about 2 or 3 weeks – very few dyed. They ran much at the Nose and coughed. Seized with the same disorder January 1760 and again at the latter-end of the Year 1767.

It is apparent from the entries scattered throughout the diaries over several decades that Richard was probably not a very good horseman, and there are numerous references to his being thrown. This must have amused his brother-in-law, who may have been 'the country cousin' but was undoubtedly a far better rider.

When it came to visiting strange sights or unusual curiosities, however, Richard was no sloth. When a handbill was posted at The Talbot Inn, just across the road from Richard's home in Southwark, in May 1752, announcing that the curious could view a 'rhinoceros or Real Unicorn', as well as a live crocodile ('such a creature was never shewn alive in the King's dominion before'), Richard not only joined the gawping throng, but pasted the handbill into his book of news clippings.

The same year what sounds like an early version of the modern caravan was exhibited:

> a very curious house which has its Roof Ends and Sides, Doors and Window Shutters covered with Plate Iron, and hath in it a very good room ... the said house goes on wheels and has been above an hundred and twenty miles and all Gentlemen and Ladies, and others, who have seen this house etc do allow it to be one of the greatest curiosities they ever saw.

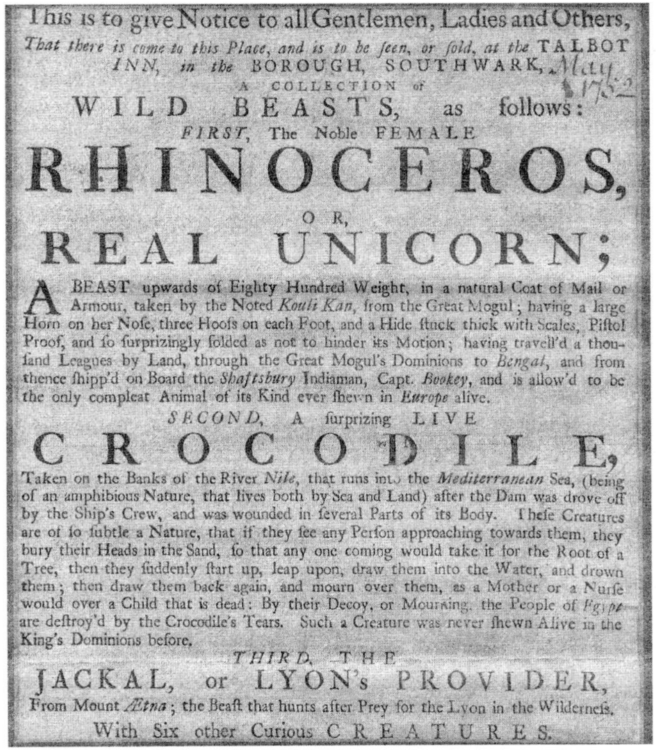

This is to give Notice to all Gentlemen, Ladies and Others,

That there is come to this Place, and is to be ſeen, or ſold, at the TALBOT *INN, in the* BOROUGH, SOUTHWARK, May 1752

A COLLECTION of

WILD BEASTS, as follows:

FIRST, The Noble FEMALE

RHINOCEROS,

OR,

REAL UNICORN;

A BEAST upwards of Eighty Hundred Weight, in a natural Coat of Mail or Armour, taken by the Noted *Kouli Kan,* from the Great Mogul; having a large Horn on her Noſe, three Hoofs on each Foot, and a Hide ſtuck thick with Scales, Piſtol Proof, and ſo ſurprizingly folded as not to hinder its Motion; having travell'd a thouſand Leagues by Land, through the Great Mogul's Dominions to *Bengal,* and from thence ſhipp'd on Board the *Shaftsbury* Indiaman, Capt. *Bookey,* and is allow'd to be the only compleat Animal of its Kind ever ſhewn in *Europe* alive.

SECOND, A ſurprizing LIVE

CROCODILE,

Taken on the Banks of the River *Nile,* that runs into the *Mediterranean* Sea, (being of an amphibious Nature, that lives both by Sea and Land) after the Dam was drove off by the Ship's Crew, and was wounded in ſeveral Parts of its Body. Theſe Creatures are of ſo ſubtle a Nature, that if they ſee any Perſon approaching towards them, they bury their Heads in the Sand, ſo that any one coming would take it for the Root of a Tree, then they ſuddenly ſtart up, leap upon, draw them into the Water, and drown them; then draw them back again, and mourn over them, as a Mother or a Nurſe would over a Child that is dead: By their Decoy, or Mourning, the People of *Egypt* are deſtroy'd by the Crocodile's Tears. Such a Creature was never ſhewn Alive in the King's Dominions before.

THIRD, THE

JACKAL, or LYON's PROVIDER,

From Mount *Ætna*; the Beaſt that hunts after Prey for the Lyon in the Wilderneſs.

With Six other Curious CREATURES.

A handbill for Wild Beasts at the Talbot Inn.

This too was visited, and the poster pasted for future reference. Likewise, he kept this newspaper cutting from 1752:

> This is to advise the curious that there is lately come to Town from Glamorgan a most curious and uncommon prodigy in Nature, being a Youth in the fifteenth year of his age, whose height is no more than two feet six inches, weighs but twelve pounds yet is in all respects proportionable...

Richard, with his thirst for knowledge and a desire to be well read, well travelled and well informed, could never resist a peepshow, an exhibition, a museum or a guided tour.

Until 1750, the only bridge across the river Thames was London Bridge ('1209 London Bridge finish'd – thirty years in the building'). Richard goes on to note: '1750 Westminster Bridge finish'd' – and later he adds: '1758 – April 11th – The temporary wooden London Bridge burn'd down Tuesday, began about 11 o'clock at Night.' This was followed in 1769 by 'Black Friars Bridge finish'd.' So, in the space of twenty years two new bridges had been added to alleviate the congestion on London Bridge.

The old bridge housed a squalid collection of tenements in disrepair, but in 1756 Parliament authorised the removal of all the shops and houses, introducing new tolls to cover the cost of demolition. It took until 1762 for all the leases to expire and for the premises to be cleared for demolition. Work had already commenced to widen the old bridge – using the temporary wooden structure to minimise congestion. It is this structure which, Richard noted, caught fire. But in the 1750s Richard would still have been able to walk across the old bridge to his shop in Red Lion Street. Well, he would have been able to walk it more easily were it not for an unfortunate accident which occurred on his way back from visiting his parents in Newington Butts. Richard attempted to jump a fence, caught his leg and tumbled awkwardly into the ditch the other side, and broke his leg.

The article in the *London Evening Penny Post* for Monday, 9 September 1751 records:

On Friday a Man, jumping over a Ditch at Newington Buts, ſlipt and broke his Leg.

The resulting injury left Richard in periodic pain for the rest of his life, and caused him to limp. As an old man, he recalls 'being follow'd around the village while the boys called out "Hobbledee-Hall".' He doubtless pretended to object and wave his cane at them, since he used a crutch, finding it a hardship to stand still. His diary for 1758 records the purchase of the crutch:

1758
Augt. Crutch Cane — 0. 3. 6

Richard's own library gives an interesting insight into the way a broken limb was treated. Rather like someone today buying *The Readers Digest Book of Home Medicine,* Richard bought Dr Buchan's *Domestic Medicine* when the second edition came out in 1785. It has the following advice:

> WHEN a large bone is broken, the patient's diet ought, in all respects, to be the same as in an inflammatory fever. He should likewise be kept quiet and cool, and his body open by emollient clysters, or, if these cannot be conveniently administered, by food that is of an opening quality; as stewed prunes, apples boiled in milk, boiled spinage, and the like. IT will generally be necessary to bleed the patient immediately after a fracture, especially if he be young, of a full habit, or has, at the same time, received any bruise or contusion. This operation should not only be performed soon after the accident happens, but if the patient be very feverish, it may be repeated next day. IF any of the large bones which support the body are broken, the patient must keep his bed for several weeks…

…And so forth. So, we can assume that Richard was fed his diet of prunes, bled with leeches, made to lie on his side, wrapped in wet leather, and told to lie still for six weeks. Try telling that to a 22-year-old! No doubt Richard counted the days, for he wrote down the familiar aide memoire: 'Thirty days hath September, April June and November, February twenty eight, Alone, And all the rest have Thirty-one.'

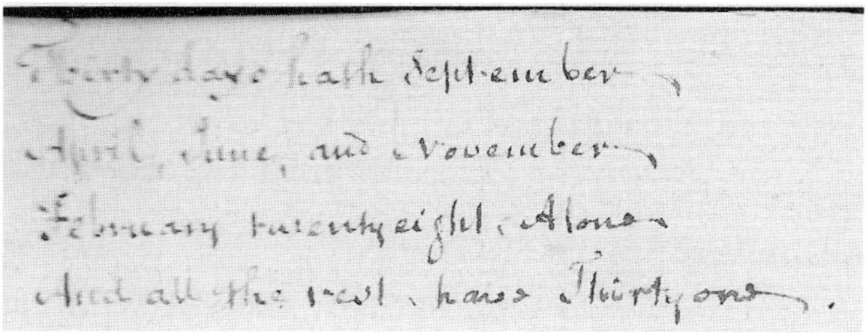
Thirty days hath September,
April, June, and November,
February twentyeight, Alone,
And all the rest, have Thirtyone.

Sounds familiar? Maybe, but there is no reference to a leap year. And what about when to change the year – we take it for granted that one year finishes on 31 December and that the first day of January marks the change to the New Year. Up until 1752 this was not the case – the changeover took place on 25 March. So 25 March 1751 was followed the next day by 26 March 1752. The problem was that there were three different ways of calculating the date in Europe – France and Russia had different calendars, which must have made it very hard for traders.

Parliament decided it was time to come into line with the main European countries where it had long been recognised that the Julian Calendar, with its lack of a leap year, had led to the date getting 'out of synch' with the lunar calendar. Parliament simply decided to 'lose' eleven days. Richard records: 'Old Stile ceased Sept. 2nd 1752. Next day 'twas Sept. 14th.' Others were less easy going about the change, and a popular cry of the time was 'Give us back our eleven days!' Richard, with a background knowledge of astronomy, and an awareness of the trading difficulties of expecting ships from the Continent to dock on the wrong day, would have had no such worries. Nevertheless, in remembering wedding anniversaries and birthdays for some years after, he would have to make corrections to his own diary entries – adding 'Old Stile' after listing an anniversary.

The calendar change still affects us today because of a curious anachronism: the Inland Revenue regard the tax year as changing on 5 April. Why? Because the tax year used to end on 25 March and the taxman simply added the 11 days, rather than following common practice throughout Europe and adopting 1 January as the New Year.

Periodicals designed to appeal to women were beginning to appear at this time. Here is an example of the fortnightly *Ladies Magazine* for 5 May 1750. It would seem from the name and date added in manuscript that such items were circulated among friends for some time after publication. It was hardly *Vogue* or *Cosmopolitan*, starting as it did with a series entitled 'History of England, by Question and Answer' and continuing with 'Broughton and Back – an entire new ballad', a fable entitled 'The Gardener and the Snail' and some verses 'wrote by Dr Swift'. All very enlightening, but nothing to give a sensitive young lady an attack of the vapours... The edition did, however, have a few useful tips about hatching chicks in incubators ('the Art of Hatching, and bringing up, in all seasons, Domestick Fowls of all sorts by means of the heat of either Dung or artificial fires in Ovens or stoves prepared for that Purpose'). It also set out suitably chilling and macabre accounts of the 'Trials and DYING SPEECHES of the eleven Malefactors who were executed at Tyburn, the 26th March 1750' and of the 'Authentick Memoirs

The LADIES MAGAZINE.

By *JASPER GOODWILL*, of *Oxford*, Esq;

Numb. XIV. From Saturday, *May* 5, to Saturday, *May* 19, 1750. Vol. I.

CONTENTS,

of the Wicked Life and Dying Words of John Collington…and John Stone, who were executed on Saturday April 7th 1750 for setting fire to the Barn and Ricks of Mr John Clarke'. The accounts serve as a reminder of how many offences – particularly against property – carried the death penalty, and show the fascination the public held with the wicked deeds of wrongdoers – and their very public comeuppance. The magazine also sought to give an answer to 'the great question concerning the Magnitude of the two capitals' (i.e. London and Paris) by listing comparative figures for marriages in the two cities. Its conclusion? That London was at least a third larger than Paris.

Richard might now have spotted such a periodical in his own household. On 21 February 1753 he married Eleanor at Badsey Church near Bengeworth – the bride just shy of twenty years old. It is unlikely that Eleanor would have worn white – it was considered impracticable as only the very rich would have bought a dress without intending to wear it on other occasions. The fashion was for bright yellow, and the dress would have been trimmed with love knots (ribbons tied in bows) – designed to be pulled off and kept by guests as a wedding souvenir – and leaves of rosemary or myrtle used as a garland round the skirt. There would have been no veil, and no wedding train. Even in those days, it was thought that wearing something blue would ensure fidelity, and everlasting love. Green would have been avoided – green was the colour of the fairies and it was considered unwise to attract their attention at a time when the bride was making the transition away from being an innocent virgin. Pink (and even scarlet) were not unusual. Grey for a wedding dress was common with the lower orders – because it could then be used as Sunday best, but is unlikely to have been worn by Eleanor who would have been keen to show herself as a fashionable young bride. Besides, her elder sister, Frances, had married the improbably wealthy William Snooke eighteen months earlier, and there would have been no way that the younger sibling would have wished to appear dowdy or poor in comparison.

Frances's wedding, on 11 June 1751, would have been a memorable family occasion as it was a 'double' – in addition to Frances Seward marrying William, her aunt Grace Seward married a Josiah Roberts on the same day in the same church. It seems likely that the actual wedding service would have been conducted by one of the bride's uncles – one of her father Benjamin's six brothers, Thomas, was the Canon of Lichfield. As a result of the union (i.e. because they had married two sisters) Richard and William became brothers-in-law – and thereafter Richard referred to him as 'Brother William' at all times.

In all probability one of the wedding party would have been the young Anna Seward, daughter of Canon Thomas. She is pictured here at a slightly younger age. Anna grew up to become a well-known 'Sapphic Poet' who devoted most of her literary output to expressing her deep love for Honora Sneyd. Honora was nine years her junior and had come to live with Thomas and Anna as a young girl. She stayed for thirteen years. Unfortunately for Anna, Honora's family then tired of the arrangement and she was sent away and within a couple of years had decided to get married. She died of consumption seven years after that, and Anna was desolate – first at the 'betrayal' and then at the death. She went into mourning and composed sad elegies for the rest of her life,

Anna Seward.

and became a prodigious letter writer. She earned the accolade of being called 'the Swan of Lichfield' and, much to his dismay, persuaded Sir Walter Scott to edit her letters. They were published in six volumes two years after her death in 1809. The poems occupied another three volumes. Many were sonnets and elegies, and her style can be seen from the opening stanza of one such poem, described as 'Written at the Sea-side, and Addressed to Miss Honora Sneyd':

> I write, Honora, on the sparkling sand! –
> The envious waves forbid the trace to stay:
> Honora's name again adorns the strand!
> Again the waters bear their prize away!

Richard makes passing references to Anna in his later journals, and one or two of her family letters remain.

A paper cut-out of a swan – though not the Swan of Lichfield!

After the wedding ceremony it appears that both the Hall and Seward families left for London. Richard therefore writes in his diary:

> I had scarcely entered into the Marriage state before I was called deeply to sympathise with my Partner in the unexpected Death of her worthy father. Mr Seward and his wife had left Bengeworth after the time of my marriage in order to visit London, where he was seized of fever which terminated

> in his death March 30th 1753. His last words were 'Sweet Jesus, Come! Come!' His remains were interred in Bunhill Fields burying ground in a vault which Bro. William and I had built for him.

The widow of Mr Seward (that is to say, his second wife, Elizabeth) remained in London until her death which occurred on 29 January 1754, at the age of fifty-eight. Her remains were interred in the same vault. 'Thus', Richard remarked in his diary, 'both left their house at Bengeworth and never returned to it. Oh how wondrous are the ways of the Lord, but he gives no account of any of his matters.' In her will Elizabeth left the income from £4,550 to various Baptist causes. This charitable trust was to be overseen by seven Baptist ministers. They included the minister at Bengeworth, Dr Gill and Benjamin Beddome from Bourton. Richard Hall and William Snooke were the executors of the will and also the residuary beneficiaries.

It is hard to imagine the financial effect that the sudden demise of both Mr and Mrs Seward would have had upon Richard's fortunes. In the eighteenth century a single woman had extensive rights to own property but those rights disappeared on marriage. In legal parlance, when she became his wife, Eleanor ceased to be a feme-sole and became a feme-covert – under her husband's protection, but equally, her husband's property. It is highly likely that before Eleanor 'entered into the married state', Benjamin Seward would have paid a dowry – and in return Eleanor would have been granted a guaranteed 'pension' in the event of Richard's death. Any property owned by Eleanor became Richard's on 21 February, and anything she acquired after that date passed to him and not to her. As a result of the law Eleanor would not have inherited from her parents – their entire estate would be divided equally between Richard and 'Bro. William'. And so it was that Richard and William became joint owners of Bengeworth Mansion House, along with all other properties and money owned by Benjamin. Given that Benjamin had built up enough of a property portfolio in London to have been able to buy Bengeworth in 1735 when he was only thirty-five years old – at a not inconsiderable price of £1,750– it is fair to assume that Richard was suddenly well-off. For William, the only son of wealthy parents and orphaned when a young child, the change may not have been as dramatic, but it appears that it was Brother William who took Richard under his wing and set about making even more money out of the inheritance.

Looking at William Snooke's diaries, with their detailed list of loans advanced on Promissory Note (for sums up to £100), on Bond (up to £1,000) and on mortgage (loans over £1,000), it is clear that he had a network of loans throughout the Gloucester, Worcester and Oxford areas – usually to established families, and generally earning him between 4 and 5 per cent per annum. His accounts show a steady income stream – some years in excess of £2,200 – an incredible amount for the day, when a farm labourer might earn £40, and a trader 'of the middling sort' might earn £400. Lending money to make money seems to have been William's philosophy, and it appears to have rubbed off on Richard. One of the assets Richard listed just before his death was 'Lady Skipworth on Mortgage £1100' and there are various references to earlier loans, mostly to titled ladies (perhaps those who had been unable to pay their haberdashery bills!).

Richard also started to dabble in stocks and shares, but it is unclear who advised him on this, and throughout his adult life he kept jottings of stock movements and changes in the Bank of England interest rates: 'An increase of One per Cent in the dividend of Bank Stock at Lady-day 1788 on which that Stock rose 10 per Cent.' Meanwhile, William's diaries show a regular pattern of stock investments purchased jointly with Richard – presumably using the income from the estate of Benjamin Seward, since this belonged to them both equally.

Bengeworth itself was a problem. The 'Mansion House' was run-down and neglected and it took time to find a willing tenant. In 1756 Richard notes: 'Mr Jenkyns rented Bengeworth House – £30.' The following year it was let to Miss Wright – £25 – and later to Mr Fortescue – £20. There then followed a succession of local vicars who were apparently prepared to pay twenty pounds a year for the privilege of living in a draughty tumbledown wreck ('1768 Revd. Mr Biddulph, 1771 Revd. Mr Beale'). The name 'Mansion House' appears to have been used to distinguish the building from the very much older Manor House, which reputedly once belonged to King Canute, and which is still standing. The Mansion House was altogether grander, having been built in the 1520s. It survives as the renowned Evesham Hotel – much modernised and extended, but still at heart the old Mansion House. The land which belonged to the mansion house would have been let to tenant farmers. Richard describes the holding: 'Bengeworth before inclosed 140 acres. Close or garden ground called the Home Close or Avon Close about 8 acres. That little Close planted with Cherry trees called Cannon's Close about two acres. One close, called Ruff's Close, three quarters of an acre.'

Bengworth before inclosed 140. Acres
close or garden ground - call'd the
home Close or Avon Close about
8 Acres.
that little Close planted with
Cherry-trees call'd Cannons Close
about 2 Acres.
one Close Call'd Ruffs Close 3/4 Acre

Originally the common land in the Vale of Evesham in Worcestershire would have been grazed by a few head of cattle owned by a number of individuals, or gleaned after the harvest by geese and ducks being fattened up for Christmas. It was to be another twenty years – in the mid 1770s – before the enclosure movement changed the face of the countryside and effectively doubled the size of the family's landholding. The area was renowned (then as now) for its fruit crops (particularly plums, cherries and apples).

Richard up a ladder pruning one of his cherry trees!

Birds and dovecote.

Richard and William were not yet ready to make their move... William contented himself with conducting trials with different seeds on his various farms – at Rissington (180 acres), Hartford (28 acres), Naunton (20 acres) and Bourton (20 acres). His favourite appears to be 'Siberian Barley' and in his diaries he notes yield and harvesting details. William would no doubt have been aware of Jethro Tull (1674–1741) and his mechanical seed drill, invented some years earlier. The controversy over this innovation, which threatened to put labourers out of work, was to last for another hundred years, though Tull was eventually vindicated and in many ways can be regarded as a forerunner of modern farming.

The picture is taken from a paper cut-out showing a ploughing scene and was made by a member of the family at the time.

In all probability Richard would have known little about farming – but Brother William had the means and the determination to experiment with new crops and farming methods. He even noted which type of peach tree he planted ('Magdalen') as opposed to nectarine ('Old Roman or Old Nevington'). His enthusiasm presumably rubbed off because in 1758 Richard notes: 'Nethercoat Grounds bought.' Nethercote (as it is more usually written) consisted of a group of houses and land just to the south-east of Bourton-on-the-Water – a couple of hundred yards from the manor house where Brother William lived. Richard obviously considered land to be a good investment – he later bought a small farm at Sedgeworth and still owned that land when he died, presumably having rented it out for some thirty-odd years.

Springtime: rabbit on the left, daffodils on the right, and a bird perched in the highest branch of the tree.

William, meanwhile, had more adventurous thoughts – like any young man with money, what he wanted was a new set of wheels, and in 1758 Richard notes: 'Mr Snooke set up his Post Chaise.' In all probability the coachwork was yellow. Later Richard was to note: 'Yellow is the most prevalent colour of the body of coaches. Most of the chariots have compass porch, prolignac springs and jacks, outside elbows and round sides. Many of the coaches are in the same taste. Bear-skin cloths are very general.' Well, there would have been one difference with William's conveyance: springs were not going to be invented for several more decades and therefore travel in the post-chaise would have been somewhat rough and bumpy.

It seems quite possible that at some stage in 1754 Richard fulfilled a childhood ambition by visiting France. There is no extant diary of his trip, but there remains a well-thumbed *Guide to Paris and Versailles* (a fascinating equivalent to today's *Rough*

Guide to Paris) with underlinings, suggesting that the guide may have been used on the trip. Travel to the Continent was not easy – but 1754 was one of the few times when England and France were not at war. Another clue is that Richard suddenly became the owner of several complete sets of books, in French, dated 1754 – the complete works of the seventeenth-century playwrights Molière and Racine. They still remain in the family and, although it is possible that these were purchased from a London bookseller, it seems more likely that they were brought back from France as a souvenir. We know that Richard was fluent in French, and could read and write in French to at least the equivalent of today's A level standard, but the evidence of the books themselves suggest that they were bought for display rather than for reading – the pages are still in pristine condition!

Richard would not have needed a passport to travel – passports were promises of safe conduct needed for more distant travels and were available both to foreigners and British nationals. There was no question of needing a passport to leave or enter the country. Up until 1772 they were written in either Latin or English and were generally signed personally by the King. From 1772 onwards they were written in French but were usually signed by the monarch right up until 1794 when this duty passed to the Secretary of State.

The *Guide to Paris* is full of helpful tips to the traveller – how to present yourself to the local governor so that you are frisked less brutally, which route to take out of town, the distance between coaching inns, and so on. It also gives advice about the local currency and warns against the local chambermaids who habitually hang the beds with damp sheets. Ironically this same complaint was made by one of George II's ministers, fed up with encountering unaired beds on his frequent trips accompanying the monarch to Hanover. Some of the advice is a trifle simplistic – the reader is exhorted to ask, not for 'The Louvre' but 'Le Louvre', although it goes on to suggest that you should simply leave all local travel arrangements to your manservant. Hints about finding rooms to rent are given, along with a cautionary tale about the unsatisfactory nature of French cuisine – particularly where soups are concerned. We may find the judgment about French food surprising – not least because fashion and taste were hugely influenced by what was happening in France – but the comments about getting 'the great looseness' and discovering that 'no place in the elegant or delicate world is so ill-provided with Conveniences to deal with the condition as Paris is' may strike a chord even with more modern travellers!

> And as for your Drink, I muſt again remind you, that 'tis dangerous either to drink much Water, or too great Draughts of their ſmall Wines, for ſo doing will moſt aſſuredly throw you into a violent Looſeneſs, and no Place in the elegant or delicate World is ſo ill provided with Conveniencies for ſuch a Condition as *Paris* is: Wherefore, that you may have no extraordinary Calls to uſe them, mix your Water always with the common Wines of about thirty Sous a Bottle, and drink no Wine under that Price, for the low pric'd Wines are only fit for Servants, and Perſons more accuſtomed to them

Also in 1754, Richard set about expanding the Hall dynasty, and a year and a half after he married was pleased to announce the arrival of his firstborn:

> September 14th 1754 I became a family man in consequence of the birth of a son who was named William Seward Hall. This event happened on a Saturday. On the following Sabbath public thanks were offered for the deliverance experienced, by Dr Maryatt. My wife was the last person that the Dr prayed for in that way because it pleased the Lord to remove him the same day suddenly by death.

Oh well, some come in as some go out...

Still in his twenties, Richard had not yet started to write a contemporaneous diary. He tended to jot down items which appeared of interest to him, as they occurred, rather than setting down a daily record of trivia: '1754 Red trunk for writings £0/12/0 [still in Richard's possession at the end of his life, when he specifically mentioned 'the papers in my Red Trunk'] 1755 – April. Was at Don Salters Coffee House at Chelsea £0/13/0.'

In fact, Richard was partial to tea rather than coffee and this was one of his few visits to a coffeehouse mentioned in his journals. The coffeehouses had by the mid-eighteenth century developed as great centres of 'intelligence' – where people could meet and discuss issues of the day, and share information about trade and so on. But the Salter Coffee House in Chelsea was something quite unlike any of its rivals! John Salter – or 'Don Saltero' as he was generally nicknamed– was quite a character and his coffeehouse was also a museum of curiosities. Salter had started as a barber, later becoming valet to Sir Hans Sloane, the physician and collector who was to give his name to London's Sloane Square. In 1693 Salter set up a coffee shop by the river, and Sir Hans gave him a number of historical oddities to display. He attracted custom from naval officers who gave him other curiosities brought back from around the world and which Salter displayed in glass cabinets or hung from the walls by the thousand. Visitors were not charged to see the 'museum' but were expected to drink coffee or buy a catalogue for twopence. We know from the catalogues – and from the auction inventory when the contents were eventually sold in 1799, that Richard would have been able to see 'a curious model of our Saviour's sepulchre, a Roman bishop's crosier, antique coins and medals, minerals, fossils, antique fire-arms, curious birds, fishes, and other productions of nature, and a large collection of various antiquities and curiosities, glass-cases, &c'. Relics included:

> King James's coronation sword; King William's coronation sword and shoes; Henry VIII.'s coat of mail, gloves, and spurs; Queen Elizabeth's Prayer-book, stirrup, and strawberry dish; the Pope's infallible candle; a set of beads, consecrated by Clement VII., made of the bones of St Anthony of Padua; a piece of the royal oak; a petrified child, or the figure of death; a curious piece of metal, found in the ruins of Troy; a pair of Saxon stockings; William the Conqueror's family sword; Oliver's broad-sword; the King of Whiddaw's staff; Bistreanier's staff; a wooden shoe, put under the Speaker's chair in James II's time; the Emperor of Morocco's tobacco pipe; a curious flea-trap; an Indian prince's crown; a starved cat, found between the walls of Westminster Abbey when the east end was repaired...

The list goes on, by turns macabre and absurd. Richard must have been in his element at such a display – a veritable treasure trove of tat embellished with improbable claims, the walls festooned with exhibits. But to pay out thirteen shillings – that's a lot of coffee!

A measure of 'public jitters' over earthquakes is shown by Richard's next entry: '1755 – Nov 1st – a Great Earthquake in Lisbon – felt in several parts of Spain. At the same time the Water in the Sea and in Fishponds in several parts of England had a surprising commotion by suddenly rising, and overflowing.' It was indeed a huge disaster. Estimated now as having a magnitude of 8.5 on the Richter scale, the quake hit the port area of Lisbon first and killed around 600 people. Many buildings collapsed, trapping others indoors. The earth shook for nine minutes but just as the survivors thought that the worst was over the city was hit by a giant tsunami which ripped through the sea defences and drowned another 900 residents. Even worse was to follow; fires triggered by the quake were whipped out of control by high winds and within hours much of the city was engulfed in flames. Ten thousand people were killed in the fire alone.

In general, Richard made very few references to international events in Europe. Thus we have the laconic 'May 18th 1756 – Tuesday – War Declared against France', to mark the outbreak of the hugely destructive Seven Years' War. Richard was much more interested in the everyday: 'Feb 1757 – Very Severe Weather – Bread very dear – much owing to large quantities of Wheat used by the Distillers.' The latter was an interesting point – Richard would have learned from this that a farmer growing barley would need good intelligence of the likelihood of war. In wartime the brewers pushed up the price of barley, with their requirement for malted barley with which to make beer. In peacetime, it was best to harvest the barley before it sprouted – and sell it to the bakers. Sometimes even the everyday can be momentous, however:

> March 15 1757 – an Exceeding Windy Day – great damage done by Sea & Land – at the Assize in Worcester a Stack of Chimneys fell, which broke into the Town Hall – killed six Persons and hurt others.
>
> 15th April 1757 – About 6 in the Evening – a Great Storm of Hail, with very loud Thunder, and Great Lightning.

18 May 1757 My Son William has the Smallpox, but through Mercy was safely recovered. A seven day pock.

The births of other children are mentioned in Richard's journals: 'March 6th 1756 my daughter Martha ... 26th December 1757 my son Francis.' By now with three young children it was clear that the family had out-grown the 'rooms above the shop' and in 1758 Richard notes: 'we moved house – Slept at our country house at Stockwell 14th May.' By this date there were already specialist carriers dealing with furniture removals – for instance the removal firm of Pickfords had been established in Manchester in the seventeenth century and by 1756 James Pickford had established headquarters in London at Blossoms Inn in Lawrence Lane, and at The Bell Inn in Wood Street, Cheapside. However, Richard is just as likely to have used the services of a local carrier, transporting his furniture on the back of a cart or covered wagon.

Eleanor may not have known it but she was already a couple of months pregnant when she moved house, and 14 May 1758 was a particularly busy and stressful day for the family. In his diary Richard recorded: 'Little son Billy breeched [i.e. put into breeches for the first time] – 3 years 8 months old... An eventful day for all of us – Daughter Patty [i.e. Martha] taken with the smallpox May 14th 1758, a seven day pock.' Poor Eleanor! – all that packing and unpacking, and on top of that your daughter goes down with smallpox – it must have been a nerve-wracking time waiting to see how the illness developed. She would have had her work cut out, since the diary for the following week notes: 'Son Billy was taken with the Measles, May 22nd 1758.' Measles was a serious illness, frequently life-threatening, but happily the lad recovered. It may have contributed to the decision by Richard and Eleanor to 'farm the boy out' to Brother William and his wife in Bourton. Certainly the journals suggest that for many years Master William would spend months at a time with his aunt and uncle, including attending the local school in Bourton and, as likely as not, this arose because of health concerns.

Reviewing his diary entries at a later date, Richard comments:

Weighed at Bourton, 11th August 1757
Papa 168 pounds
Mamma 123 pounds
Self 111 pounds

Weighed at Blandford 4th September 1789
Self 122 pounds
Wife 118 pounds

So, we have Richard weighing in, as a 29-year-old, at a shade under eight stone – and even thirty years later he was still under nine stone. We have no record of his height but presumably he would have been around five feet tall – certainly no more than five feet two inches. Definitely short and skinny – neither of which adjectives would be used to describe members of the family in subsequent generations!

Signs of growing affluence started to appear in family life. Richard listed various items which he bought at this time in his life:

1756 June. 12 silver coat buttons £0/14/6

Very fashionable and ostentatious. Nothing wrong with a bit of conspicuous wealth to impress the customers! Buttons would be transferred to successive garments as the old ones went out of fashion – leaving the discarded garment to be relined, re-buttoned and sold on down the clothing 'chain'.

1756 January – Frame for marble slab 2 guineas

It was not uncommon for traders to 'round up' prices by 5 per cent from a pound to a guinea – that is, from one pound to one pound one shilling. Guineas, incidentally, took their name from the gold from the West African country used to mint them when they were first introduced in 1661.

1756 October Silver canasters and sugar dish £5/4/0

A canister was the original name for what became the tea caddy.

Canisters were usually sold in pairs. One would contain Green Tea (*Thea viridis*) and the other Bohea (*Thea Bohea*). The tea would then be mixed by the hostess, using the cap of the silver canister as a measure. Boiling water would then be added from the tea kettle (later to be replaced by the tea urn, with its own tap to avoid the need for tilting, but this did not become fashionable until the following decade).

1756 December A pair large China Jarrs & a pair branches £3/3/0

The 'branches' were presumably candelabra.

1756 August Mr Wayman doing Mahogany bookcase £1/10/6

1757 July Mr Buskin for Deal Book-Case on wheels £1/18/0

The latter is an indication that from his mid-twenties Richard was collecting books – and presumably referring to them – hence the advantage of a case on wheels.

October 1757 – Two two-handled pewter Cups and 2 plates gave to Bourton Meeting

These were presumably for use at the communion table.

Mr Phillips Chipping Norton Mahogany Elbow Chair £1/7/0
1758 small arm chair £0/6/0

By this time nearly all the furniture bought by Richard appears to have been made of mahogany, no doubt replacing the far bulkier 'family' pieces which would have been made from oak.

1758 February – gave Master Parsons for drawing Billy & Patty's picture 5/-

1758 5th July – was at Windsor Fair £1/1/11

1758 November Son William's miniature picture drawn £1/11/6

(This was very probably commissioned as a memento to give the boy's aunt and uncle – that is, for when he was not staying with Brother William and his wife).

The diary for 1758 starts with a reference: 'January began a General Mourning for Princess Caroline.' It may well be that Richard's interest in her demise was occasioned by the need to close the shop for a number of days. With an expanding royal family, and frequent deaths, this must have been a considerable interruption to the job of making money!

Other items in 1758:

> July 2 1758 – was Graciously preserved. Wife, Self, and young Billy in our single horse chaise – the harness broke and the horse ran away. Through great Mercy neither of us received hurt.
>
> July 14 – Remarkable for high winds in the night and much Rain
>
> [July] 21 & 22 – Remarkable for exceeding heavy and long Showers of Rain
>
> Aug 18 – great rejoicing on taking Cape Briton
>
> Aug 24 – About 7 in the evening a very great Storm of Thunder – very terrible lightning which lasted about an hour and a half – much Rain.
>
> Sept – Son Francis taken with the Measles

The journal goes on to record: 'November 12th 1758 my daughter Frances was born – she died ... 23rd December, 1758. A most sorrowful Christmas for us all.' Later on Richard was to recall: 'So, in total my dear Eleanor bore me four children, apart from ten miscarriages.' Pregnant fourteen times in twenty-seven years – but perhaps with the prevailing lack of contraception the surprise is that she was not pregnant more often!

The year 1758 saw the reappearance of Halley's Comet –

predicted by Edmond Halley in his lifetime. It would, however, be unfair if Halley were remembered only for his astronomy – he would merit a place in history anyway for his work on barometric pressure, on magnetic variations and on the movement of trade winds and oceanic currents (among other things), and for having the wisdom to fund the publication in 1687 of Isaac Newton's *Principia* out of his own pocket. Oddly the appearance of his eponymous comet is not alluded to in Richard's diary, especially as he was usually so aware of what was going on in the heavens.

The year 1759 began sadly. 'Jany. – a General Mourning for the Princess Dowager of Orange.' But of far greater significance to Richard was the death mentioned later the same month: 'January 8th 1759 at the age of 60 died my father Francis Hall after a declining state of health.' On 14 January Richard would have wearily put his hand on the latch to the front door of his parents' house in Newington Butts. He would have covered the couple of miles on horseback from his shop in Red Lion Street, wrapped in his own thoughts. It had been six days since word had reached him from his mother to say that his father had died in the night. There was much to do. Richard had been to see the undertakers – the people who 'undertook' all the things which needed to be arranged. He had written a dozen letters to his distant relatives in Berkshire advising them of the death. Postal collections from Southwark were every two hours and by 14 January he would have expected replies from anyone intending to attend. He had been to the jewellers and had a set of mourning rings made, engraved with his father's name and date of death, for handing out to close friends and family (in the same way as Richard himself was to specify in his own will, half a century later, that each of his nieces was to receive 'a Mourning Ring of a guinea value'). He had filled in the time and place of the funeral on some fifty tickets bearing the heading 'Memento Mori' ('Remember you must die') and named the recipients who were to be the funeral guests, and sent these by hand to his father's friends and business colleagues. And he had helped his mother dress the house from top to bottom in black crêpe. The crêpe, developed by the Huguenot weavers some 40 years before, was used to cover the windows and drape the doors. The mirrored wall sconces had been covered and the looking glasses had been turned towards the walls so that, on entering the house, barely a glimmer of light could be seen.

We can imagine the scene. Richard's mother, dressed in her 'widows weeds' of black with a black cap peaked over her forehead, was in the front room by the open coffin. And everywhere Richard could smell the all-pervading aroma of the dear-departed. The corpse of his father lay on a bed of bran lining the coffin floor – bran to absorb the fluids from the decomposing body. Parliament had passed a law at the end of the previous century (designed to protect the nation's woollen industry) insisting that all bodies should be wrapped in woollen cloth, without a stitch being used, on pain of paying a fine of £5. His father would not have wanted the family burdened with such an expense but Richard would have been adamant: fine or no fine his father's shroud should be of finest white Holland. Not in a winding sheet tied top and bottom, but in an embroidered garment resembling a long nightshirt, the edges trimmed with black silk both at the sleeves and down the front. Richard himself would have overseen the stitch-work of his apprentice. His father's darkening face was not yet covered. The mourners would be due at nightfall and all who attended would inspect the corpse before it was finally covered and carried to the hearse.

The funeral procession would then walk to the burial ground, to escort the corpse on its final journey. But first there were the final arrangements to be made – the guests would expect drinks both before and after the burial. Fresh rosemary had been bought from the market and arranged in baskets either side of the front door – sprigs to be collected by each guest and held as a nosegay to disguise the smell of death, until finally discarded over the coffin as it was lowered into the ground, as a final mark of respect. No doubt Richard would have liked to have seen the coffin covered with the thick velvet pall bearing the coat of arms of the Haberdashers Company, but his father was denied that honour because, as we know, he was not a Guild member. Instead, a simple black square, emblazoned with the Hall family coat of arms, would cloak the coffin for its journey.

His stepmother would have deferred to Richard in all the

arrangements for the funeral – in effect she would now carry on in the house on sufferance. She would presumably need to take in lodgers to cover the cost of running the household. However, Richard was good to her and treated her as an honoured parent and saw to it that she finished her days in comfort. The maid, who would have been bewildered as to what would happen to her, would have been attired in black from head to foot. She would have been given clear instructions to heat the currant wine and add cinnamon before the guests arrived. It is unlikely that she would have attended the burial, but would have waited in the empty house for the return of the funeral guests – for more drinks, and the reading of the will.

Richard dealt personally with the administration of his father's estate, as is apparent from the following newspaper clipping:

> Publish'd in the London Gazette, Tuesday February 20th to Saturday February 24th: 'Any persons who have any demands on the estate of Francis Hall, late of Newington Buts in the county of Surry, sometime of Red Lyon Street, in the Borough of Southwark, Hosier, deceased, are peremptorily to apply to Mr Richard Hall of Red Lyon Street aforesaid with an Account of such their demands on or before 1st Day of May next.

ALL Persons who have any Demands upon the Estate of Francis Hall, late of Newington Buts in the County of Surry, sometime of Red Lyon Street, in the Borough of Southwark, Hosier, deceased, are peremptorily to apply to Mr. Richard Hall, of Red Lyon Street aforesaid, with an Account of such their Demands, on or before the 1st Day of May next.

The Will of Francis was interesting because it bears all the hallmarks (no pun intended) of having been 'home-made'. Just as Richard had an interest in home medicine, so he was interested in the law, and his books included *The Law of Wills and Codicils* by Tomlins, bought by Richard for half a crown. He also bought *Lovelass on Intestacy and Wills* for 4s. 6d., complete with a handy appendix listing precedent forms – much like something the Post Office sells today to those who wish to dispense with the services of a qualified adviser.

The will itself is fairly straightforward and is set out in Appendix II. But what gives it away as the work of an amateur is the fact that there were no witnesses to the will. It contains the words 'witness my hand' but then omits any witnesses! It rather looks as if Richard saw the precedent in the law book ending with the words 'As witness' and did not realise that this was legal shorthand for the very much longer standard clause: 'As witness the hand of the testator affixed in the presence of two witnesses who in the presence of the testator and of each other have duly appended their signatures the day and year first before written...' A lawyer would have realised the importance of this – and indeed if it had been made after the Wills Act of 1837 the flaw would have invalidated the will. Richard was fortunate – prior to 1837 a will could be admitted if two people who knew the deceased and recognised his signature attested to the fact. Therefore the Probate records were endorsed to show that it had been 'retrospectively validated' by John Crouch and Jonathan Bond who were both friends of the family.

Whether or not Richard was embarrassed at the palaver (and, presumably, expense) of having to get his father's friends to validate the will before a notary public is not clear, but it may have left Richard with an abiding interest in the law of wills and intestacy – years later he wrote out a reference to a Chancery Court decision: 'Lord Chancellor – it is the duty of all Courts to give effect to a Will, as far as the intention of the testator can be made out in that will.'

After her husband's demise Richard's stepmother removed from Newington to South Lambeth. Richard inherited the business and premises in Red Lion Street and set about expanding the business. From making and selling silk hosiery he progressed to selling all manner of fine silks, brocades and damasks as well as silver buckles, buttons and like fashionable items. It was a time when gentlemen were taking to wear elaborate and much-embroidered waistcoats, sometimes woven with metallic strips designed to sparkle in the candlelight, and these would have been displayed at his shop (more commonly called a 'warehouse') so as to attract the public, whether they were simply buying their silk stockings or acquiring the materials for a full outfit.

If Richard received a consignment of lace or calico or embroidered silk from abroad, he would inform his customers of that fact in the newspaper, buy a copy to make sure the notice had appeared, sometimes putting a ring around the box in pencil, and then consign it to his bottom drawer where it remains to this day! Richard clearly appreciated this relatively novel way of bringing his wares to the attention of the public. The growth in the number of newspapers was phenomenal – the earliest daily appeared in 1702 but by 1782 there were no fewer than eighteen appearing every day, as well as weekly and monthly periodicals. Many carried advertising, and for the first time this enabled traders to do more than rely on mere passing trade. Just as with the growth of internet shopping, the public could actually find out what was on offer without entering the 'warehouse'. Hence we see the *General Evening Post* carrying an advertisement from a (rival) hosier:

> Silk Stockings – Men's White and Black Ribb'd Knit Silk Hose, at so low a price as £5 per dozen pair, are now selling at Smith's Warehouse, at Sam Clark's in Bread Street. Their wear and cheapness renders them by much the best Stockings of any as yet offered to the Public, and indeed the large demands for both Home and Foreign Consumption is a sufficient confirmation of their Goodness.

For centuries tradesmen had relied on hanging signs outside their premises to show the trade that they followed – we are still familiar with the 'barber's pole' but in the eighteenth century there was a whole range of hanging signs. It was not until 1760 that a law was passed prohibiting overhanging street signs – presumably as a result of people being injured in high winds. Thereafter signs were fixed to the façade of a building – in turn leading to the type of shop fascia which we are familiar with today. In the 1750s it is safe to assume that Richard's premises would have been marked by a stockinged leg – or possibly a woolpack (the sign for a haberdasher).

The list of expenses for the final year of the decade include:

> 1759 July – Paid Farmer Ford for one hundred (weight) Cheese £1/8/0

Richard regularly bought cheeses by the hundredweight and

would then divide the cheeses into smaller units and share them with Brother William. The family consumption was prodigious. William's diaries confirm this. His entry for 19 June 1775 shows a purchase of over five hundredweight of cheeses – he kept eighteen whole cheeses, of which two were sage. Richard took six cheeses weighing a total of 82 pounds. The rest was distributed among mutual friends.

The year seemed to end more happily than it had begun:

> 1759 – Oct 13th – Was Mercifully preserved when going to Stockwell when my Horse ran away with me. I received a fall, and some hurt, but not what I might have expected.
>
> 1759 Nov 29 – a day of General Thanksgiving observed for the great and plentiful Harvest and the train of Successes the Lord has been pleased this year to give us over our Enemies, in Europe, Asia, Africa and America.

The year 1759 marked the high-point in Great Britain's battle for ascendancy against the French. After arduous campaigns across four continents, the French were defeated on all fronts. Each month the newspapers seemed to bring reports of fresh successes – it was indeed an 'annus mirabilis' and it must have been mighty reassuring to people like Richard that the Lord had decided to grant the British invincibility throughout the world!

A cut-out showing a warship in harbour, with soldiers on guard and cannons pointing out to sea.

6

The 1760s

'1760 October 25th – Our good King George the Second departed suddenly in the 77th year of his Age, and 34th of his Reign. His Royal grandson, now King George the Third, was proclaimed October 26th.' It appears that Richard was fond of the royal family, because his entry for May 1762 reveals that he purchased a picture of the new King George III and his queen, alongside a likeness of George II – fond enough, indeed, to pay one and a half guineas for it (the equivalent of £90 in today's money).

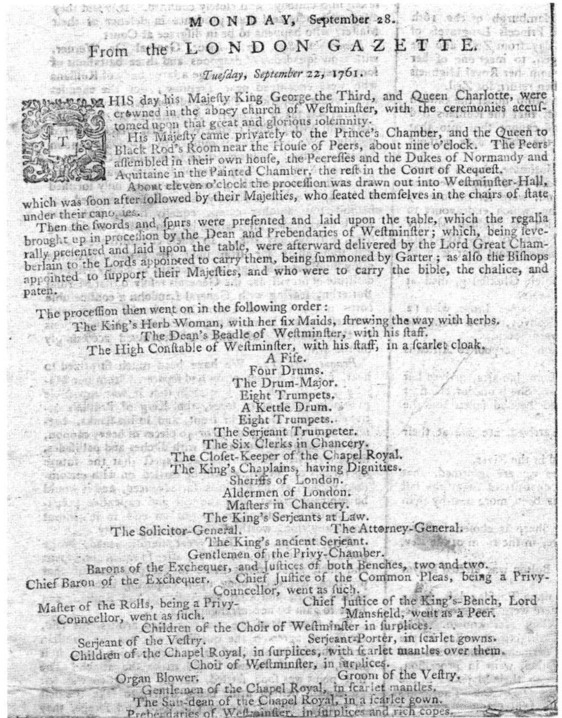

MONDAY, September 28.

From the LONDON GAZETTE.

Tueſday, September 22, 1761.

THIS day his Majeſty King George the Third, and Queen Charlotte, were crowned in the abbey church of Weſtminſter, with the ceremonies accuſtomed upon that great and glorious ſolemnity.

His Majeſty came privately to the Prince's Chamber, and the Queen to Black Rod's Room near the Houſe of Peers, about nine o'clock. The Peers aſſembled in their own houſe, the Peereſſes and the Dukes of Normandy and Aquitaine in the Painted Chamber, the reſt in the Court of Requeſt.

About eleven o'clock the proceſſion was drawn out into Weſtminſter-Hall, which was ſoon after followed by their Majeſties, who ſeated themſelves in the chairs of ſtate under their canopies.

Then the ſwords and ſpurs were preſented and laid upon the table, which the regalia brought up in proceſſion by the Dean and Prebendaries of Weſtminſter; which, being ſeverally preſented and laid upon the table, were afterward delivered by the Lord Great Chamberlain to the Lords appointed to carry them, being ſummoned by Garter; as alſo the Biſhops appointed to ſupport their Majeſties, and who were to carry the bible, the chalice, and paten.

The proceſſion then went on in the following order:

The King's Herb Woman, with her ſix Maids, ſtrewing the way with herbs.
The Dean's Beadle of Weſtminſter, with his ſtaff.
The High Conſtable of Weſtminſter, with his ſtaff, in a ſcarlet cloak.
A Fife.
Four Drums.
The Drum-Major.
Eight Trumpets.
A Kettle Drum.
Eight Trumpets.
The Serjeant Trumpeter.
The Six Clerks in Chancery.
The Cloſet-Keeper of the Chapel Royal.
The King's Chaplains, having Dignities.
Sheriffs of London.
Aldermen of London.
Maſters in Chancery.
The King's Serjeants at Law.
The Solicitor-General. The Attorney-General.
The King's ancient Serjeant.
Gentlemen of the Privy-Chamber.
Barons of the Exchequer, and Juſtices of both Benches, two and two.
Chief Baron of the Exchequer. Chief Juſtice of the Common Pleas, being a Privy-Councellor, went as ſuch.
Maſter of the Rolls, being a Privy-Councellor, went as ſuch. Chief Juſtice of the King's-Bench, Lord Mansfield, went as a Peer.
Children of the Choir of Weſtminſter in ſurplices.
Serjeant of the Veſtry. Serjeant-Porter, in ſcarlet gowns.
Children of the Chapel Royal, in ſurplices, with ſcarlet mantles over them.
Choir of Weſtminſter, in ſurplices.
Organ Blower. Groom of the Veſtry.
Gentlemen of the Chapel Royal, in ſcarlet mantles.
The Sub-dean of the Chapel Royal, in a ſcarlet gown.
Prebendaries of Weſtminſter, in ſurplices and rich copes.

When George III had his coronation on 22 September 1761, Richard went to observe the royal goings-on, and bought his souvenir edition of the *Evening Post* to commemorate the occasion. Note particularly the importance of the King's Herb Woman, who had the job of strewing the way with herbs, aided and abetted by six maids! It gives a lovely picture – Handel's *Zadoc the Priest* being blasted out by the choir and orchestra as Mrs Lavender and her maids dart to and fro, scattering seed heads and rose petals, to help minimise the aroma of the common people...

Richard also shows an interest in maritime goings-on. So, for 15 February 1760 we see a reference to the sinking of the *Ramilles* (off Hope Cove in Devon) in a violent storm: Later that year he notes: '1760 May 1st Din'd at Mr Foljambs – saw a Ship launched.' Richard does not mention the name of the ship but England's merchant fleet was in the middle of a period of great expansion. From a fleet of 3,300 ships and a tonnage of 260,000 in 1702 the merchant fleet had almost tripled and would reach 9,400 ships and a tonnage of 695,000 by 1776. London was a major shipbuilding centre and the whole port area by the docks would have been heavily congested. Delays in unloading became a major problem, with ships queuing for days to unload their cargoes. Theft was prevalent. Barges wanting to go upriver could only go under London Bridge for three hours either side of high tide, adding to the congestion and chaos. Richard's own book of contemporary prints (the one opposite of Amsterdam) shows boat building of the time.

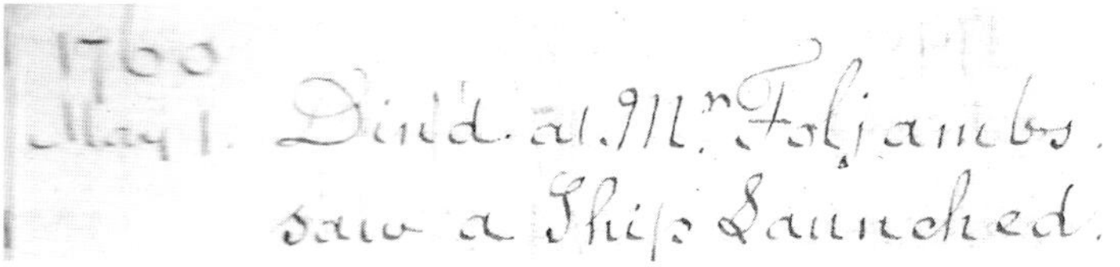

Richard was generally curious about what was going on, especially anything new or innovative.

1760 October 8th – Went with Mr Crouch to see British Museum

Richard must have been one of the earliest visitors to the British Museum, housed in the recently acquired Montagu House. It had only opened the previous year, having been funded by a Lottery launched by Pelham (then First Lord of the Treasury). Tickets had to be applied for weeks in advance of the visit, which would have been a half-hour guided tour of the exhibits. Only later were visitors allowed to wander around unaccompanied. The nucleus of the museum was the library of Sir Hans Sloane (50,000 volumes!) together with his collection of curiosities, which had been gifted to the nation in 1753. His avid collecting has already been referred to in connection with Don Saltero's Coffee House. Richard must have loved the new museum.

> 1761 June 14th – Went with Miss Boswell to Vauxhall Gardens

Vauxhall Gardens encapsulated all the extremes of London at the time. A twelve-acre park, laid out with chequerboard pathways, it held fifty supper boxes, some decorated by Hogarth, as well as Chinese pavilions and a large bandstand and various 'theatricals' – including an imitation cascade of water constructed from long narrow sheets of hammered tin, against which carefully concealed lights would flicker. Richard and Miss Boswell would have been able to wander the pathways listening to popular songs played by a small orchestra, while sneaking a view into the supper boxes to see who was dining there, the fashions, and the display of dinnerware. Entrance was a shilling and the Gardens attracted the nobility and even royalty – the Prince of Wales was a regular visitor. It was also a haunt of prostitutes and pickpockets, and straying into the quieter alleyways was as ill-advised as jostling through the crowded thoroughfares. Quite who Miss Boswell was, and why she was out walking with Richard, is not clear!

Richard also appears to have been interested in what was going on in the theatre – where half the fun and spectacle seems to have been taking place in the auditorium rather than on the stage!

> 1763 January 25th – Went to the Theatre Royal at Drury Lane – 'Elvira' a play by David Mallett.

It would have been a 'lively performance' as appears from the write-up in the *British Magazine*:

> Wednesday January 26th: Last night there was a disturbance at the Theatre Royal Drury Lane on account of the managers refusing admittance at the end of the third act of the play for half price, and the play was not suffered to go on. And this night when the third music began the audience insisted on 'Britons Strike Home' and 'The Roast Beef of Old England'; which was played accordingly. Mr Holland, coming in to speak the prologue to Elvira, he was hissed off. Mr Garrick immediately came on but could not obtain a hearing. After a confused uproar which lasted some time, during which he remained on the stage in a state of mind that may be more easily conceived than expressed, a hundred voices calling out 'Hear him. Hear him' while others called out 'Hear the Pit'. He was asked from the Pit whether he would answer the questions that would be put to him? He respectfully said he would. The following question was then put: 'Will you, or will you not, give admittance for half price, after the third act, except during the first winter of a new pantomime?' Mr Garrick wanted to explain the reasons of his conduct in asking full prices during the first run of a new play, but could not obtain leave. He was required to give an explicit answer: Yes or No. After again attempting to speak to explain his conduct he called out in some agony,

> not without a mixture of indignation we may suppose, at the uncandid treatment he had received: Yes, and the audience expressed their triumph in the manner they usually express their applause. Mr Ackman, an actor who had incurred some displeasure on the preceding night, was next called upon to make an acknowledgement, which he did. Mr Moody another actor was then called for, but not being rightly understood on account of the noise, he was supposed to be refractory, and the audience, insisting upon him going on one knee, he went off and Mr Garrick was obliged to come in and promise while Mr Moody laboured under the displeasure of the audience, he should not appear on the stage.

It must have been an unusual evening's entertainment, the mob proving more memorable than the play itself.

Other excursions were more run-of-the-mill but fascinating nonetheless:

> 1761 August 20th – Rode with Mr Snooke & Mr Edward Seward to Sedgeberrow.

Edward was uncle to both Frances and Eleanor, and it appears that both William and Richard had farming interests in Sedgeberrow at that time, possibly inherited along with the Bengeworth estate when Benjamin Seward died.

> 1761 August 20th – Went with Brother and Sister Snooke to see Fairford Church and Mrs Lambs – slept at Mrs Turners.

Fairford's St Mary's Church would have been famous then, as now, for its spectacular stained-glass windows, made some three hundred years before Richard's visit. The church had been built in the perpendicular style in the fifteenth century and it houses the only complete set of windows to have survived both the Reformation and Cromwell's Protectorate. During the Reformation the windows were whitewashed to disguise them, and in the time of Oliver Cromwell they were taken down and hidden so that they could avoid destruction by his more zealous Puritan followers. The twenty-eight stained-glass windows are a vivid storybook – designed to illustrate the Bible and spread its stories to a largely illiterate populace.

The education of Richard's children was by now uppermost in his mind – William was seven years old. The decision was made to send him to Mr Damonlin's school at Peckham. Richard makes no direct comment about the school, but it appears not to have been a success. Writing in 1764 (two years later) the boy's aunt, Frances, writes to Richard: 'I wish you may hear of a suitable place to fix Dear Billy at; as you can't see an Improvement, a Removal seems necessary, tho' 'tis not agreeable to change Schools.' Reading between the lines, 'Dear Billy' was quite a handful, with various references to the cost of repairs to broken panes of glass, and so on. His uncle (William Snooke) comments: 'I hope he retains his usual liveliness, which renders him so very engaging.' Mmm – a young hooligan, more like . . . Intriguingly, the same letter shows that Richard's daughter Martha (known as Patty) was already 'farmed out' to the Snookes: 'Your dear Patty [then aged six] is very brisk and well, and so grown that we were oblig'd to cut the Silk hanging Sleeves to let down her Slip, which is still too short.' It rather sounds as if living on a farm may have fattened out the child: 'I hope her Shape rather mends. We don't confine her [e.g. in a corset or stays] lest that might be injurious.' In an era when it was almost universal to keep girls in tightly fitting stays – frequently causing breathing difficulties and internal injury – it must have been a great relief to Patty that she was allowed to grow freely. Frances adds a postscript to a later letter: 'Patty's stockings are got very thin, should be glad to have a pair sent by the first conveyance, also her new shift. She desires her Duty' (in other words 'she acknowledges her duty to you as her parent').

All in all, there is a pattern of each of Richard's children in turn spending increasing amounts of time with their aunt and uncle. It may in part have been for the health of the child. It may have been because Eleanor could not cope with having had three children in as many years. Or it may have been that the Snookes, then childless, desperately wanted to have children to share their lives, and badgered and cajoled Richard into letting them 'borrow' theirs. The latter seems quite probable, given the correspondence which has survived.

In April 1762 Richard comments on what appears to have been an influenza epidemic:

> April. 1762. People in general were seized with sore throats, swelled faces, and bad coughs, and colds. – a sickly time very dry season, scarce any Rain for a Month and more.

There was remarkably little interest in the medical community in defining specific illnesses because there was no understanding of what caused infectious diseases to spread. The word 'influenza' (which was first used in the eighteenth century after an outbreak of the illness in Italy) got its name because it was believed that the illness was caused by the 'influence' of the planets.

There are passing – very passing – references, too, to European wars affecting England: 'War Declared against Spain January 4th 1762' – followed by 'A General Peace Proclaim'd' a year later on 22 March.

> War Declared against Spain. Jany 4th 1762.

> Tuesday March 22d 1763 A General Peace Proclaimed.

The winter of 1762/73 was an especially harsh one and our weather-obsessed diary keeper records this. On 8 January 1763, the *British Magazine* noted:

> The Thames was frozen over so hard at Isleworth that a fair was held on the ice. This lasted all day and many people attended from far and wide, with beer and other liquors on sale from a large booth erected on the ice. A round-about was put up for children and a keg of mutton was boil'd up for the assembled company.

It is likely that the 'roundabout' involved sitting on wooden 'vehicles' pushed round and round a circuit by a team of boys. Richard would doubtless have been able to keep himself from getting too cold at night, comforted by the warming pan filled with charcoal which the maid would have slid between the sheets before he retired to his bedchamber. The warming pan, intricately decorated with paisley shaped swirls, and with a long plain handle, survives, though in poor condition.

What Richard does not record is that the hard frost caused considerable damage to London Bridge. Work in clearing the old buildings had finished, and the central span of the bridge had been widened by removing one of the 'starlings' in order to create a single 'Great Arch' midway along the bridge. In the cold snap the river froze and blocked all the other arches, causing a far greater force of water through the central gap. This in turn damaged the foundations of the Great Arch. Londoners must have started to despair of the endless repair costs.

1764 marked the year that houses were given street numbers for the first time. But for many years afterwards letters were sent with a more general set of directions – or else were delivered to a chosen address (such as a coffee house) from where they would be collected. The envelope shown here is from a letter posted to Richard in 1771 – 'To Richard Hall, Hosier, The Corner of Thames Street opposite Magnus Church London Bridge'.

Religion continued to play a central role in Richard's life. Reviewing his father's life at the start of the following century Richard's son Benjamin records:

> 1763 [Father] was baptized by Dr Gill under whose ministry he had sat with much pleasure for several years. This circumstance took place at the Barbican chapel on 14th December and on the 18th he was received into full communion with Dr Gill's Church at Carter Lane Southwark.

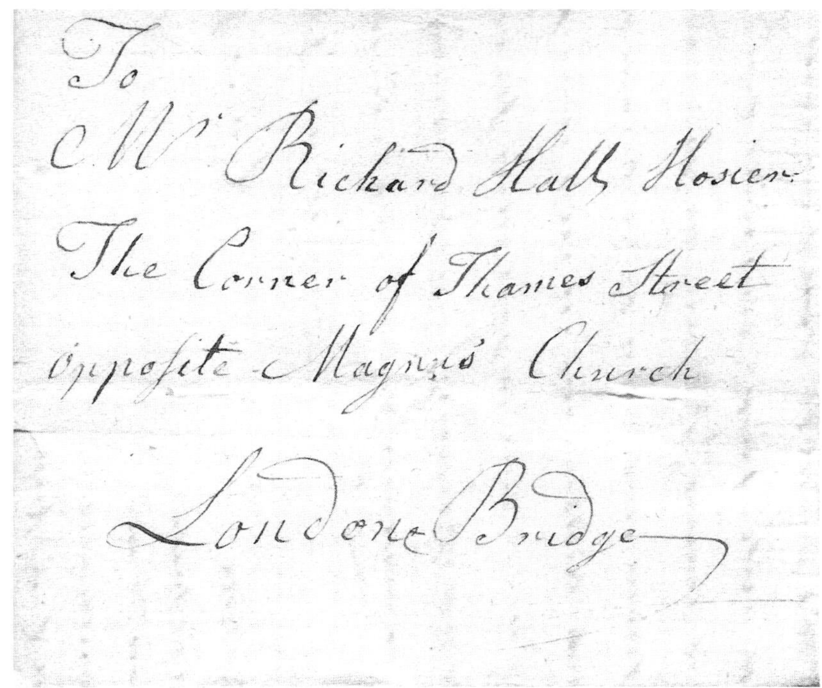
To
Mr Richard Hall Hosier
The Corner of Thames Street
opposite Magnus Church
London Bridge

Richard himself writes: '1763 December 5th –Gave experience into Dr Gill's Church 1763 December 14th – was Baptised at Barbican by Dr Gill.' 'Giving experience' meant explaining before the whole church how he had come to faith in Christ. This does not appear to have been a sudden decision – Richard had been, as we have seen, a devoted follower of Dr Gill for many years and an earlier entry reads: ' 1757 March 17th – gave towards Dr Gills new Meeting £20/0/0' – a generous gift by any measure, linked to Dr Gill's move to Carter Lane. Carter Lane Meeting Place was just a few hundred yards from Red Lion Street, and Richard attended services there on Friday evenings as well as once (sometimes twice) on Sundays.

A surviving letter from Frances Snooke dated 29 March 1765 shows that Richard's wife appears to have been suffering religious doubts – or at least, doubts as to her own faith. 'I am sorry you complain of such a dark and uncomfortable frame of Soul ... you seem my dear Sister to have the desires of Faith tho' you have not the Joys of it. It is a great Mercy to experience the former and a strong Encouragement to hope that in the Lord's time you will possess the latter.'

A little later Richard was interested to hear how the new chapel at Bourton was progressing. Frances wrote on 13 July, prefacing her letter with the comment: 'Mr Snooke's unavoidable engagements with the Meeting obliges him to imploy me as his secretary.' She went on to explain that the pulpit was ready to be installed, 'which I think may be call'd elegantly plain and neat as it has no carving about it'. Evidently Richard had announced that he would donate the pulpit cushion, and she asks: 'please to send it next week as we have some thought of using the Meeting the Sabbath after next. If not the pulpit and desk must be made agreeable to the size of the Cushion.' Richard presumably visited Bourton to inspect his new cushion a couple of months later, because the entry for 4 September reads 'Took Mrs Snooke behind me to Aylworth, when she fell off from the Horse on my opening a gate, but received no hurt.'

It is clear that William Snooke was much involved with the building of the Baptist meeting place. He also saw it as his duty to look after the preacher – his diaries show that he paid the Minister Benjamin Beddome two guineas every Quarter Day as well as contributing at Christmas to the cost of cleaning and heating the building in which he preached. William's philanthropy has to be seen in the context that he was never actually baptised, although he attended the services twice and sometimes three times every week. Beddome was to become an important spiritual adviser to Richard. He was, after all, pastor at Bourton for over half a century. He was four years older than Richard, wrote over eight hundred hymns and was a quietly spoken but effective preacher of the gospel.

Later the same year, on 21 December 1765, Richard lost his 'mother in law' (that is to say, stepmother) Martha Hall, aged sixty-three. A further harsh loss was to follow: '1766 May 25th died Frances my beloved sister in law of the smallpox. She had but recently visited us in London and on her return to Bourton fell ill and died in her 34th Year.' The actual exchange of letters between William and Richard during the period of the illness is most poignant. The news of Frances's illness must have come as dreadful shock to Richard and his wife since they had been entertaining the Snooke family in London just days before. The letters start with William commenting that Frances felt poorly during the journey back to Witney – that she was unable to come down to dinner, but had some bread in her wine and water, that she felt 'feverish, with a weariness in her Limbs'. He suspected that she had caught a cold. But the next day William writes: 'Oh my dear Brother and Sister – the cause of my dear Wife's disorder too clearly appears to be the Small Pox – the doctor makes no doubt about it. Our Distress is inconceivable. Pray remember her in your Prayers.' Daily updates followed – the description of her constant vomiting, and of the pocks covering her face chest, arms and legs.

> May 21 – Through Divine Goodness my dear Wife slept last night very comfortably and is now pretty cheerful, though blind and greatly swell'd. The pock begins to fill and to run together in the face, where 'twill be in One. 'Tis really a very awful distressing sight. She complains of her Throat, and the great soreness.

More letters followed, and then: 'May 24 – Yesterday morning very early I sent to Tewkesbury for a Physician, (Dr Perrold) who has been very successful in the Small Pox. He came before dinner and stayed all night. A blister had been put on the Back ... he ordered another last Night on the Arm.'

The same letter shows that Richard's eleven-year-old son Francis was staying with William – 'Franky sends his Duty – he is in no way troublesome – the little rogue is now my bedfellow.' William even found time from his troubles to recount that Franky 'needed some Green worsted stuff to lengthen his sleeves, which can't be wore without some Crimson is made Use of.' He also confirms that the boy was attending school in or near Bourton:

> The Master gives him a very good Character as to his Spelling, Writing, and Temper, that all the Boys love him ... Mr Huntley show'd me a specimen of Franky's writing – some of the letters are pretty well made; I dare say he will write a good hand soon. This was his first essay in joining hand, when you see it I dare say you'll think it a smart performance.

Sadly May 25th brought a letter from a mutual acquaintance Mr Palmer:

> Dear friend I must acquaint you about twelve a clock last Night without any material alteration the Lord was pleased to take Dear Mrs Snooke to Himself. I doubt not these will be heavy tidings to good Mrs Hall and your self... Dear Mr Snooke is so much oppress'd but desires me to lett you know the interment is designed for Wensday evening. If you can come down to pay your last respects to your valuable sister 'twill be very Agreeable to Mr Snooke tho distressing on so Mournfull an Occasion.

For the next two hundred years the full exchange of letters was incomplete – because all that remained with the Hall family papers were the letters from William to Richard. Thanks to a remarkable coincidence the full set of letters can now be reconstructed. In the 1970s two complete strangers met in British Columbia, each unaware of the other's family history. The talk turned to genealogy, and they discovered that one of them (my aunt) was descended from Richard Hall, and the other from William Snooke. More amazingly both sides had kept the original letters and in due course photocopies were exchanged completing a sad record of a devastating illness.

Back in 1766 Richard and Eleanor set off from London immediately – it must have been a hideous journey. Later Richard was to give details of the plaque which the family put up in memory of Frances. He states: 'A handsome tablet is erected to her memory at the chapel at Bourton.' From time to time (when it is not covered by 1970s plasterboard) it can still be seen:

> In a vault beneath is deposited all that was mortal of Frances Snooke, wife of William Snooke of Bourton-on-th-Water, Gentleman. The immortal part dismiss'd about the dawning of the Sabbath, from a body perishing by that dreadful disease the small Pox. She was the eldest surviving Daughter of that eminent Christian Benjamin Seward of Bengeworth in the County of Worcester, Gentleman. In whom the Divine Graces planted in the best of soils, a most amiable sweetness of Temper sprung up and flourished. And far wide diffused their fragrance.

> The daughter was the exact Portraiture of her much valued father Every Alliance to whom Was an Honour – a Blessing.

The death of Frances is a reminder of what a potent killer smallpox was in eighteenth-century England – it was the equivalent of cancer and heart disease today, being responsible for perhaps one in three of all deaths.

A portrait of Anne Snooke shortly after her marriage to William Snooke.

One year later, on 4 June 1767, 'Bro. William' remarried. His bride was his cousin Anne Snooke from Chipping Sodbury, who thus achieved the unusual distinction of marrying without changing her name. Before her marriage to William, Anne had gone to Evesham to be inoculated against smallpox – William notes in his 1768 diary for 3 March: 'Mrs Snooke and her sisters came home ... from being inoculated after an absence of almost six weeks, a year ago today.' Inoculation had been introduced into England in 1721 by Lady Mary Wortley Montagu after she had witnessed the custom in Turkey. It involved introducing scab material from someone with a mild form of the disease into a scratch, usually made on the arm. This, it was hoped, would give the 'patient' immunity from more lethal strains of the disease. The process was known as variolation and doctors found it a lucrative sideline. It was, however, a very inexact science, and many people died from being variolated.

William and Anne were to have five daughters – the first being named Nancy, born 7 December 1768. William's diary records his evident delight, the more so because he had had no children with his first wife, Frances. He writes: 'My Dearest Mrs Snooke made me a present of a Daughter about 11 at night. Paid Dr Paxford for delivering my dear wife 3 guineas. Paid the ringers on account of my little girl 2d. Mrs Snooke – put into her purse Three Guineas' He then paid franks on no fewer than twenty-six letters written to notify the birth of his daughter.

Nancy pictured as a young girl.

Nancy was a bright child, full of laughter, but, alas, short-lived. There appears in Richard's diary, Wednesday 7th April 1773: 'Heard the Melloncholly Account of the Death of poor Nancy Snooke, three days since. She was but four years old.' It is hard to imagine the horror of what happened – Nancy saying goodnight to her father before going upstairs to her bedroom to get ready for bed, expecting her mother to follow shortly afterwards to say prayers and extinguish the candle. The maid had just taken up a boiling hot cup of milk and a crust of bread for Nancy's supper. The child presumably started to eat the bread and while drinking the milk scalded herself. This caused her to choke on the bread. She was already dead when her mother came upstairs, minutes later. To lose a child with such suddenness must have been truly awful – and no doubt afterwards every single 'bed-time ritual' for the other children must have reminded William and Anne of that fateful night.

Going back to the start of 1767, Richard's diary opens with the sad news for 2 January: 'My Wife Miscarried in the Evening – the Lord is Gracious to her.' He notes that it was cold and foggy all week – it must have been a miserable time. But a week later he states that Eleanor was better and the diary turns to other events – 'Ale tapped January 14th.' It was Richard's birthday on the fifteenth ('The Lord has spared Me to ye return of another Birth Day – may I live more in his Fear, and to his Glory'). Perhaps he drank too much of the ale – the whole of the next week was taken up with references to 'taking Physick'.

Around this time Richard appears to have decided on a change of direction for the business – following the death of his father he apparently felt able to move the business into new areas. From manufacturing and retailing silk stockings he branched out into the wholesaling of stockings, as well as diversifying into the sale of other silk items. The shop was not well placed to promote the sale of fashion fabrics and it is likely that Richard was keen to take advantage of the incredible appetite of Londoners for fashionable garments of all sorts. Astonishingly, Londoners were willing to part with a quarter of their income on clothes and fashion accessories. Trade must have increased significantly and Richard wanted to move nearer the more fashionable parts of town where he could sell to a wider, more discerning audience. The ideal compromise appears to have been to move to the end of the newly refurbished London Bridge – only a few hundred yards from the Red Lion Street premises but in many ways a world away. For Richard moved not to the Southwark end but the City end – suddenly he was aiming at a totally different clientele. Passing trade was constant and he could expand his business to include the sale of the whole range of silk clothing – waistcoats in particular. If Richard hankered after something prestigious then 'Number One London Bridge' must have sounded good (although in practice street numbering was still not commonplace).

That address is now used to describe the site of a giant marble and glass edifice on the Southwark end of the bridge, but Richard makes it clear he is talking about premises in Lower Thames Street 'opposite St Magnus' Church' – that is, north of the river. In the late 1760s the address would have been just as prestigious

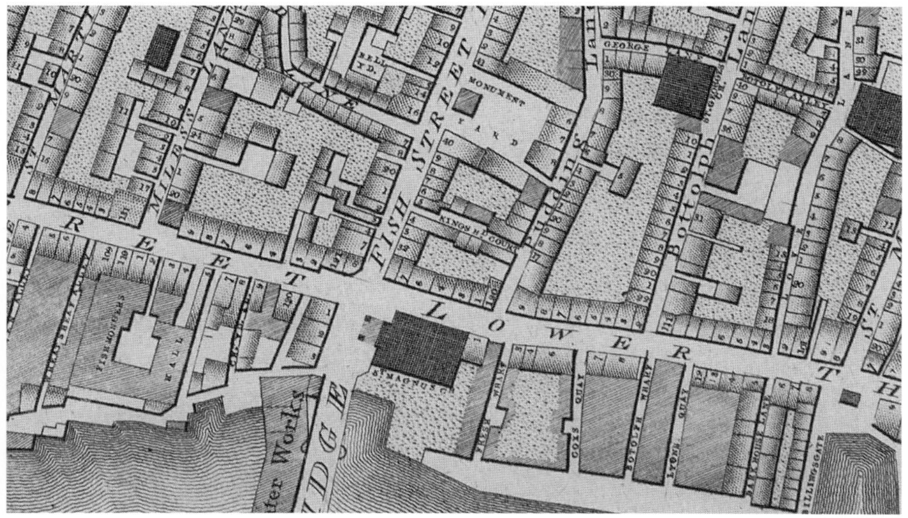

as it is today. All other houses on the bridge having been demolished some years previously, this was almost the first building which a traveller would encounter, having crossed the river from Southwark. The detail from the Horwood Map on the previous page (courtesy of Motco Enterprises Ltd.) shows the entrance to Number One London Bridge immediately opposite the church, in a row of three behind the waterworks. As mentioned earlier, London Corporation had made improvements and repairs to the bridge, rebuilding it with a larger central arch to facilitate the flow of water and the easy passage of shipping, and the removal of all the old buildings had meant that bridge users were no longer funnelled into a narrow gap some twenty feet wide, but could use the full width of forty-six feet. The authorities were, however, prepared to allow new building on the approach to the bridge – that is, constructed on the riverbank rather than on the bridge itself. Richard entered into an agreement for a lease of sixty-one years with the Corporation, enabling him to sign a building contract with a Mr Poultney for the completion of the building. He notes: 'November 1766 – entered into an agreement for finishing a new-built house on the corner of Lower Thames Street London Bridge.'

Richard's account book contains the following details and expenses for the change of premises:

Lease 10th Dec	1765	
Lease	61	
Expires	1826	
Agreement not to exceed		£850.0.0
Sundry extra Bill, surveyor etc		228.7.7
		£1078.7.7
Papering		5.16.0
Purchase of £4.5.0. [ground rent]		
of Mr Poultney		91.15.6
		1175.19.1.

There still exists the insurance policy – covering fire only – in the sum of £800 with Royal Exchange Assurance describing the house as being 'under construction'. It took four months to finish off the building works: '1767 April 3rd Remov'd shop Goods to my New House, the Corner of Thames Street. April 6th opened shop there.' Richard was much honoured – his friend and spiritual adviser, Dr Gill, dined with Richard that night ('Spent a little time in Prayer').

Richard had previously been involved largely in the manufacture of stockings – mostly in silk since no one of fashion would wear woollen stockings – but now he was able move more towards general haberdashery, with the sale of general fabrics such as lace, damask, linen and so on. One or two display cards still remain, one for velvet and another for 'Bat' – the name for the

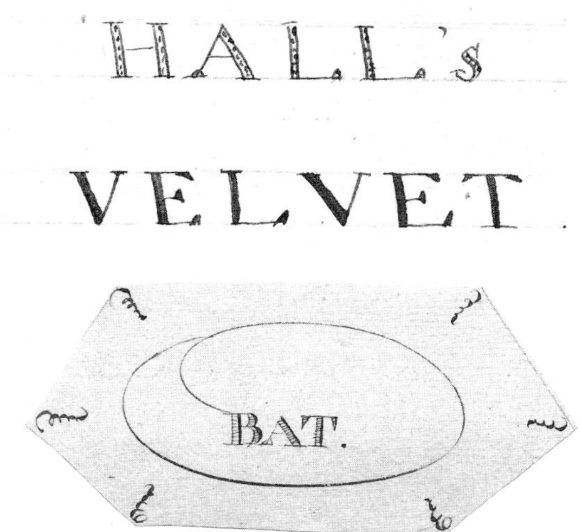

cotton wadding used to fill quilts and padded garments. Displays were discreet rather than 'in your face' and consisted of small drawings showing the fashions of the day, or occasionally of fashion dolls – showing current fashions in miniature. Modern-style shop displays, with mannequins and display models, simply did not exist.

Some idea of the quantities and range of stock held in the new shop appears from an auction list which was issued by one 'Thomas Dalton, Sworn Broker, of Warehouses at No 4 Bishopsgate Within' in around 1770. It probably reflects a bankruptcy sale of a similar haberdashery and hosiery shop and the fact that Richard kept the list suggests that he may have attended the auction – but unfortunately it is incomplete because Richard cut it up and used it as a temporary book binding, and all that remains are details of Lots 151 to 230. These refer to:

4 superfine Winchelsea clear lawn
10 double silesias
5 two and three coloured cottons
4 superfine ditto and laylock striped
3 chints
Sundry red and white printed linen handks
Ditto fine lawn
2 yard-wide figured dimities
2 Damascus
12 silk waistcoat pieces
12 pair spun silk hose
23 dozen pairs white silk hose
10 mottled ditto
8 dozen pairs black plain knit worsted hose
2 dozen black ditto
24 pair white China silk ditto
71 two thread worsted breeches pieces
5 dozen silk mits.

This demonstrates that items such as trousers and waistcoats were bought in as pieces and then 'finished to fit'. 'Dimity' was a type of coarse cotton or flannel. 'Damascus' or damask got its name from the city of Damascus and was the name for finely worked – and often glittering – silk fabric. 'Laylock' was a dialect form of 'lilac' and 'silesias' were fine linen sheets originating from the region in Germany of the same name.

The diaries indicate that Brother William came up to London in April 1767 – but without the whole family, being accompanied only by 'his Boy Robert' (actually his young cousin). There was the usual round of 'taking tea', and a visit to Westminster Abbey, but the lack of entertainment suggests that Richard's energies were taken up entirely by business – including provisioning Francis Kearse for his Kent trip (27 April). Francis was Richard's uncle and appears to have been involved in the business – as will be explained later on. Richard also had the worry of an attempted break-in ('The past night had an attempt of Rogues upon New House. Cool. Began New Medicine').

At much the same time as the shop move Richard and his wife decided that the accommodation in Stockwell where they had been living was not to their liking and they 'removed to a fine house …

leased in Peckham in Surry': '1767 June 13th Slept at New House for first Night.' Peckham was a prosperous village well known at the time for its market-gardening activities. In a time before refrigeration, fruits and vegetables needed to be transported quickly to the markets in the City, and Peckham was ideally situated. There are even records of figs, grapes and melons being grown in the locality. The entry for 23 June suggests that there was finishing off to be done at the kitchen of the new house – 'a very hurrying time putting up the smoak jack' – followed by a hectic round of visitors coming to take tea and inspect the new premises. The 'smoak jack' would have been installed up the chimney and would have been in addition to the more common crane used to lower pots and pans above the flames of the open fire. The simple crane was capable of being swivelled so that pans suspended from it could be retrieved. The smoke jack was altogether more complicated. First described in a drawing by Leonardo da Vinci, it sought to harness the rising air from above the fire to turn a complex set of gears and pulleys in order to rotate the spit on which meats were roasted – the invention owes a great deal to the clock-making industry with its teethed wheels and gearings. The alternative was to employ a servant to turn the spit, which meant hours of drudgery. Fixing the jack, with its spiral-shaped vane inserted in the neck of the chimney (i.e. where it was at its narrowest and the force of hot air strongest) was not easy. Few of the jacks survive and they were generally regarded as being as expensive as they were inefficient!

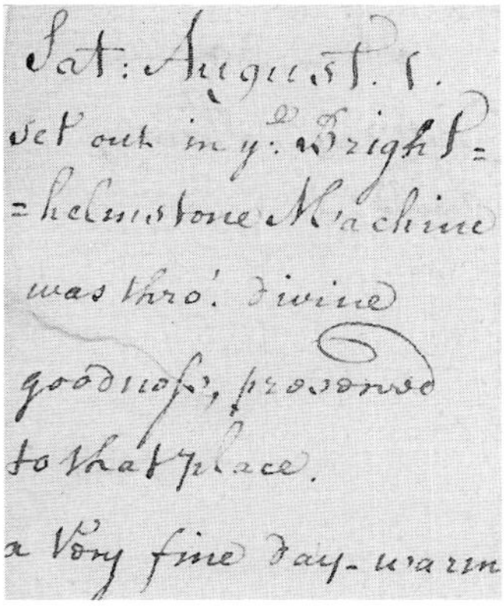

Richard appears to have been persuaded that his health would be improved if he went to the seaside, and 1 August saw him 'setting out in ye Brighthelmstone Machine' (i.e. for Brighton) and on the following day he 'bathed in the Sea, and through Divine goodness was carried through it better than I feared'. In fact, there was no stopping the intrepid swimmer and he took to the waters for the next three days before noting 'went again to Bathe but it did not agree with me' and that was the last of that nonsense! Instead, he 'went to sea on board the Packet with Wife – returned safe. Pretty fine Day – not so Hot'. But when the week was up, they left Brighton and 'set out for London – breakfast at Lewes, dinner at Godstone. Got home about 6 o'Clock'.

The following week after the trip to Brighton Richard notes: 'Went to Haberdashers Hall – partly agreed to come upon the Livery in a twelve month.' This would appear to be a reference to the fact that Richard had previously been trading (in Southwark) without actually taking up membership of the Livery Company – but now that he was trading from new premises at the City end of London Bridge he was caught by their long arms. So a year later we see the entry 'Friday 8th May – Fine morning, very mild. Went and took up my Freedom of City'. Freedom came at a price and his expenses book for the year contains the entry:

Taking up Freedom of City	4.5.0
Livery Fine –	25.14.6
Septr. 9. 1768 –	29.19.6

£25 14s. 6d. was a hefty penalty (the modern equivalent of perhaps £1,500), but paying the fine was inevitable if he wanted to run a business within the City boundaries. 'Taking up Freedom' of the City at a cost of £4 5s 0d meant that he was recognised as a free man entitled to vote at Meetings of the Livery Company – but he was also bound by their rules. He could grant apprenticeships to men who would automatically also become free on completion of their training. Richard retained the paper handed him by the Chamberlain of the City outlining what a free man should and should not do.

Richard retained his interest in royal events and on 24 November 1767 'went to Westminster to see the King go to the Houses [of Parliament]'. After that he stayed indoors for most of December and the entries for the year end with complaints about 'not being very well ... poorly with my face ... out of sorts with pain to my face and ears.' All that and worries about a dangerous conflagration, no doubt clearly visible in the night sky because he notes that on Christmas Day there was 'at 9 in the evening a great fire in Hounsditch – dreadful appearance'.

A

C H A R G E

Proper to be given by the

CHAMBERLAIN of the City of *LONDON*

T O A

PERSON on making him F R E E.

YOU ought to revere God and his holy religion, and not to *blaſpheme* or turn any part of his ſacred rights into *ridicule*; but eſpecially that part of it called the *Lord's Prayer*, or any other ſacred portion of the ſervice of the church of England: but above all, you muſt not directly nor indirectly, write, print, or publiſh, *in your own houſe*, any thing of evil tendency, to the bad example of others. You muſt carry yourſelf *affectionately* towards your *wife*, and your family and domeſtics. You muſt not *diſſipate* your fortune, in *whoring* or *gaming*, nor contract more debts than you are able *fully* to pay, without the aſſiſtance of either *ſocieties* or *individuals*. You muſt not deſtroy any of the bills, *bonds*, or notes of your creditors, or any other perſon, who, in unſuſpecting honeſty, may at any time intruſt you; and muſt apply *all* your property in the firſt place, towards the ſatisfaction of your creditors demands, without *ſecreting* the ſame to their prejudice and detriment.

You muſt not *embezzle* any money you may be intruſted with, whether it belongs to *hoſpitals*, *ſoldiers*, *orphans*, *foundlings*, or others. You muſt not obtain goods under *falſe* pretences, to the *ruin* of any perſon, his widow and Orphans. You muſt not let any perſons ſuffer by your *litigiouſneſs*, when they attempt to recover their juſt property from you. You muſt not write *libels*, or diſturb by *falſe pretences*, the peace and order of good government, as by law eſtabliſhed. You muſt engage in ſome *commerce*, *trade*, or *manufactory*, for the good of the community in general, and of this city in particular. You muſt alſo keep the peace towards all his majeſty's ſubjects, *without finding ſureties for your ſo doing*. And you muſt, in all other reſpects, conduct yourſelf as a good ſubject and citizen ought to do.

F I N I S.

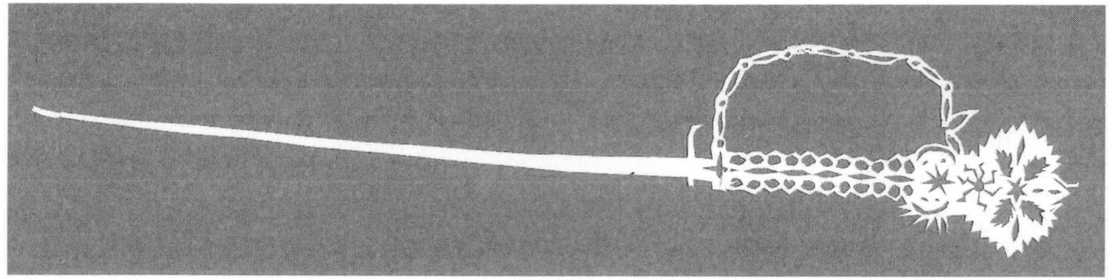

A paper cut-out of a suitably regal sword!

Meanwhile there was a succession of dinners to be given to impress friends ('September 18th Mr Hill Mr Marriott Captain Devon and Mr Stead dined at Peckham on a Haunch of Venison. Fine morning – very Dull afterwards, warm and Muggy. Francis Kearse returned from Sussex journey'). But most of the entries for the remainder of the year focused on either the weather (it was almost invariably 'Foggy' unless it was 'very Foggy') or his health ('Very much out of sorts with Pain in face and Ear' … 'Did not go out being poorly with face'). On fine days Richard records that he was enabled to walk from Peckham to the shop, and it was on one such occasion 'when the family were Mercifully accompanying me' that he suffered a Robbery, recorded thus in the *Daily Advertiser*:

> 1768 Saturday September 3rd WHEREAS on Saturday the 20th August last the home of Mr Hall of Peckham in Surry was broke open and robbed of two yellow silk and worsted Damask window curtains, the Furniture of two beds, one a red check the other a blue and white cotton with large figures, a fine white calico Quilt, a counterpane worked with a variety of colours, a small running pattern with a knotted fringe round it, a Toilet worked with yellow silk, a Scallop'ed Japanned Tea Board with a Shepherd and Shepherdess and a Basket of Fowls painted thereon, a Japanned waiter, a pair of fluted French metal candlesticks sundry sheets and table linen, some marked with EH, some with S, a Pair of Silver Salts with three feet marked REH, 2 table spoons marked REH. Whoever brings the above things to Mr Hall's. No. 1 London Bridge shall receive Five Guineas Reward, and a proportionate reward for any part thereof.

He never did recover the goods, but the description of the stolen items is entirely in keeping with prevailing tastes and fashions.

Each of the main bedrooms would typically have contained a four-poster bed. It would have been equipped with damask or linen curtains, and, as Richard describes, with a large white calico quilt and embroidered counterpane over monogrammed sheets and coloured, patterned blankets. The room would have included a washstand and a table for the 'toilet worked with yellow silk', along with a linen press where clothes would be kept. Typically the house would have contained a number of formal rooms with a high standard of comfort and decoration – parlour, drawing room and dining room. Walls would have been covered with wood panelling, particularly the dining room, whereas other rooms may well have been wallpapered. Britain was by then the leading manufacturer of wallpaper, exporting throughout Europe. Carpets would have been in use in all the main rooms, including the bedrooms. Pairs of curtains (in this case of yellow silk and worsted damask), which would be drawn across to meet in the middle, were comparatively recent, and wooden shutters would have been used – both to keep out the light at night, and to ensure privacy and cut out noise. Lighting was by means of candles – beeswax if Richard could afford it – and these would have been placed in front of wall-mounted mirrors or sconces. Heating would have come from fires – open grates burning coal, which needed to be cleaned out by the servants first thing every morning. Richard would have found that his new abode in Peckham boasted a kitchen with its own open fire for cooking on – previously food would have been prepared in the kitchen but then be taken through to the sitting room where it would have been boiled, steamed or spit-roasted over the fire. In Peckham, the food stayed in the kitchen until it was ready to be served.

Educating his growing family was an abiding concern of Richard's thoughts: '1767 – went with Wife & Patty in a Post-chaise to see Dear Billy at Pinner' ('Dear Billy' had been unwell, and the entry suggests that he had been sent away to a boarding school). He recovered and an entry shortly afterwards notes that Billy was able to return to school, 'the Lord having restored him'.

Term ended on 16 December, because the diary notes that 'Billy came home from Pinner' on that day. No other details of his schooling are given. In March 1768, Richard records: 'enterence fee son William learning to dance £1/1/0.' Dancing was not just a social grace – it was an opportunity for a young gentleman to learn how to move gracefully – how to bow, how to doff his hat, how to hold himself in public. In September 1768: 'A pair of Wainscot drawers for Patty for school £1/4/0' ('Wainscot' meant that it was made of wood panels). Evidently Patty started at her new school (Lamb's) the same month – at a fee of four guineas for the term, half a guinea for writing and five shillings for learning French. Her elder brother wasn't the only one to learn how to move gracefully in society: in 1769 Richard recorded 'Entrance for Patty learning to dance £1/1/0'. Mind you, she had started much earlier, as an entry six years before read: 'November 3rd – My daughter Martha began to learn to dance'. It is clear that as a girl Martha was expected to be able to read and write – although her education was nothing like as good as Richard had received and her letters, as an adult, are poorly written. As a child she was expected to know how to behave in polite company, to embroider samplers, compose silhouettes, and use her nimble fingers and fine eyesight to make pictures from paper cut-outs. Many of the cut-outs have been used as illustrations in this book.

The youngest child, Francis, was still staying at Bourton with William Snooke. The diaries note: '1768 Franky's pocket money 2d per week – reimbursed Wm 4s6d. 16 Jan – Franky returned to School behind John, being detained a week by the Weather. The horse fell with him in the Snow, but no injury received.' 'John' was Brother William's manservant, John Twining. Interestingly, William Snooke's own diary for the year showed that John was paid 'a year's wages due 10th October £6.0.0' (clearly he got board and lodging and clothing over and above this – but still not a lot to compensate for the delights of taking a young whipper-snapper like Franky on the back of his horse through the snow in the depths of January). The same diary shows that John agreed that the next year he would be paid an extra £2 'in lieu of victuals' – an indication that he probably had a smallholding of his own. John's clothing appears either to have been gifts from William of his older suits or took the form of a livery made by J. Payn: 'making coat and waistcoat for John 9s6d. Ditto frock 3 shillings'.

Like all parents, Richard would have been pestered by his children to have a pet, so in September that year the family acquired 'a glass globe for Fish' at a cost of six shillings and sixpence.

It had become customary for the Snookes to come up to town once a year to see Richard, usually in April but staying for as long as seven or eight weeks. It must have been quite a challenge keeping everyone occupied. Thus Richard writes: '1768 April Showing Brother & Sister Snooke and her Sister the Tower – 6 shillings.' Strictly speaking, it was not 'her sister' but rather the 25-year-old Elizabeth Snooke, sister to William Snooke. She was a cousin of William's (second) wife, and features more in the years to come... It appears that then, as now, the Tower of London was a major attraction, holding, among other things, the Crown Jewels. Besides, if the visitors tired of seeing the regalia, and the buildings themselves, there were always the wild animals to see. The Tower was the original home of the King's Menagerie (the last animals were to be relocated to London Zoo in 1834). Lions, elephants, zebras – all were to be found in cages kept within the compound of the Tower.

Another member of the family came to visit later in the year: 'October – Shewing Polly Snooke the Tower and Wax work £0/3/11.' Let us hope that the Snooke entourage were dressed for London society, and that William did not venture up to town in his new 'suit of clothes (viz. Wilton Coat, Red Knap Waistcoat & Black shagg breaches)' which he had just acquired for £4/8/0 and which sound far more suited to life back on the farm!

William's own diary of the April visit gives a better idea of the hectic schedule of visits and suggests that William picked up most of the expenses (perhaps not surprising since his income that year was a whopping £2,060 – far, far greater than the figure Richard earned):

> 1st April – went to the Chapel Royal. Saw the King & Queen, afterwards the zebra (two shillings) and elephants (three shillings). Gave the Chapel keeper five shillings.

A LIST *of His Majesty's* Regalia, *besides Plate and other Rich Things, at the* Jewel House *in the Tower of* London.

1—THE *Imperial Crown*, that all the Kings of *England* have been Crown'd with, from the Time of *Edward* the Confessor.

2—The *Orb* or *Globe*, held in the Kings Left Hand at the Coronation, on the Top of which is a Jewel near an Inch and a half in Height.

3—The *Royal Scepter* with the *Cross*; which has another Jewel of great Value under it.

4—The *Scepter* with the *Dove*, the Emblem of Peace.

5—St. *Edward's* Staff, all beaten Gold, carried before the King at His Coronation.

6—A *Rich Salt Seller of State*, the Figure of the *Tower*, used on the King's Table at the Coronation.

7—*Curtana*, or the *Sword of Mercy*, born between the Two Swords of Justice, Spiritual and Temporal.

8—A Noble Silver *Font*, double Gilt, that the Royal Family are Christened in.

9—A large Silver *Fountain*, presented to King *Charles* the Second by the Town of *Plymouth*.

10—THE Rich *Crown of State* His Majesty wears on His Throne in Parliament, in which is a large *Emerald*, seven Inches round, a Pearl the finest in the World, and a Ruby of inestimable Value.

11—His Royal Highness the Prince of *Wales's* Crown.

12—Queen *Mary's* Crown, Globe and Scepter, with the Diadem she wore in proceeding to her Coronation.

13—An *Ivory Scepter*, with a *Dove*, made for the late King *James* His Queen.

14—The *Golden Spurs*, and the *Armillas*, wore at the Coronation.

15—The *Ampulla*, or *Eagle of Gold*, which holds the Holy Oyl the Kings and Queens of *England* are Anointed with, and the *Golden Spoon* that the Bishop pours the Oyl into; which are great pieces of Antiquity.

Price to see the whole with Company One Shilling each Person, or a single Person One Shilling and Six-pence.

Well, it is good to see he got his priorities right – first go and see the King and Queen, then the wild animals … he would have reached the Chapel Royal through the State apartments inside St James' Palace. Later the same day:

> Coach from Cheapside to the Horse Guards half a crown, and from St James to Harley Street the same amount.

> Turnpike 2d. Dined and drank tea with Mrs Vanderwall and came home in her coach betwixt 9 and 10.
>
> 4th April – went with party to Covent Garden after dining with Mr Pearson – Dr Faustus – (15 shillings) followed on the next 2 days by the Lord Mayors Procession. Saw the Preparation for the Dinner at the Mansion House on Wednesday 6th April and on 9th April saw the wax-works in Fleet Street (3 shillings for three). After seeing the wax works went into Lancaster Inn Gardens. The following day (Sunday) coach to and from the Magdalen 3/6d (plus one shilling each as a donation to the church) to hear Mr Dodd's text on Luke 7.47. Monday 11th April we went to the Town again in the morning. Afternoon to the theatre in Drury Lane to see Romeo & Juliet (3s.9d, coach 2s., oranges 6d.). The next day at the Tower seeing Lions & keepers 2s.3d. Regalia 4s., Warden 1s., cakes 3d. and seeing Neville's Machine (5s. for the five of us). Later went again to Covent Garden and had the pleasure of standing the whole Play (Hamlet). Play and coaches 9s.6d., macaroons another 8d.

In fact macaroons were William's weakness – he bought 'eight penn'orth' just about every other day!

> 22nd April – went to Westminster Abbey and the following day went to see Old Bancroft in St Hollins Church who had been buried this forty years. (Paid sextoness at Great St Hollins 1s., Mansion Vault 2d.) 27th April accompanied the party to Ranelagh Gardens, a most enjoyable diversion. 29th April – went to Greenwich with 4 horses. Mr William's chaise came for us about 10. Saw the Hospital. Dining at Greenwich 10s.6d.

This was a popular outing – Defoe, for example, writes of his visit to Greenwich in glowing terms:

> I took boat at Tower-Wharf, sending my horses to meet me at Greenwich ... which is the most delightful spot of ground in Great-Britain; pleasant by situation, those pleasures increased by art, and all made completely agreeable by the

> accident of fine buildings, the continual passing of fleets of ships up and down the most beautiful river in Europe; the best air, best prospect, and the best conversation in England.

And still the sightseeing went on:

> 2nd May went to the Museum in the afternoon – 2 coaches 3s. Seeing Birds & Beasts in Holborn (nine of us at sixpence each – 4s.6d.) 4th May went to Sadlers Wells and saw a rehearsal – 5 of us – 12s.6d., coach 5s., coachman 6d.

Dick Sadler had started his 'musick house' a hundred years earlier. When the enterprising Sadler discovered a well on the site he changed the name of his premises to Sadlers Wells and promoted the idea of 'taking the waters' while being entertained by musical performances, plays and exhibitions of juggling and tumbling. It had no connection at that stage with ballet.

> 9th May – went again to Ranelagh (going in 10s.6d., coach 10s.6d., coachman 2s.)

Ranelagh was altogether more select than Vauxhall – perhaps because of the entrance fee of half a crown. However, this included either tea or coffee. There was no alcohol. The gardens adjoined the Pensioners Hospital at Chelsea and it was used to house balls, concerts and dinners. The most visible attraction was a giant rotunda – 150 feet in diameter – housing a bandstand. Music was played every evening. Had they gone four years earlier the party would have been able to watch a young Mozart playing a duet with his sister.

And then there were the gifts William made:

> Gloves for Mrs Snooke and Betty 2/6. Put in Mrs Snooke's purse 5 guineas. Necklace and ear-rings for Mrs S £1/0/0, ditto for Mrs Pearson £1/1/0. Paid Messrs Third & Picket for 4 silver salts, spoons Glasses and engraving as a present for Mrs Pearson £6/16/0. Mr Mighell for a Paste Sprig for the hair for Mrs Snooke (asked 12s) 10/6d. Hairbrush and hair-pin for Mrs Snooke 4/6d ditto for Betsy 5/0. Ring with

> my hair set in a tress in it, with garnets, for Mrs Snooke 18/-. Paid Mrs Slade for Mrs Snooke's bonnet 16 shillings and handkerchief £1/10/6 Paid Mr Langton for Mrs Snookes Head Handkerchief 5/4d. Ditto for handkerchiefs for Betsy & Polly 9/-.

There was also his personal grooming: 'shaving at Greenwich – once – 1/- Barber at Newington ditto' as well as his more regular barber ('shaving 44 times 18 shillings'). There were the odd breakages 'repairs to coach having broken a whole Glass by shutting the door 10/6d.' Finery for his head-wear involved 'paying for gold band, button and loop for my Hat 18/-' There were presents to the servants, too: 'Brother Hall's servant 2 shillings. Brother Hall's two maids 2 shillings. Mrs Pearson's two maids each 7 shillings, boy 7 shillings, and Man Robert 4/6d.' Presumably the servants' gratuities reflected the different length of time spent with each of the Pearson and Hall households (and incidentally establishes that Richard had two maids and a manservant, and that 'cook' was not a separate title in Richard's house).

Visits to London provided an opportunity to have repairs carried out at William's home ('Grinding knives and scissors 10d, cleaning Mrs Snooke's watch 4 shillings, mending box one shilling') and of buying useless oddments ('paid G Ribright for a pocket camera obscura (of no use to me) 10/6d'). There were the expenses of travel – 'horses at livery in Aldermanbury £1/7/0, ostler 2/-, turnpikes, payments to waterman (4d) visits to the coffee house (4d) payments for three places in the Stage[coach] at 1/3d each 3/9d'. There was always the risk of encountering the mob and having to buy them off ('gave Wilkes' mob as a passport 1/-'). There was money to be lost at games of chance ('Lost by Mrs Snooke, Self and Betsy at the game of the Goons 2/5d'). There were Lottery tickets to be bought and of course, before returning to the Cotswold wilderness he needed to replenish provisions: 'Currant jelly bought of Mr Filstead 2/8d A dozen of rum £1/4/0 Almond powder for Mrs Snooke ninepence.' Crockery for the Manor House needed replacing: 'Messrs Wood & Lamden for China £8/5/0.'

In all, William paid out over £150 during his seven-week stay in London – but it was money he could well afford since his investments during that same period yielded him nearly £200. These investments included interest on a loan made by him to Richard – which looks very much as though Richard borrowed £350 towards the cost of constructing and fitting out the new shop from his brother-in-law, paying it back by payments of principal of £100 per annum and interest at 4 per cent. That year he was one month late with the instalment – and had to pay William an additional two shillings by way of interest for the thirty days' delay. He may have been 'family' but business was business!

All good things come to an end, and the time came for the visitors to go home. 'Bro. William and his Wife left London to return to Bourton 17th May at 9 o'clock. My Son William accompanied them, travelling via Oxford to visit the Colleges and then to Woodstock – they could not see the House, the Duke being there.'(Brother William was not always so timid – there is a later diary entry in which he mentions that he arrived at Blenheim after six o'clock, when the Palace would normally close, but asked if the Duke would kindly allow him to view the house and grounds and that the Duke graciously granted an audience.)

Three months later Richard and Eleanor got the chance to visit William at Bourton, as is apparent from William's diary entry: '9th August 1768 – Went in the Chariot alone to Oxford to meet Brother & Sister Hall and Patty. Got there about 7 o'clock. Found 'em safely arrived.' William celebrated their arrival by buying six pounds of eels at Witney ('wanting one ounce') for 4s. 5d. – plus a further sixpence for the basket to put them in. They ate well: William ordered 'half a hundred crayfish' from T. Reynolds (2s.), paid John Phillips half a crown for a goose, and 3s. 6d. for a pig (plus 2d. for killing it). Sunday 14 August involved consuming tongue (bought from Giles Thomas for 1s. 6d.), then loin of veal followed by rice pudding. The party visited Evesham, dining at Badsey and no doubt visiting the Bengeworth estate. Then it was back to Bourton for another half hundred of crayfish (sounds more like shrimps!) bought from Mr Reynolds for 2s. and a three-and-a-half pound trout costing 2s. 7½d. That appears to have been consumed with bread pudding and a fillet of veal – no doubt washed down with some of the three dozen bottles of 'mountain wine' bought on 5 August for £2 18s. 6d.

William was no doubt feeling flush with money – he had just

completed the sale of Compton Abdale Rectory to Lord Chalfont for £1,141 (2 August). The cash was not idle for long – within days he had lent Mr Beale one thousand pounds at 4-per-cent interest, 'secured by his mortgage of his estate at Bourton'. That left more than enough in hand to buy 'ten yellow dishes, 36 plates, 2 yellow mugs, 12 small plates (yellow) a quart mug and 3 flower pots' for a total of two guineas.'

The days seem to have been taken up visiting local worthies, taking tea, going in the chaise to Stow, Fairford and Letchlade, receiving a haunch of venison from Mr Ansell and yet more eating ('Beans – the last and young – and bacon, loin of veal, followed by Aunts Pudding'). They went to Oxford but forgot that it was race week and found that 'all was confusion there'. But the following day (31 August) 'Brother Sister and Patty set out about 7 o'clock for London in the Machine (Kemp's)', leaving William to return to Bourton via a shopping trip in Oxford to buy two shuttlecocks, two shuttledores, a brush for jewels, a toothpick case, two sticks, two butter-patters and 'a padlock for Nora' at a cost of 13s. 6d. Another thirteen shillings went on buying cream cheese, paying the turnpikes, hiring horses at Burford, buying dinner for John and tipping the ostler.

That weekend the Snookes invited their friend William Clifford 'and all his family' round for lunch where they dined on shoulder of veal, cold buttock of beef and apple dumplings. History does not record what Richard and his wife ate after they emerged from Mr Kemp's 'machine', but maybe it was the 42lb Cheshire cheese he bought for fourteen shillings earlier in the visit!

Late in the decade we find Richard visiting a 'bagnio' to find relief from his health problems: 'December 7th 1768 Cupped at the Bagnio Newgate Street £0.3.6.' This somewhat unpleasant treatment involved heated cups being placed upon the back, causing the skin to blister. This, it was believed, would draw out the toxins. The blisters were then pierced and the serum extracted. Cupping is still used today as an 'alternative' medicine. Anyone visiting a 'bagnio' needed to know what they were letting themselves in for – at best, they were reputable places where people would go for hot baths and treatments such as cupping. More generally, however, they were simply brothels, where rooms could be rented by the hour, so knowing which one was respectable was perhaps like knowing which massage parlour to go to today.

7

The 1770s

The decade started with more purchases, more visits and more changes for Richard:

> 1770 January 6 – A Japan'd kitchen £2.2.0

The word 'kitchen' was sometimes applied to a utensil used in the kitchen. This was probably a tea urn, finished with black lacquerwork.

> 1770 July 6th Bound my Son William Seward Hall Apprentice to me.

William would have been just under sixteen years old, much the same age as Richard when he had been apprenticed. In time, he would inherit a very different business from the one founded by his grandfather Francis Hall.

> 1770 October Showing Polly Snooke the Tower £0.3.11 Ditto The Wax Work 1771 April 25th – went with General Whitmore Mr and Mrs Snooke, Mr Gifford and my wife to see the Mint at the Tower.

The Mint had been based at the Tower since medieval times, but in practice there was very little activity at the Mint in 1771 – a few gold coins were being minted – guineas but no half-guineas. There was no silver minted at all in that year – contributing to a drastic shortage of silver coins. The price of silver had risen to such a degree that the Mint simply could not afford to buy the ingots, because they would make a loss on each coin. Silver prices had soared between 1756 and 1763 (the duration of the Seven

Years' War) because output from the main silver mines in Germany collapsed. This coincided with the exhaustion of the mines in the west of England, where silver had been separated from lead since Roman times. The problem was compounded when Spain terminated all trade between Great Britain and Spanish America – thereby closing off the stream of silver which had flowed into the country in the previous centuries. The chaos this caused would last throughout most of the reign of George III, and was only ended in 1816 when Lord Liverpool decided to move the currency onto the gold standard and to make silver into a token currency (i.e. the intrinsic value of the metal in silver coins became substantially less than the face value). Silver was thereafter intended to be reserved for coins of low face value.

Meanwhile, the effect of the lack of activity at the Mint – by then the only one in the country – was to cause all sorts of difficulties for tradesman like Richard. Those coins which were in circulation were becoming increasingly worn – many coins from the reign of William III ninety years earlier were still in use and they were badly flattened or worn – so much so that there was a risk of forgery by unscrupulous counterfeiters issuing mere blanks of silvery metal and passing them off as coins of the realm. Alternatively, lighter coins of a similar size were brought in from abroad and passed off as the more valuable shillings and sixpences. Banknotes were never in general circulation at this time – not surprising since the minimum value was £10. To make matters worse, shopkeepers could be faced with having to accept payment of sums of up to £25 in silver. But things had been even harder – up until an Act of Parliament in 1774 there was no limit on the amount of poor-quality (i.e. badly worn and clipped) coins which could be palmed off on a trader such as Richard – sometimes as much as 30 per cent below its correct weight. The copper coinage was little better – only the halfpenny and farthing were minted in 1771. There was a shortage of copper, although unofficial tokens were issued in later years – for instance using copper from the mines in Anglesey. These tokens were technically illegal – they infringed the royal prerogative. Worse still, the tokens were often of use only within a very limited area and a token given to Richard in Oxford might be unacceptable (and hence valueless) by the time he reached Evesham.

* * *

In October 1771 Richard lost his revered pastor the Reverend John Gill D.D. aged seventy-three. Of this bereavement he writes:

> Great is his loss in the Church and much felt by me. It is a great affliction when we know the worth of our privileges by the want of them, especially our spiritual mercies. It is possible to set too great an esteem on man – perhaps I did not prize my faithful Minister as I ought to have done. I wish I had improved more under his sound Ministry. I now will greatly miss him. Will the Lord be pleased, as a token for good to me, to bring me into a good fold and give me an appetite for His Word and Ordinances. I desire to be thankful I have my pastor's works to consult, which I much value.

Indeed he did have the pastor's works to consult, for Richard had written out every sermon which he had heard from the good doctor over the past twenty-five years and had these bound up. In January 1772 Richard decided to have printed – at his own expense (£1 14s 6d) – two hundred copies of *What I Remember of Dr Gill*, which he then proceeded to hand out to his friends and acquaintances.

But Richard's hope that he was to be 'brought into a good fold' was not to be fulfilled. Richard seems to have been much vexed by the goings-on at his church – he refers to his sadness at matters being 'very quarrelsome' and starts to go on early-morning walks: 'Walk'd over London Bridge and Black Friars Bridge before Breakfast' (30 July). He was still attending Mr Rippon's services – and indeed having him round for tea – but matters were coming to a head and on 16 August he records 'was at Church meeting. Very disagreeable disputes and contentions'. Later in the year (11 October) he records: 'Was at Church Meeting – things very confused. A protest against the proceedings delivered in – signed by 19 persons. Very fine day. Like Summer. Cool.' There is a reference to Mr Rippon being ordained (11 November – 'to my great concern'). Later his son was to write:

> In consequence of a division in the Church on the death of their Minister my father's mind appears to have been very

> unhappy and for a time he was unsettled. Much animosity and contention existed in consequence of the majority of the Church choosing Mr Rippon, (afterwards Doctor), who was ordained to the pastoral Office November 11th, 1773. My father was one of the minority who signed the protest against this step, and with that minority chose Mr Button to be their pastor, for whom it appears that they built a new Place, but owing to some shyness between the members he discontinued his attendance and in 1776 was set aside by the Church.

Richard always viewed this as most ungenerous conduct on the part of the Church. He never forgave Rippon, who must have been as different from Dr Gill as chalk from cheese. John Rippon was a mere twenty-one years old when he succeeded the great scholar, and in Richard's eyes he had neither the talent nor the learning of his High Calvinist predecessor. Born in Tiverton in 1751, Rippon brought a lively, impressive and popular style of preaching which would have horrified the more solemn, thoughtful Richard. Besides, the family diaries show a much more personal slant on the discord. John Rippon took a fancy to Richard's daughter Martha – then just sixteen years old, and Richard was having no Devonshire hothead messing with her affections! Spurned by the family, John Rippon turned his attentions elsewhere and soon found an alternative bride.

Richard's son's diaries take the story further:

> On 20th August, 1776 my father was much pleased by the baptism of his beloved wife at Leominster by Mr Thomas and on the 6th November, 1777 that pleasure was enhanced by his daughter [Martha] giving in her experience to the same Church and being baptized by the same minister on the 20th of the same month.

Such pleasure was short-lived because two years later daughter Martha 'defected' – back to Dr Rippon's church! Richard was horrified. His relationship with his daughter deteriorated. It looks as though Richard regarded her as something of a 'wild child'. Matters improved in time but at some stage after 1785 (when she got married) contact dwindled to the extent that they barely spoke or corresponded. For the last ten years of his life they never met or wrote to each other, and Richard was to die without resolving their differences. It appears to have been a one-sided silence to begin with – there still exists a sad letter from Martha to her father, pleading for forgiveness and understanding, and ending with the words 'I remain your affectionate though afflicted unhappy & distressed daughter.' Richard was apparently unmoved, and he also bore the grudge against John Rippon to his grave. He made his distaste for Dr Rippon clear to all and sundry. A letter from a friend who was the Baptist minister in Bedford dated 16 February 1773 reads: '...you complain in your letter you are like a sheep without a shepherd. May the great Head of the Church afford you support, relief, direction and consolation. But I always think it must dismay a humble minister to think of succeeding the great Dr Gill of precious memory.'

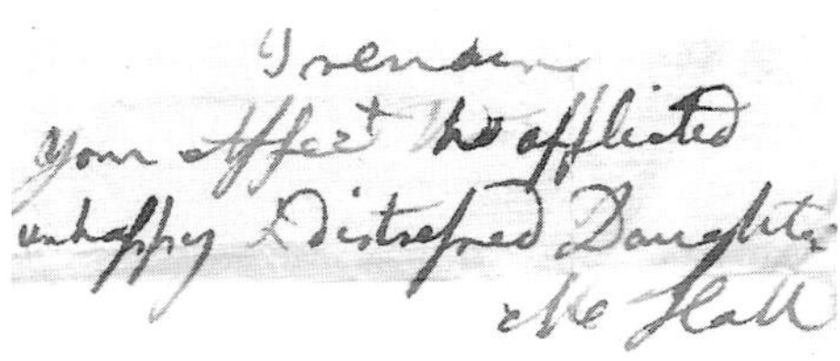
I remain
Your Affect tho afflicted
unhappy Distressed Daughter
M Hall

The dislike was reciprocated – at Richard's funeral Dr Rippon wrote a short eulogy, not, as was normal, praising the deceased for his fine qualities, but stating: 'Mr Hall was certainly not distinguished among his religious connections for the felicity of his disposition but we are given to understand that he has left behind him the testimony of an affectionate husband a kind father and a sincere friend.' In other words, 'somehow his family put up with him, but to everyone else he was a pain in the neck.'

In general the year 1773 seems to have started extremely cold – after a 'dribbling sort of day' on January 28th it turned 'very cold' then 'very hard frost – sharp' and 'exceeding hard frost, very sharp' until 10 February – 'Snow in Morning. Very dark. Afterwards the sun broke out. Very cold.' So the next day he was able to walk into 'high Park (Hyde Park) and see them skate'. Ever alarmed by fires out of control, Richard also notes 'Thursday February 18th 1773 – a Terrible Fire this morning at Bishopsgate Street – 8 lives lost. How awful.'

On 21 February Richard and Eleanor celebrated their twentieth wedding anniversary – there is no record of any family celebration but Richard records: 'Sabbath 21st. Spared to see the return of another Wedding day, which is now 20 years. What cause to set up our Ebenezers...' ('Ebenezer' is a biblical reference meaning 'Up until now the Lord has helped us'). '... Past night windy with Rain, today turn'd out fine, not cold.'

The pair made a journey to see Waltham Abbey on 25 February ('set out early in the Post Chaise') but otherwise Richard seems to have had his time taken up with visits to the Guildhall 'about the Carts – to no avail' (a reference to a disputed access-way adjoining Richard's property). It was Richard's birthday on 16 March ('Spared to see the return of another Birth Day... Franky dined with us today on a Hare and a piece of Salmon'). Whether or not it was a birthday present is not clear, but two days later, 'Mr Melton gave us a Dog.' Presumably Richard liked his present – he even drew the dog and preserved its cut-out among his papers!

Richard often seemed pre-occupied with the state of his digestion, and wrote of his frequent discomfort: 'Sabbath Day 9th May 1773 was confined at home on account of pain in my bowels. May an absence from the House of God increase my appetite to His Holy Word.' No doubt an unbalanced diet exacerbated the problem, and also affected his teeth. Later the same year he writes:

> 1773 Thursday 9th December – was pretty much confin'd with Tooth Ach etc, through Mercy the pain abated. Frost. Fine Day Very Cold. Friday 10th – Face still poorly. Frost. Very Cold. Sat 11th. The past night very painful with my Tooth etc. – got up between 3 & 4 o'Clock. Today very bad with it likewise. Frosty, dull, very Cold day. Sabbath Day, 12th Dec. Was confin'd from the Public on account of my Face etc – may the Lord Grant absence. Monday 13th – through Mercy, my pain was abated. Wed 15th My Tooth Ach returned. Thurs 16th Had a very indifferent night the past – with my Tooth. Today was enabled to go through

> the Operation of having it drawn out which gave me great relief. Part fine, part dull, not very Cold.

Poor Richard! Dentistry at that time was somewhat brutal. The tooth would have been tapped gently with a hammer to loosen it, and the equivalent of pliers would then have been used to extract the tooth sideways. Richard makes no mention as to whether he had the tooth replaced – mother-of-pearl and silver was popular, as was the use of ivory, bone or even human teeth. There was always a trade in teeth from cadavers. An entry in the *British Magazine* for January 1763 gives the following explanation of a tooth extraction:

> 1st in drawing all teeth, the patients head should be held by an assistant in the required position. 2nd The forceps is always to be held in the right hand, and the fulcrum in the left. 3rd The tooth after being first freed from the Gums, if the surgeon thinks it is necessary, is to be griped as low as possible by the forceps ... covered with leather...

A detail from Hogarth's *A Midnight Modern Conversation* from 1733 showing a pipe-smoker about to light his pipe from a candle. Note the broken stems and discarded pipes on the floor – the long stems were delicate and easily broken. © The Trustees of the British Museum.

There are then another nine stages describing the actual removal of the tooth, with the admonition that it is important not to break the offending tooth '...the force that is necessary here, as it cannot be expressed, should be learned by experience on the dead subject.' All surgeons needed to experiment on corpses – and there was a trade in stealing bodies from undertakers and graveyards for onward sale to the teaching hospitals.

Despite such hardships as the

toothache, life went on – Richard occasionally 'spent some time at the Boars Head, Eastcheap' or 'smoak'd a pipe with Mr Rogers.' Richard would have been smoking a clay pipe – indeed, there were several factories making clay pipes close by to Richard's house. The prevailing fashion was for pipes with small bowls and extremely long stems – the 'Churchwarden' being around thirty inches long! As usual he drank a lot of tea and occasionally – very occasionally – he took a bath. Hence 31 May was noteworthy: 'Resum'd my Bath and through Mercy was carried very well through it.' Bathing appears to have been seen as a continuous operation, albeit suspended for weeks or even months at a time. So the next time a bath is mentioned is on 3 August: 'Resum'd my Bath'!

On 4 June 1773 the diary entry relates how 'Wife, Billy, Patty and Franky went to see the Fireworks at Mr Harris's and through Mercy were Preserved.' At the end of that month Richard and his wife set out on a journey through Hampshire. 'June 30th – Wife and Self set out in Coach. Breakfast at White Hart Cobham, Dinner at White Hart Guildford and Supper at White Hart Alton.' The next day saw them take breakfast at The Swan at Alresford before making it to The Dolphin at Southampton for dinner and The White Horse at Romsey for supper. After a few days sightseeing and calling on friends the Halls moved on to the Wallops and Broughton before setting out for Salisbury ('went to see Wilton House and Stonehenge. Supp'd and lay at the Bear at Devizes'). From there they travelled to Chippenham, and on to Tetbury, leaving the next day (8 July) and getting to Bourton just in time for Dinner! It was a hot summer, and Richard was able to visit his estate at Bengeworth, take tea with all and sundry, and to visit Burford Races with Brother William

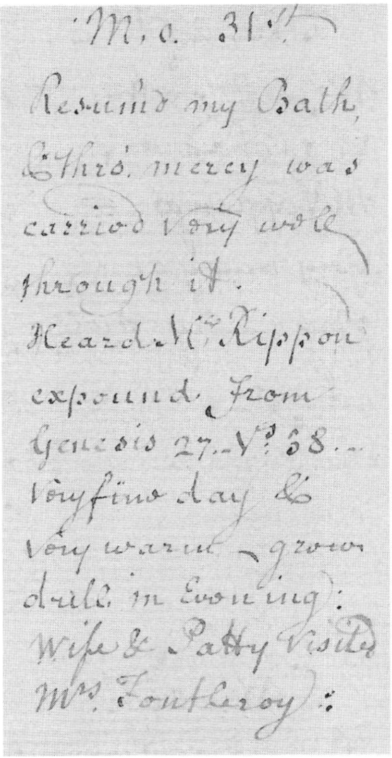
Mo. 31st
Resum'd my Bath,
& thro' mercy was
carried very well
through it.
Heard Mr Rippon
expound from
Genesis 27.-Vs 38..
very fine day &
very warm – grew
dull in Evening:
Wife & Patty Visited
Mrs Fontleroy:

(20 July). They started their return to London two days later but it must have been a slow journey because 'the Coach broke down'. In the days before a breakdown service passengers just had to be patient and wait – in this case for half a day while an axle was replaced.

'1773 Thu 29th July – Wife & Patty visited Mr Cooper, Coachmaker.' Richard does not mention whether the family bought a chaise or were merely window-shopping. Previously, while he was living at Red Lion Street, he appears to have had a two-wheeled carriage and was required to pay Carriage Tax – a copy of the receipt was kept by Richard but he used half of it as scrap paper.

There appear to have been other distractions, too:

> 1773 August 17th – Began Whitewashing the Shop etc
>
> 1773 Fri 5th October At 11 last night was alarmed by a great Fire, near Dowgate – through a Merciful & Divine hand, it did not come near our dwelling.
>
> October 20th – entered upon my Business as a Grand Juryman at the Old Bailey

It was to be a four-day trial, although, strangely, Richard makes no mention of either the cases being tried or of the verdicts.

Other places of interest attracted Richard and his family: '1773 Tue 2nd November Went with Wife to see Mr Wright's Waxwork in Chidley Court Pall Mall.' Mr Wright appears to have been a forerunner of Madame Tussaud, who did not come to London with her travelling collection of models until 1802, a year after Richard died. But the public already had a fascination for wax effigies, some of which were death masks – that is, modelled on the heads of the recently departed, particularly those whose notoriety had captured the imagination of the public. There were walks to Camberwell, to Peckham and to Rotherhithe and, on 9 November, they 'saw the Lord Mayor's Show by water – wet in the morning, was fine at the time of the Show.'

The 7 December 1773 entry records, in rather bolder handwriting than any of the other entries: 'Mr Rippon Married.'

* * *

In April 1774 William set out for his annual pilgrimage to London to stay with Richard. 'Took four horses to Burford. Sent Jack back with a pair. Went with the other pair to Witney from whence I hired horses.' He lists the expenses:

> 6 horses from Witney to Oxford (10 miles) 7/6d. Driver one shilling. Ditto to Benson (12 miles) 9/-. Driver one shilling. Ditto to Henley (11 miles) 8/-. Driver one shilling. Ditto to Maidenhead Bridge (9 miles) 6/9d. Driver one shilling. Ditto to Hounslow (16 miles) 12/-. Driver one shilling. Ditto to London Bridge (15 miles) 11/3d. Driver two shillings. Total 73 miles £2/14/9d Turnpike from Witney to London 4/7d.

They reached Richard's a little after five o'clock on Thursday 7th April, but not before the party had paid for cleaning William's boots (3d.), greasing wheels at Henley (1s.), a 'woman on Henley Hill' (2d. alms) and purchase of two cucumbers (price not recorded).

Their first excursion seems to have been to view a house at Upper Clapton (north of the river, beyond Bethnal Green and near the marshes of Hackney and Bow) with brother-in-law Richard ('not agreeable') – perhaps an indication that the Halls were thinking of moving again. It would also appear that Mrs Snooke had an upset stomach ('Magnesia Alka & Manna for Mrs S. 1/10d'). They visited various museums and on the afternoon of 22 April 'went to hear some singing at the Jewish Synagogue'. Above all, William and his wife hit the shops:

> Silver spectacle frame 12/6d
> Mrs Snookes Riding Dress & Hat of Parlins & Co £6/15/0
> 3 yards superfine Pompadour cloth 3 guineas
> Mr Smith for a pair of shoe buckles 6/-
> 18 yards silk for negligee £7/13/0d [a negligée being an outer garment, worn out of doors and not a garment for the boudoir. To have needed eighteen yards it must have been made of gossamer...]
> 6 dozen broad lace @ 8d each
> One yard catgut
> Mending smelling bottle and ear-rings 2/6
> Books 13/6d

Silk for waistcoat 19/-
Paid to Mr Brewer, coach maker £17/3/6d.
Stockings £5/0/6d
2 dozen Port £2

...And a lot more. In between shopping trips the Snookes fitted in visits to Kensington, Blackheath, Greenwich and Ealing. Richard simply records: '1774 April 27th – Dining at Greenwich with Mr & Mrs Snooke £0.10.6.' and later in the year: '1774 July 23rd Went with Miss Warne, Miss Hall, Miss Talbot to see Lord Tinley's House on Epping Forrest.'

When William returned to Bourton in the summer of 1774, his diary records that he purchased 'porter' (so called because it was a beer favoured by the porters at Billingsgate Market, who fancied a strong beer after a day's work) and also 'light Guinness'. Arthur Guinness had started brewing a light ale in 1759 –but company records do not show any exports from Dublin until 1796, and even then, not of light ale. At that stage Guinness had moved over to producing porter (where roasted barley is added to the sprouting barley grains to give it a dark colour) but the product William bought was clearly 'light' and therefore not porter. How did he come by it if it was not exported? And how did he already know it by specific name (as opposed to the more general 'bought beer from Witney')? The diaries give no explanation, but the entry is one of the earliest on record to show that a Guinness product was being consumed beyond the Irish borders.

In the summer of 1774 Richard appears to have made a return visit to Bourton: '1774 9th August – went to stay with Wm. Met us at Oxford and rode to Woodstock for breakfast – arriving Bourton at 6 o'clock. Visit to Evesham, Fairford. Returned 31st Aug.' Brother William would no doubt have acquainted him with the latest bit of village gossip, as recorded in William's diary for 11 July 1774: 'Farmer Parker married his favourite servant, pregnant by him after engaging himself to the widow of George Lawrence, for whom he had bought the ring which he gave her, and she had made him some shirts.' The rascal – to do that to your fiancée – after she has gone to the trouble of making you some shirts! A shame Richard did not wait a day longer – he could have stayed on to witness the wedding of the year at

Bourton: '1st September – Will Farmer married to Forty's daughter – Rough Musick at Night.' [I have no idea what Rough Musick was, but it sounds as if it involved traditional country tunes played badly on fiddles and drums!] But at least Richard would have been able to share in William's extravagant dinner party on 10 August – the day after his arrival. 'Our Dinner: Ham, 2 chicken roasted, Colly flower, Cabbage and carrots, Leg of Lamb boiled, pudding baked, ground rice, beans, 2 chickens boiled, sirloin of beef, kidney beans, cheesecakes, butter, tarts. N.B. Lobster and Crayfish were also introduced.' Meals like this were usually dominated by meat – in this case at least five different meat dishes as well as two of fish. In general vegetables were little used – and there was certainly no presumption that a decent meal was 'meat and two veg'. Vegetables were often prepared with a mixture of butter and flour, but in this case there is a surprising number of vegetable dishes. Much of the produce would have been grown locally, and the sirloin of beef would have been the highlight of the meal.

In a way it is strange that venison was not chosen, for this was generally used as a way of showing off. Neither Richard nor William could pass up on itemising in their diaries whenever they ate venison – it was a sign of wealth that you had your own deer park – or that you had influence with someone else who did. So William

mentions in his diary that he 'paid Lord Chedworth's keeper half a crown for delivering a shoulder and side of buck venison' (25 July 1768) – and in much the same way Richard proudly recorded that when he had moved house in London he had invited his friends to 'dine on a haunch of venison'.

Many thought that eating uncooked fruit was a cause of the plague – or, at the very least, chronic indigestion – and it was late in the century before the English navy understood the importance of vitamin C and started dispensing lemons and other citrus fruit as part of the sailor's diet in order to ward off scurvy. It would have been a rare dinner party which included any fresh fruit at all – and whatever William grew on his estate would have been preserved or made into jam.

Meanwhile back in town: '1774 Tues 9th November saw the Ld Mayor's Show by Water. 1774 Received from Wm £7 for 28 yards chintz 1774 November 7th – Went with Betty Snooke (sister in law) and Mr Kearse (wife's uncle) to see Cox's Museum.'

1774 Nov. 7 Went with Betty Snooke
and Mr Kearse to see Cox's Museum
1775 April 25. Went with Wife to
see Cox's Museum.

This was not Richard's first visit. Earlier in the year the entry for 22 April read: 'Went with Mr & Mrs Snooke, Wife & Patty to see Cox's Museum.' Nor was it the last visit – it was evidently a huge attraction and the following year he returned, this time again with his wife: '1775 April 25th – went with Wife to see Cox's Museum.' Given that it cost half a guinea per person to enter the museum, what was the attraction? Fortunately Richard kept the admission brochure listing the exhibits. The premises in Spring Gardens, Charing Cross, it seems, contained a number of salons, each with its own collection of bejewelled automata. The foyer was dominated by giant portraits of King George III and his wife Queen Charlotte, painted by Johan Zoffany. 'Before the portraits, upon a Throne of gold 32 feet in circumference of six steps, stand two rich and finely adorned altars of silver, border'd and embellish'd with gold.' The exhibits were on the grand scale – twenty-three in all – with elephants nine feet high, and tigers made of silver and set with precious stones, alongside much more dainty clockwork models, usually based on animals or birds. One exhibit was a 'magnificent Asiatic

Temple, ornamented with gold, jewellery, Palm trees and other rich embellishments, out of the dome of which gradually rises a pagoda to the Musick of its chimes. The temple itself stands on a Rock, adorned with various Animals, Shrubs, Flowers, Fossils etc. The stand or pedestal upon which it is placed is composed of Palm trees of a beautiful transparent green, growing on a Rocky ground; upon which Crocodiles, Plants, Corals and other aquatic productions may be seen: in the centre is a pool of artificial water, surrounded with bull-rushes, and within the pool water Fowls are seen, variously sporting on the surface. This piece is ten feet high.'

Nothing subtle about that! Another item, featuring humming birds hovering over ornate flowers, is described as having 'upwards of one hundred thousand stones of different colours, by which the shades and tints of the flowers are beautifully expressed.'

The undoubted star of the museum display was a life-size silver swan, first exhibited in 1772. It created a sensation in London and became a 'must see' for all those of fashion and taste. It is now exhibited at the Bowes Museum at Barnard Castle in Durham and it is perhaps best to quote from their own website:

> The Silver Swan is perhaps the best known and best loved object in The Bowes Museum. It is a musical automaton in the form of a life-size model of a swan, comprising a clockwork mechanism covered in silver plumage above a music box. It rests on a stream made of twisted glass rods interspersed with silver fish. When the mechanism is wound up, the glass rods rotate, the music begins, and the swan twists its head to the left and right and appears to preen its back. It then appears to see a fish in the water below and bends down to catch it. It then swallows the fish as the music stops and resumes its upright position. The whole performance lasts about forty seconds. In reality the fish has been concealed lengthways on a pivot in the swan's beak and returns to this position. In real life swans do not eat fish.

There are in fact three separate mechanical parts to the swan. It was originally enclosed in a glass case, and it is interesting to imagine the wonderment on the faces of the visitors upon seeing such a stunning novelty. Even today, audiences frequently burst into applause at the end of each showing. It certainly captured the imagination of Mark Twain. Writing in *The Innocents Abroad* he remarks:

> I watched a silver swan which had a living grace about his movements and a living intelligence in his eyes – watched him swimming about as comfortably and unconcernedly as if it had been born in a morass instead of a jewellers shop – watched him seize a silver fish from under the water and hold his head and go through all the customary and elaborate motions of swallowing it.

The Silver Swan. Courtesy of the Bowes Museum.

Examples of James Cox's craft are still to be found in the Chinese and Russian Imperial collections, and in a sense were the forerunners of the Fabergé eggs. Known as 'sing-songs', the elaborate mechanical pieces were produced in huge quantities for sale in the Far East. It appears to have been Cox's undoing – his business grew too big too fast. At one stage it is reported that he was employing nearly a thousand jewellers and skilled craftsmen in London alone. The value of his unsold stock items rose to an incredible £750,000. Unfortunately trade with China and the Far East took a downturn, payments were not made and therefore Cox was unable to meet his debts. He ended up petitioning Parliament to be allowed to dispose of the museum stock by public lottery, on the grounds that the items owned by him were designed so much with the Far Eastern tastes in mind that they could not be disposed of 'by the common way of sale'. Cox may have got permission from Parliament for his lottery, but the subsequent ticket sales were sluggish and proved insufficient to stave off his bankruptcy. Poor Cox, having to submit all his bejewelled automata to a lottery, but lotteries were the flavour of the moment. The nation seemed to be obsessed with anything involving gambling. An entry in William's diary throws an interesting light on the popularity of the State

Lottery. In 1774 he notes that Richard had bought a lottery ticket ('numbered 37–956') for £13 2s. and that William had agreed to go halves on the expense. Thirteen pounds – that was quite a flutter! The numbers did not come up on that occasion, but that did not deter the pair of them having another go the following year. William records that on 11 February 1775 he received his share of a prize – amounting to just under twenty pounds. Richard retained the handbill. Note the final sentence

STATE LOTTERY, 1775.

S C H E M E

No of Prizes.		Value of each.		Total Value.
2	of	20,000	is	40,000
6	—	10,000	—	60,000
8	—	5,000	—	40,000
18	—	2,000	—	36,000
36	—	1,000	—	36,000
60	—	500	—	30,000
300	—	100	—	30,000
870	—	50	—	43,500
18,700	—	15	—	280,500
20,000 Prizes				596,000
First Drawn for the first Three Days 1,000*l.* each.				3,000
Last Drawn				1,000
40,000 Blanks.				
60,000 Tickets.				£600,000

Only Two Blanks to a Prize.

The Price of Tickets and Shares.

	l.	*s.*	*d.*		*l.*	*s.*
Ticket	12	18	6	may gain	20,000	0
Half	6	10	0	———	10,000	0
Quarter	3	5	6	———	5,000	0
Eighth	1	13	0	———	2,500	0
Sixteenth	0	17	0	———	1,250	0
Thirty-second	0	9	0	———	625	0
Sixty-fourth	0	4	6	———	312	10

The Price of Chances.

	l.	*s.*	*d.*		*l.*	*s.*
Whole Chance	9	4	0	may gain	20,000	0
Half	4	13	0	———	10,000	0
Quarter	2	7	0	———	5,000	0
Eighth	1	4	0	———	2,500	0
Sixteenth	0	12	6	———	1,250	0
Thirty second	0	6	6	———	625	0
Sixty fourth	0	3	6	———	312	10

If Tickets should rise or fall in Price, a proper Allowance will be be made.

TICKETS and SHARES and CHANCES of
TICKETS and SHARES,
From a Half to a Sixty-fourth Part,
Are now selling in great Variety of Numbers at the very lowest Price,
By JENKINSON
AND THE REAL
GOODLUCK,
At their Old STATE LOTTERY OFFICES, *viz*:
No. 57, Cornhill, nearly opposite Bishopsgate-Street;
No. 41, in the Poultry, near Cheapside, and No. 1, in the Old Jewry.
No. 2, Sparrow Corner, the bottom of the Minories.
No. 3, Ludgate-Hill, near Fleet-Market.
No. 8, Temple Barr without, near Butcher Row.
No. 438, in Oxford Street, opposite Tottenham Court Road, and
No. 4, and 5, the Corner of Chequer Court, opposite Northumberland House, Charing Crofs.
Resident upwards of Seventeen Years
Remarkable in former Lotteries for sharing and selling most of the Capital Prizes,
The following Numbers have been Sold Shared and Registred.

No. 1,437, a Prize of 20,000l.	No. 29,266, a Prize of 10,000l.	No. 19,896, a Prize of 5,000l.
No. 29,266, ——— 20,000l.	No. 21,344, ——— 10,000l.	No. 44,464, ——— 5,000l.
No. 30,672, ——— 20,000l.	No. 25,614, ——— 10,000l.	No. 27,666, ——— 5,000l.

Other Prizes such as Two Thousands, One Thousands, &c. too numerous to insert.

N. B. A saving of near 4*l.* per Ticket is made by purchasing Chances of Tickets and Shares, at the above Offices, a Share of a Ticket entitles the Bearer to such part of any Prize, from 15*l.* to 20 Thousand and a Chance from 50*l.* to 20 Thousand. We have upwards of 100 Tickets divided in Shares and Chances, the Purchasers of which is as Safe in their Property as if they were Possessed of the Original Ticket, as the Tickets divided in Shares and Chances at our Offices is secured in so particular a Manner that must satisfy the most credulous Adventurer.

As there are other Office keepers in Town make use of the Name of Goodluck, we find it necessary to acquaint the Publick that all the Tickets, Shares and Chances of Tickets, Sold at our Offices will be stamp'd on the Back Jenkinson and the real Goodluck. Messrs. Jenkinson and Goodluck, respectfully return Thanks to their Friends and the Publick in General, who have honoured them with their Commands, in the last and many former Lotteries and hopes for the Continuance of their favours in the present Lottery as they flatter themselves their just and upright dealing heretofore, may be sufficient Recomendation.

Country Correspondents favouring us with their Commands may depend on having Tickets, Shares or Chances on the same Terms as if Personally Present.

All Business relative to the Lottery transacted on the most equitable Terms.
Begins drawing the 13th of November next. Only Two Blanks to a Prize.
Schemes given gratis. Letters Post Paid duly answered.
Tickets and Shares insured from Blanks.

– purchasers could take out an insurance against individual numbers not being drawn!

Richard was keen to expand the business at the shop. It looks as though trade was good when people with money came up to town 'for the season' but slumped when the visitors returned to their country estates. The remedy? Employ a person to visit customers at their homes in the country. Richard entered into an arrangement with his cousin Frank Kearse, who for many years had been engaged in business as a tailor. He was the son of George Kearse (brother to Richard's mother, she having been born a Kearse). He commenced travelling for Richard, taking samples and stock, as evidenced from the following entries for 1773:

> Monday 11th January – Frank Kearse set out for his West journey.
>
> Thursday 18th February – FK returned from his West journey, through Mercy safe.
>
> Saturday 20th Gave FK 6 bottles of Red Port.

Mind you, he could spare it – in the previous month Richard had bottled off a 'Quarter Pipe' of port: 'it ran ten and a half dozen bottles'.

> Thursday May 13th FK set out for Kent journey –a very fine day, not cold. (He returned one month later, while my Wife and I were away on our Hampshire & Bourton journey.)
>
> Mon 13th September FK set out on his Sussex & Kent journey.
>
> Sat 16th October Mr Kearse returned from his Sussex & Kent journey.
>
> Tue 16th November Mr Kearse set out on his Essex journey. Very fine day. Cool.

> December 1st Mr Kearse Retd. From Essex journey. Wife went to Miss Warners. Morning fine, afternoon dull, some rain. Cold.

The pattern seems to have been for his cousin to spend a month on the road, return for a month, and then set off on his travels again. Frank was not only selling clothing and materials, he was able to make alterations as well: 'June 17th – Bro. William paid Mr Kearse for Betsy's stays £1/5/0. Ditto for altering a pair for Polly 3 shillings.' The stays were a form of corset and were worn by all women regardless of age or class. The material (usually cotton or linen) was stiffened by overstitching and reinforced with bone, wood or ivory inserted in the panels at the front, to keep it rigid. It would have been worn over a shift – never next to the skin – and would have required adjustment if the wearer 'filled out' as the young Polly was presumably doing!

A pair of stays exhibited at the Museum of Costume, Bath, dating from around 1775. It had adjustable shoulder straps and eyelets down the back so that the wearer could be laced up. Photo courtesy of Fashion Museum, Bath and North Somerset Council/The Bridgeman Art Library.

Both Betsy and Polly would have worn a stout linen petticoat, reinforced with cane hoops, and silk stockings held up by garters, and each ensemble would have been finished off with a dress of silk brocade, often worn with a decorative lace apron during the daytime. The fashion in the 1770s and 1780s was for dresses to be just short of ankle length – and stockings therefore became more elaborately embroidered with 'clocks' on the ankle. The ladies would have had leather-soled fabric shoes – double strapped and buckled at the side. Out of doors, back at Bourton, they would have topped off their ensemble with a straw hat, or a bonnet. However, by the 1770s the fashion in town was for enormously high hairstyles (buoyed up over pads of hair or wool), the hair greased and then powdered, worn under a hat tilted over the forehead. If they were not to feel like 'country cousins' on their trips up to London it is highly likely that the

Snooke women would have had to spend hours on their coiffure before venturing outside – particularly in the evening.

Richard, meanwhile, would have been no less the peacock than the ladies. He would have worn a wig, though not necessarily a full-bottomed one. It would have required regular maintenance – particularly because the curls would 'drop out' in the rain. When he travelled he would take several wigs with him, and as part of his daily visit to the barber his entire head would have been shaved. ('Shaving and dressing wig – one shilling'). If he was attending a formal gathering his wig would have been greased and powdered, and he would have worn a three-piece suit consisting of a knee-length coat, elaborately decorated waistcoat, knee breeches – and of course a pair of his own silk stockings. Waistcoat buttons and shoe buckles were silver, and the fashion still veered towards the ostentatious, with lace ruffles worn at the wrist. Indoors he would have removed the wig and hidden his bald pate under a night cap (probably the seven-shilling velvet number he bought the year before!), and worn a loose full-length gown called variously a morning gown, night gown or India gown, probably of silk damask. Paintings of the time often show gentlemen wearing these unfitted garments, but it was not the done thing to be seen out in polite society attired in 'undress wear'.

On his forays to the country Richard would have worn riding gear, and, as the decade progressed, there were more and more trips to Bourton, and from thence to Bengeworth, to consider what best to do with the land he jointly owned with William. The decision was made to petition Parliament to pass an Act of Enclosure – allowing them to fence off the area technically belonging to the Mansion House, but used by a number of local farmers for sheep grazing, fattening off livestock in the summer months and so on.

To achieve their goal, first of all they had to ensure that 'their man' got elected to Parliament as member for Evesham. In 1774 Richard took the trouble to assemble a list of all members of Parliament (duly pasted in to his scrapbook!). William was assiduous in his wining and dining of those who might help him and in particular seems to have made various trips to

Evesham to attend meetings throughout 1774. His diary mentions one particular feast, attended by John Bushant, where 'only 19½ dozen bottles of Port Wine were consumed – besides Punch and Beer – 2 courses for Dinner.' Their homework paid off:

> 1774 October 17th – Mrs Snooke and Self set off in the Chaise for Evesham. Dined at Mr Dunns. Mr Bushant, Mr Freeman, Mr Savage and Mr Cloverly also dined. October 18th – I dined at the Craven with Mr Hammesely and Mr Seymour's representatives. Mr Bushant and Mr Seymour returned by a great majority – chaired amidst the acclamation of the people in general. Lord Melvington and Mr Dinant unsuccessful.

Having got 'their man' elected, a Private Members' Bill was introduced to the House and in 1775 their Bill received assent and was entered on the statute book. Richard writes: 'Award of Inclosure at Bengeworth bears date 11th November 1775 and is inrolled with the Clerk of the Peace for the County of Worcester.' Richard paid 'Charles Welch balance in full due for my proportion of the charges for Bengeworth Inclosure £68/17/5½d', while William paid the same person £65 14s. 9d. for his share of these parliamentary expenses. They were now free to commence fencing the land.

Award of Inclosure at Bengworth
bears date 11 Nov: 1775.
and is inrolled with the Clerk
of the peace for the County
of Worcester.
Feb. 6. 1787. Paid £7. 2. 6
for the purchase of the Kings
Rent, that used to be
annually paid for the Land
at Bengworth.

Richard and William resolved to be fair to those who had previously grazed sheep, foraged with pigs and so on, and appointed commissioners to agree rents and to handle disputes. William had to make numerous trips up to Bengeworth to discuss matters and his diaries contain various references to 'dining with the Commissioners at the Unicorn'. He had also been involved in mapping and recording the land in some detail. The diary entry for 12 June 1775 reads:

Mr William Reeve's Bill	
To: Measuring Bengeworth & expenses	£3/2/6
Valuing & measuring trees	10/6
Measuring walls on the hill	2/-
Total	£3/15/-
Paid for a skin of vellum	2/3
	£3/17/3

Later that year, about 14 December, William recorded that he had paid 'Mr Wm Acton for nails 5/4d, Mr Wm. Fisher on Account of Fencing £50, J Walton, smith, in full for Irons 13/-, Mr Henry Smith for gates etc £4/16/0, Mr Staple for the lead pump etc £2/7/6.' Richard then repaid his half share of those expenses – and fifty pounds for fencing was quite a considerable cost. The 'skin of vellum' was a superior form of parchment made from calfskin and was for writing out the formal deed of ownership, together with its map or plan.

Meanwhile there was Land Tax to pay (£92 6s. 4d.).

92.6.4. The whole amount of the Land-tax at Bengworth.

'February 6th 1787 – Paid £7.2.6 for the purchase of the King's Rent that used to be annually paid for the land at Bengeworth' – in other words they paid a small capital sum to buy out the original 'rent' due each Michaelmas amounting to a penny over ten shillings, charged on the freehold interest in the estate. Unfortunately Richard's own diaries are silent as to whether he paid William the 10s. 6d. which William had paid to 'Mr Clark, surveyor, on Brother's account which perhaps he might think of paying'. What is clear is that between them, William and Richard paid out a lot of money, but presumably the exercise was worth it.

For some years William received the rents and forwarded to Richard a moiety (i.e. one-half). But in due course they entered into a Deed of Partition and William took one half of the land and Richard took the other. The Partition deed was still with his papers when Richard died, and his half of the land was transferred to sons William and Francis.

Back in London, 1774 saw the opening of Josiah Wedgwood's showroom in St James Square at York Street. It was a sensation, being one of the very first shops which we would recognise as such, since the goods were on display and available for purchase (as opposed to being made to order). The showrooms became a fashionable place for ladies to meet and examine Josiah Wedgwood's wares. He had already developed 'creamware' and his 'bone china' was to come later.

In 1775 Richard records a number of purchases – gravy spoons in January, watches for Francis and Martha in October and December (each costing two guineas) and, the following year, a new Wilton carpet for the dining room costing nine guineas. In all Richard mentions three different types of carpet – Brussels (where the woollen top surface was woven onto a backing of stout linen thread); Wilton (where the rib of the woven fabric was cut to make a velvet pile); and Turkey (with a deep pile,

1775 Oct..	Metal Watch for Son Francis .	2.2.0.
–	Gave Mr. Beddome 1 & 2 Vol Nonconformist Memorial	0.13.6
– Dec.	Metal Watch for Daughter.	2.2.0.
1776. June,	Wilton Carpet for Dining room	9.9.0

usually richly coloured, on a backing of flax or hemp). The names were already generic rather than denoting a specific place of origin but show that it was already fashionable to have carpets laid in the main rooms. Clothing was still elaborate and ornate ('November – Buff laced Waistcoat') and there are signs of deteriorating eye sight when in the same month he notes: 'Green Spectacle case Four shillings.' Presumably it had nothing whatsoever to do with the growing consumption of port: 'Bought of Mr Baughan Quarter pipe of port £9.0.0.'

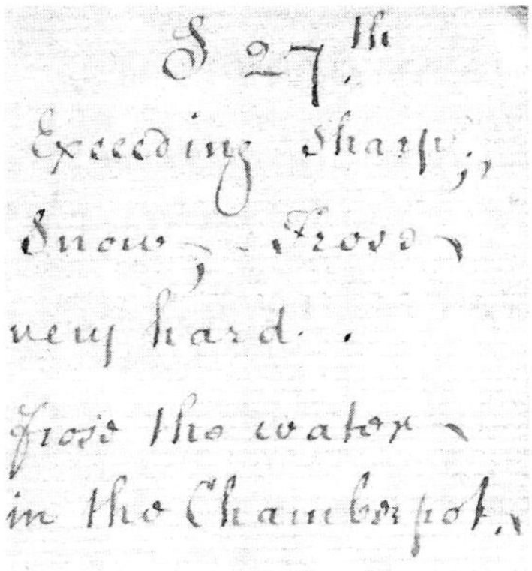

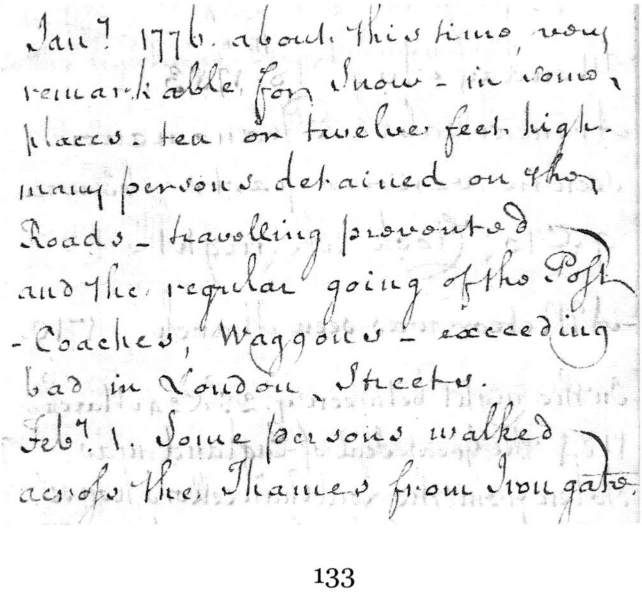

1777 had started with an unusually settled period of very cold weather – day after day Richard noted 'severe frost', 'snow very thick' and, when the thaw set in, 'streets exceeding dirty'. But the freeze returned and 27 January saw the lovely entry: 'Exceeding Sharp; Snow, froze very Hard. Froze the water in the Chamber Pot.' Thanks for that, Richard. Nice one! It remained cold into the next month and Richard noted that 'persons were able to walk across The Thames' on 1 February. Later he was to look back on the period and note that it was 'a remarkable time for Snow – in some places ten or twelve feet high. Many persons detained on the roads, travelling prevented and the regular going of the Post Coaches and Waggons. Exceeding bad in London Streets.' The nightmare of being stuck in a stagecoach in a ten-foot snowdrift for several days is hard to comprehend.

As spring approached, Richard seems to have been busy with the local Charity School ('March 7th – attending School Board' and 'March 28th Din'd at the King's Head with the Managers of the Horsly-down School'). Later he records that he 'was chose Treasurer' of the School – an excuse for another supper with the Governors at The King's Head! Thereafter he appears to have attended managers' meetings once a month. One of Eleanor's uncles came and stayed in London for a few days in May, prompting the family to visit him. He returned on 20 May and Richard noted 'some rain in morning. Clear'd up – was in general pretty fine in afternoon. Not cold. Washed Feet.' Richard had problems with the drains and the next day 'went to ye Commissioners for Sewers about the drain being stop'd.'

On most days Richard took tea with friends, either 'home' or 'away', and at the end of each year he compiled a list headed 'Visited Us: Visited by Us'. There are various mentions that he 'took Physick' – either for stomach pains or for his gout, or for Toothache. He was, however, well enough to plan a trip to Worcester at the end of July: 'Took places in the Worcestershire Machine. Very fine day, very warm. Breakfast at Home, Dinner at Red Lion High Wickham, Supper at Kings Head Oxford – was Graciously preserved.' He visited Bengeworth, stayed a few days at Leominster at Mr Marlowe's, 'rode out a little in ye Carriage', but complained that the roads were 'indifferent'. It appears to have rained torrentially for most of his time – until 12 August when he notes that there was 'a fine and Beautiful Rainbow about 7 o'Clock in the Evening'. He 'Din'd with Lord Bateman and Captain Allen' and, on 20 August, witnessed his 'Dear Wife's Baptism by Immersion' at the hands of Mr Thomas, early in the morning. As if that wasn't enough

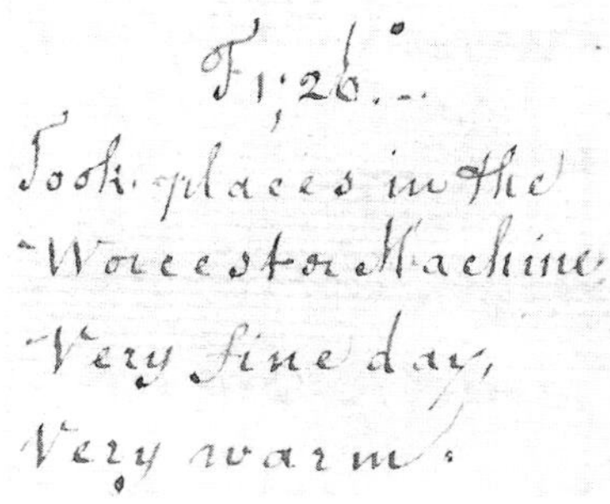
Took places in the
Worcester Machine
Very fine day,
Very warm.

of water it continued to pour down day after day, occasioning the comment 'very bad wat'ry roads'. But it relented in the afternoon of 4 September, enabling the party to go to Leominster Fair. A visit to Worcester ('Supper at the Hop Pole') was followed by a 'very hurrying unpleasant time on account of the Music Meeting' (no explanation given). They returned to London in stages, pausing for 'B[reakfast] at Bengeworth, D[inner] at Chappel Heath, S[upper] at King's Head Oxford', before proceeding to Town the next day via Tetsworth and Uxbridge.

Richard continued to enjoy ill-health – being 'confin'd at home on account of my Eyes being so Poorly' on 22 September. He took 'physick' all the following week, complained about the dull and foggy weather, dined on a haunch of venison and commented that 'Patty was very ill' but without giving details of the ailment. At the end of October Billy and Patty went with Miss Smith and Mr Clugh to 'see His Majesty Robed' (Franky was staying at Bourton at the time). Mr Clugh had a son, Dick, and on 3 October 1776 Richard states that he 'enrolled Dick Clugh' – that is, took him on as an apprentice. Richard would appear to have started taking more interest in his professional responsibilities, dining at Drapers' Hall in November, before going with his son to see the Lord Mayor's Show. Again, there is mention of the foggy weather.

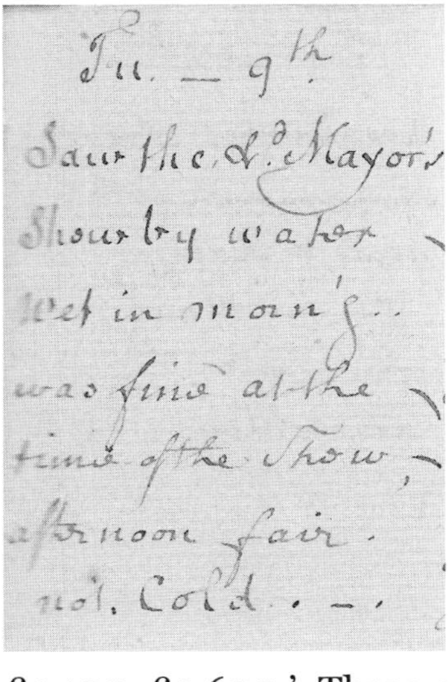
Tu. — 9th
Saw the Ld. Mayor's
Show by water
wet in morn'g
was fine at the
time of the Show
afternoon fair
not Cold. —

Fire was an abiding concern of Richard's – as well as of all Londoners: '1779 – October 31st – Our house at London Bridge was preserved when in great danger from Fire' Richard kept meticulous records of his fire insurance: 'Union Office No. 21065 dated 24th December 1778 on household goods books plate& apparel £500 Utensils and goods in Trade £2,100 £2,600.' Three years later he had amended the split between house and shop so that we see: 'October 10th 1781 Household goods etc £300 Goods in trade and trust £2,300.' At that time he noted that the stamp duty on the policy (£2 8s.

9d.) had been paid up to 24 December 1783. He held a quite separate policy with the Hand in Hand Office: 'Policy dated November 3rd 1781 No. 85657 – £900, stamp duty paid to November 3rd 1783.'

The point was that unless you could show that you held a current policy (usually indicated by exhibiting the insurer's plaque on the outside of the building, rather as we might display the name of a security company on a burglar alarm) people would not come to help – the volunteer fire crews would only put out a blaze if they knew that they were going to be paid.

Union Office
No. 21065.
Dated 24 Decr. 1778 –
on Household Goods
Books, Plate, & Apparel.
. . . . 500.. –..
Utensils & goods
in Trade 2100.. –..
2,600 . –.

Octr. 10. 1781.
alt. Household
Goods &c.. 300 –
Utensils &
goods in Trade 2 300 –
and Trust 2,600 ..

Hand in Hand Office.
Policy Dated Novr. 3. 1781.
No. 85657. £900.. –
Stamp Duty.
pd up to Novr 3. 1783.

at Union
Duty . 2. 8. 9. –
Pd. up to 24 Decr. 1783.

Later on Richard reviewed the diary entry and went on to write:

> This Evening experienced the Lord a very present help in a time of great need, by his preserving us, and our habitation from devouring flames, a fire having broken out about 8 o'clock at the Hop warehouse behind our house, which consumed it and the Water-works. Oh may I never forget this kind appearance when in imminent danger.

The artist William Marlow recorded the scene in his painting *The Waterworks at London Bridge on Fire 1779* – with the

The Waterworks at London Bridge on Fire 1779 by William Marlow. Courtesy of Guildhall Art Gallery, City of London.

flames illuminating the church of St Magnus the Martyr. The hop warehouse in question belonged to Messrs Judd and Sanderson – hops were grown in Kent and for centuries had been brought up to London, stored in warehouses either side of the bridge, and sold on to the brewers. The fire destroyed the warehouse and reduced the waterworks to the level of the river in under an hour. It was to be another ten years before the water wheels and pumps were rebuilt.

The year was to end tragically for the family: '9th December – Death of Mr Snooke'. Richard later wrote:

> After a short illness of about five days of a paralytic stroke departed my worthy friend and brother-in-law William Snooke Esq. aged 49. My dear wife and self went to Bourton on hearing of his illness but he died the day before we got there. We stayed the internment which was on the 17th.

It must have been a huge blow to Richard – William was all the things which Richard was not – rumbustious, charming, always laughing at his own mistakes ('Leg of Pork for Dinner – an unfortunate choice for Mrs Cox as she eats no pigmeat and this I forgot' – or 'Paid one penny to have the bruise knocked out of the kettle, occasioned when I dropped it'). Richard, always pious and invoking the Lord, must have envied William his simple faith, his generosity – and of course his enormous wealth. William had never been baptised, but attended regularly (two or three times a week) at the Baptist church in Bourton under the ministry of Benjamin Beddome. After William died his widow Anne maintained the tradition of paying the good preacher eight guineas a year. Anne remained at the Manor House for the rest of her life. It was then occupied by her fourth daughter, Eliza, who married Dr Nathaniel Stenson (the man who gave his name to Stenson's Duct, the salivary gland).

The year 1779 also marked the death of Captain James Cook in far-off Hawaii. Originally Cook had set sail in the *Endeavour* in 1769 with a mission to go to Tahiti. He took with him a party of astronomers sent by the Royal Society in order to observe the passage of Venus as it passed in front of the sun. This was considered to be the best opportunity of making exact measurements of the distance between the earth and the sun. Afterwards, Cook went on to chart the shores of New Zealand and the eastern seaboard of Australia. In 1772–75 he undertook a second epic voyage, to chart the waters of the Atlantic. But the third voyage, in command of the *Resolution*, was to be his last and he was clubbed to death in a brawl (on Valentine's Day 1779) after he had kidnapped the local king. Richard appears to have read of his exploits because in one of his diaries he remarks on the fact that the first edition of the *Journals of Captain James Cook on his Voyages of Discovery* had sold out and that the book was being reprinted.

Also in that year Richard notes: 'Our Nation much alarmed by the Combined Fleets of France and Spain lying off Plymouth Saturday August 14th 1779 – continued there till Wednesday August 18th then they went off.' It was a worrying time – with the English fleet sorely stretched trying to keep up its supplies

Our Nation much alarmed by the Combin'd Fleets of France & Spain laying off Plymouth Saturday Aug.t 14th 1779. Continued there till Wednesday Augt 18th they then went off.

to America, fighting the French in the Caribbean, trying to defend Gibraltar (which remained under siege by Spain until 1783) and generally trying to keep the French fleet bottled up in port. Small wonder that this country started to tire of trying to defend its interests in the American colonies. It may have been another couple of years before peace was finally reached with the United States, but the desire for peace (and with it the ability to defend Britain's interests nearer home) was clearly already in the minds of Richard and his contemporaries.

8

The 1780s

Two books spanning five years.

The year started positively as Richard took his son William into the family business: 'January 1st 1780 – This day took my son into Partnership. Gave him half my Trade ... A hard frost very Cold, some part morning fine, after very Foggy. My Son was 25 years old, 3 months 17 days.' The actual Articles of Partnership were signed on 19 January, backdated to the start of the year: 'May the Lord give a Blessing to it. Fine in morning, hail in afternoon. Cool'.

However, within days, tragedy struck. Several versions of his diary entry covering this event exist (Richard seems to have written contemporaneous diaries and often rewrote). In one he writes: '11th January, 1780. O the affliction of this day. My very dear and affectionate wife departed after so short an illness as about six or seven hours, to my great grief and sorrow, having lived together in the conjugal state 27 years, all but 41 days. Blessed be the Lord.' Other members of the family confirm that 'She was remarkable for her piety, an affectionate wife and tender parent' and that her 'complaint was apoplexy and paralysis' – in other words she suffered a fatal stroke.

The Halls' younger son, Francis, then described as living in Portsmouth, came back up to London three days later and stayed until 7 February. William was already in London, with his sister, and they all attended the burial at Bunhill Fields on 18 January. Eleanor was interred alongside the remains of her late father. On the original tombstone was added the following inscription: 'Underneath this tomb are also deposited the remains of Mrs Eleanor Hall late the beloved wife of Mr Richard Hall of London Bridge and daughter of the above named Benjamin Seward Esq.'

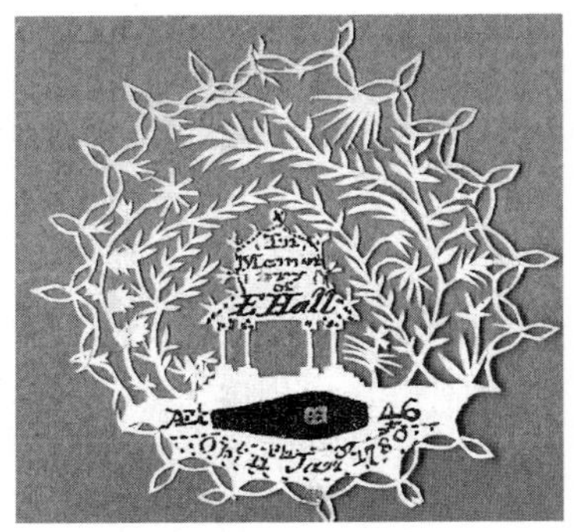

'In Memory E. Hall – Aet. (aged) 46 – Obit. 11 January 1780' The paper cut-out is shown twice actual size and was possibly made by Richard's daughter Martha (though the writing is Richard's own).

It was obviously a miserable time for Richard – there were endless visitors calling to pay their respects and express their condolences, and attendances at prayer meetings four or sometimes five times a week. Slowly, however, life returned to normal. Hence on 3 February we find the entry: 'Sons went to see the British Museum.' And then, slightly oddly, within a couple of months of the death of his first wife Richard decided that his priority was to acquire a new wardrobe! His diary records: '1780 March 20 – Mahogany Wardrobe £9.7.0.' It is interesting that he uses the word 'wardrobe' and not 'linen press' (or even 'armoire') which were the names more commonly given to the item of bedroom furniture used to store clothing. As with all his purchases of furniture, it was made of mahogany, a newly introduced wood from South America. The account books kept by Richard point to a complete re-fitting of the whole house with mahogany furniture, no doubt influenced by the likes of Chippendale, Sheraton and Hepplewhite.

Richard's year settled down to the same old rhythms: business was presumably good, with Mr Kearse setting out on more and more visits to Sussex, Kent and the West Country, often turning round and setting forth on his next journey within a couple of days of returning from his previous trip. There are indications that travel on England's roads was getting better – hence on 23 March Richard mentions that he 'set out in the Gloucester Coach after Dinner to travel all night' – something not to have been entertained twenty years earlier. But it was still enough of an adventure for Richard to remark that he 'experienced Journeying Mercies, which call aloud for Praise'. He spent three weeks at Bourton, staying with his brother-in-law's widow and sister, before returning via Oxford, where he 'caught the Post Coach back to London, via Maidenhead'. He appears to have started attending the Anglican church at St Magnus, becoming Church Warden on 12 May whereupon he 'went to see the poor at the Workhouse at Mile End'. Later in the year he comments that he was engaged in 'attending a Vestry to make a Poor Rate' and 'to give away the Coal and the Money' to the poor of the parish. The fact that he was a Baptist did not mean that he was unwilling to attend Church of England services – just as long as the gospel was being preached. In much the same way, John Wesley maintained that he remained an Anglican all his life, notwithstanding his 'Methodism'.

Richard mentions going with his son Billy to see the exhibition of pictures at Spring Gardens (18 May) and a fortnight later comments upon 'a vast concourse of Persons Assembling and going to the House of Commons, with a Petition to repeal the late Acts made in favour of the Papists.' The situation worsened and 7 May sees the entry 'Sad Rioting last Night with the Mob. Set fire to the Inside of Newgate and let out the Prisoners – pulled down Lord Mansfield's House etc. An awful time.' In fact, Richard is describing the Gordon Riots which had begun as a protest march from St George's Fields, Southwark, to the House of Parliament. Led by the Protestant activist Lord George Gordon, MP, the marchers intended to hand in a petition complaining at the attempt to end discrimination against Catholics. The mob of some 50,000 got out of control and many went on the rampage. Newgate, Clerkenwell, the Fleet and the Clink prisons were burnt down. Some 850 people died in the rioting. Twenty-one ringleaders were found guilty and hanged and, although George Gordon himself was charged, he was acquitted, largely due to his brilliant defence lawyer. The rioting continued for several days with Richard noting that 'Marshall Law' took place on 8 May. 'We had Soldiers in the Vestry Room to guard the Toll House and Waterworks.' Richard was sufficiently alarmed by the mob to say that he 'went and slept at Mr Roberts' for a couple of nights. By 11 May 'our Neighbourhood and City quiet', so Richard came home, resumed drinking tea with his friends – and 'showed Mrs Wilkins St Pauls and the Waxworks'.

However, it was apparent that Bourton held attractions for Richard – although he never mentions what they were – and he set off for the Manor House on 16 June, staying with the recently widowed Mrs Snooke. Indeed, so frequent are the mentions of Mrs Snooke that the reader might assume that he was hoping to promote his cause with the wealthy widow. Maybe he tried. He stayed a month and returned to London on 20 July, again via the post coach. The soldiers were still billeted around town – 'went with Patty to see the Camp in the Museum Gardens August 1st'. They stayed another ten days, when Richard notes: 'the soldiers left us. A fine day. Very hot.' Ever the dutiful daughter, Patty seemed to accompany her father everywhere. On 3 August he went with her 'to Greenwich to eat Whitebait'. There was the shop to decorate ('August 28th began to whitewash the Shop and Counting House ceilings and to paint the front of the Shop').

Meanwhile Billy paid his membership for the Guild of Haberdashers and thereby was able to take up the Freedom of the City (6 September). Curiously the diary then jumps an entire month – from 7 September to 7 October – restarting with the words: 'Set out from Oxford in Post Coach. Dined at Maidenhead, got to London safe and found the Family well'. In other words, he slipped in another visit to Bourton, but left his diary at home. He returned to take Billy to the British Museum, Patty went off to see the Lord Mayor's Show at Mr Fox's on 9 November, and then the following day he set out in the Oxford stagecoach – for the fourth visit of the year to Bourton. This time he notes that 'the Roads are Exceeding Good'. Once more there is mention of Mrs Snooke, but not of any other family members. Certainly there is no mention of any romantic intentions – simply an odd comment on 8 December that he had had 'an unpleasant day on account of my proposing to set out for London for which I sent for a Chaise, but afterwards discharged it and stayed. A dull cold day.' That was on the Friday. And then, without any explanation, the entry for Thursday 14 December reads 'This day entered into the Solemn and very important engagement of a second marriage with Betty Snooke.' Betty Snooke was not the widow of William Snooke – she was his younger sister. Ominously it continues with the words 'may it never lessen the Happiness of my Dear Children' – it was to prove a vain hope.

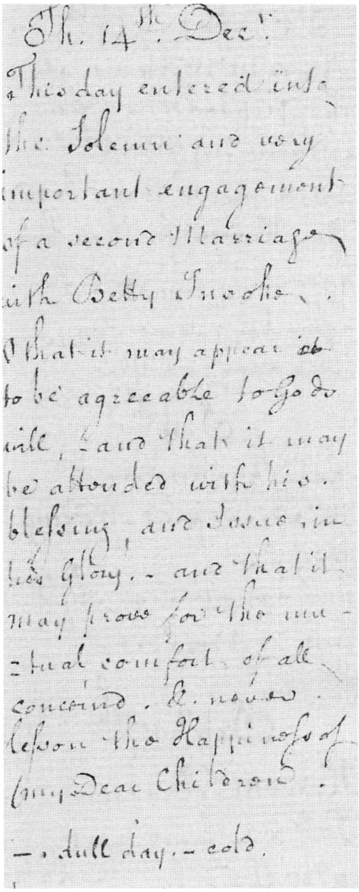
Th. 14th. Decr.
This day entered into
the Solemn and very
important engagement
of a second Marriage
with Betty Snooke.
That it may appear to
be agreeable to God's
will, and that it may
be attended with his
blessing, and Issue in
his Glory. – and that it
may prove for the mu-
-tual comfort of all
concerned. & never
lesson the Happiness of
my Dear Children.
– dull day. – cold.

Given that Lord Hardwicke's Marriage Act had come into force in 1753 (outlawing weddings unless banns had been published over the preceding three weeks), the wedding must have been planned since the latter part of November. So why no mention of the planned nuptuals? Why had he even contemplated going back to London a mere six days before the wedding was to take place? One possibility is that Betty Snooke wavered, after having consented to become engaged, forcing Richard to act the spurned suitor and 'head for home' – only for Betty to relent. It had been her birthday on 15 November – her thirty-seventh and it is easy to imagine that theirs was a birthday engagement. Richard was fifteen years her senior – but it seems unlikely that he would have made reference to the 'unpleasantness' of 8 December if all had ended well. Subsequent events suggest that the problem lay not with his bride but with Richard's children. It seems entirely possible that Richard had proposed, realised that his children back in London were likely to disapprove, and had written to them asking them to attend the wedding. Perhaps he got the reply on the Thursday saying that Billy and Patty were having nothing to do with the union, forcing Richard to consider returning to try and explain his case.

For the new bride, agreeing to marry the older and somewhat serious-minded Richard may have been a case of choosing the lesser of two evils. While Brother William was alive she would have been left to do as she wished within the household. But on his death she would have been reduced in status almost to that of an unpaid governess looking after his five children and being answerable to William's second wife – her much younger cousin Anne. An escape to London may have seemed an easy option, but in any event marrying for the first time at thirty-seven must have been an enormous upheaval for her.

The diaries give the firm impression that Richard's decision to remarry was somewhat calculated: it does not come across as a 'love match'. For many years afterwards, Richard would duly note in the diary his wife's birthday (meaning Eleanor's) and never mention Betty's. He remembers his wedding anniversary to Eleanor, and even details the anniversary of her death. It is not until another ten years have elapsed that Richard starts to express love and devotion for Betty, and it is hard not to feel sympathy for a woman who must surely have had to put up with knowing that she was 'second best'.

Why might Richard's family have disapproved? Not, one suspects, because less than a year had passed since Eleanor had died – remarriage within the year was commonplace and indeed both Richard's father and grandfather had followed the same course. The traditional mourning period for a man was six months (as opposed to one year and a day for a woman), so it seems unlikely that the wedding would have appeared impetuous. There are various other possibilities: the most likely one is that the family may have suspected that Richard had been courting his other sister-in-law – William's widow, Anne – and had turned to Betty when his suit was declined. This may have appeared unseemly and somewhat calculating. Or, possibly, Betty may have been the target of his son Billy's affections. He was after all twenty-six, and hence closer in age to his new stepmother than was Richard. He had been brought up for many years as part of the Snooke household with Betty more like a big sister to him in his formative years. The problem could perhaps have been, more predictably, money. Perhaps the three offspring, anxious to guard their Seward inheritance, thought it more appropriate that Richard should marry 'an old widow' for companionship – one who was way past child-bearing! They may have realised that with young Betty, her biological clock ticking away, there was a very real chance that their anticipated inheritance could at best be diluted and at worst be dissipated entirely.

Whatever the reason, none of the children attended the wedding, and it would have been with a strong sense of foreboding that the couple made the journey by Mrs White's stagecoach back to London on 20 December. Richard found 'his Dear Children well' and commented that this year he 'had travelled 689 miles to and from Bourton in safety', There was time to show off his new bride – Lady Harrington and Mrs Rice paid a wedding visit and innumerable friends came to take tea. But Richard notes on 4 January 1781 'Son went to Mr Fields – stayed all night' – perhaps an indication that Billy was not happy being under the same roof as the newlyweds. Later it was 'Son went to Battersea – dined and slept there.' But there were attempts at joint outings ('February 8th – went with my son and Betsy to see the Museum' and later 'Went to see the Exhibition of Pictures with Wife Son and Daughter'). There were other visits – without the children – to see St Paul's, Westminster Abbey and the House of Lords.

Shortly after this the business appears to have suffered a downturn – possibly when one of their trading partners folded, leaving them in the lurch: 'April 6th met with a frowning Providence by the failure of Messrs Ginos.' A month later Richard 'went to the choice of Assignees to Ginos & Atkinson' and, on 22 May, 'went to the Navy Office, Exchequer Bank, to the last meeting of Messrs. Ginos.' This would suggest that Richard and his son had been involved in some way with a naval contract – very possibly the supply of silk stockings (which were an essential part of a naval officer's uniform) via the firm of Ginos on some sort of agency basis and the failure of Ginos would have cost the Hall firm dear if it had also meant the loss of the navy contract itself. A possible confirmation of a naval connection is that the second son, Francis (also in the family business), had previously moved down to Portsmouth – the home of the British Navy. Maybe this was so that he could personally deal with the supply end of the naval contract, eventually taking over the role of Ginos & Atkinson as local agent.

Then, on the last day of May, Richard 'set out with Wife in Oxford Coach for Bourton ... 'a fine day, very warm and dusty.' Later entries for June mention 'a violent storm of Thunder, Lightning, Hail and Rain – very terrible weather' after they had accompanied Mrs Snooke to a sale of goods at Oddington. But no explanation was given in the diary as to why they were attending a goods sale in the first place, let alone one in the pouring rain. The clue is that, when 22 June came, Richard 'set out in Mrs Snookes Chaise – tea at Burford. Mrs Snooke and my Wife then returned and I came on to Oxford... Got home in safety.' In other words, Richard's wife was never to return to London – the decision had already been made that Richard would go back on his own, sell up, leave the business, and settle in Bourton complete with his newly acquired furniture. Reviewing the events years later, Richard was to write 'The Lord in whose hands are all my times and ways, has suffered a further change to take place – my dear children being dissatisfied that we should continue to live together I removed to a small house at Bourton on the Water, where we slept the first night November 19th 1781.' Not for them the grandeur of the Manor House – they were to move into 'a house opposite the New Inn' – rented from ... Mrs Snooke.

First, however, Richard had to spend time in London tidying up loose ends. It cannot have been helped that he got called again to do jury service – first on Monday 9 July ('Attending at Guildhall being summoned on ye Lord Mayor's Court Jury but there was not sufficient to make a jury') and then a fortnight later ('Attending again at the Guildhall – was there about ten in the Morning. Returned about 20 minutes past six in the Evening. Tryed 13 Cases'). He resigned as Church Warden, having attended a meeting where his replacement was appointed and his accounts approved, before heading off to the delightfully named George and Vulture for a spot of dinner.

There were domestic arrangements to make – 'July 30th Maids Dolly & Martha left us' – presumably having been told that their services were no longer required. He fitted in visits to his lawyers to swear various business papers, and he found time to note his son's birthday on 14 September ('Son now enters into his 28th year – may the Lord grant that as he grows in days he may grow in Grace'). He bought items to take back to the country: '1781 September A new carv'd gilt frame to an Old Glass 1.11.6.' There was still time to note the weather, despite all the packing up to be done: 'November 1st – very buisy packing to go and send to the country. Rain in night. Not cold' and 'November 6th – very buisy in preparing for the journey. Very heavy showers today. Not cold.'

At last he set off ('November 7th – set out for Bourton in the Oxford Coach. Slept at Oxford. Breakfast at Burford, got to Bourton for Dinner') and soon after arrived at his new home town ('November 9th – very busy in putting things away at the New House, Mr and Mrs Wilkins drank tea'). Separately he refers to paying 9d. for help with the unpacking,

And eventually, when the happy couple did move in on 19 November:

> O that the Lord will be pleased to make this a peaceable and quiet dwelling' [a clear reference to the tempestuous times of the past few months]. December 28th – Mr, Mrs & Miss Palmer, Mrs Beddome, her Sons, Mr Boswell and Richard Boswell, Mrs Snooke and Sophy din'd. Very stormy with wind. Rain – our Parlour smoaked so I was oblig'd to put out the fire and dine without one. Had a fire made upstairs.

Fortunately the day was 'not cold' but no doubt Mrs Snooke as owner of the freehold of the building would have muttered something about the chimney being fine with the previous tenants...

It was not, however, a 'clean break' in the sense that Richard was still entitled to half the profits of the business, even though William was left to do most of the work, and clearly this remained as a source of contention for many years. Finally Richard insisted on a valuation of the shop, its stock, and all the contents of the house at London Bridge in order to establish what was his and what rightfully belonged to his son. The inventory of the house goods appears in Appendix II. It is also clear that Richard still picked up the expenses for the shop throughout the 1780s and 1790s, of which details appear in later chapters. And, as will be seen, the split was never entirely healed. Father and son appear to have 'agreed to differ' but were never close again. They still met and William came to see his father on his final illness, and maybe there was a deathbed reconciliation (other family diaries hint at this) but too late to undo the damage caused by Richard's own will, in which he pointedly refuses to allow any papers to be passed to the children of his first marriage.

There is one surprising omission from the 1781 diary, given Richard's interest in astronomy, and that was the discovery of a new planet by William Herschel (reported on 26 April). Since antiquity man had known of the five planets – because they were visible with the naked eye. Then along comes a German-born musician, earning a living teaching music to the good burghers of Bath and who, using a home-made seven-inch telescope, discovers 'Georgium Sidus' (George's Star). It created a sensation: overnight doubling the size of the known solar system. The name never caught on – for a start it was incorrect to term it a star when it was a planet, and years later it was renamed Uranus. But the attempt to flatter the King worked, and George III appointed Herschel as his private astronomer, gave him an annual income of £200, and subsequently made grants of many thousands of pounds, enabling Herschel to build the world's largest telescope (forty feet long) in 1789. Herschel enlisted the support of his sister, Caroline, and together they catalogued stars throughout the universe. He discovered the rotation of Saturn's rings and two of its satellites. He even (1797) detected the existence of a ring orbiting Uranus – but this discovery was overlooked and it was to be a further two centuries before modern astronomers 'discovered' the feature (1977).

What was remarkable about the Herschels was their breadth of knowledge. William came to England as an oboist in the

Hanoverian Guards; he taught the organ, he composed symphonies, choral works and chamber music; and as an amateur taught himself to make instruments of the highest calibre; and at the same time vastly increased our knowledge of the solar system, the Milky Way and of the nebulae. Caroline published a star catalogue in 1798, as well as discovering eight comets and several star clusters. They were all the more remarkable because they were entirely self-taught.

The book containing the diaries for the three years 1782–1784 marks a complete change in Richard's life. In a way, with little or no involvement in the day-to-day running of the business, and with no visits to see the sights, the diaries become much more of a description of the weather, details of sermons listened to, and the minutiae of country living.

Fitting into a tiny house (probably a two-up, two-down semi) would have been a major upheaval for the pair of them – let alone when Betty became pregnant and produced Anna, the first of two children, who arrived in the world on the eve of Richard's fifty-third birthday on 15 March 1782. Betty had been married just over a year – oddly there is no mention whatsoever of her pregnancy, but it must have been a huge 'shock to the system' for Betty having a first child at thirty-eight, and for Richard embarking on a second family (all those soiled clothes and sleepless nights!) just as he had started his 'retirement'.

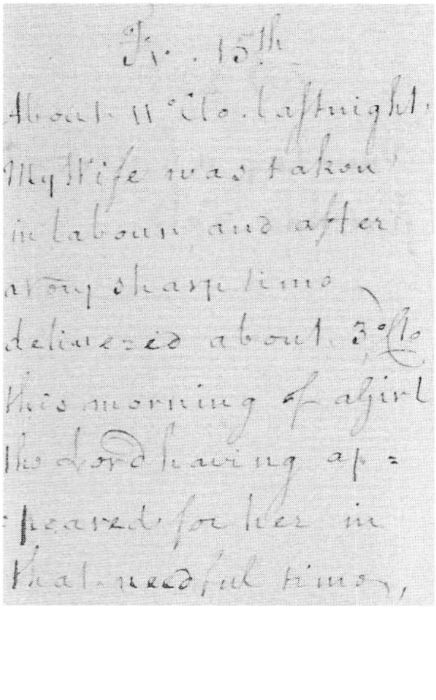

As was the custom of the time, Betty remained in her bedroom for the first two weeks after the delivery– Richard noting on 9 April that 'Betty came downstairs this afternoon for the first time'. Richard seems to have had little or nothing to do with household matters – indeed he resolutely went and 'Din'd with Sister' on most days in the first few weeks of Anna's life. Either Richard or his sister-in-law were still in the mood to buy furniture and household affects – together they attended Lord Chedworth's Sale on 2 May. There then seems to have been a 'family exchange' – Richard went up to London on his own to visit William, while his elder daughter Martha ('Patty') came down from London to Bourton. Possibly it was intended to heal the family rift. But it was a sickly time – Richard remarks 'The Present a Remarkable time for the Lord visiting more or less most Family's in London with Coughs and Colds, with which many are confin'd'.

June 5th sees the entry: 'Son William went with Mr Wrench to St James's – kissed his Majesty's hand.' Well, that must have been nice, for all of them. But William does not appear to have given his father his undivided attention – 'setting off for Margate by Water' on 27 June, returning two weeks later. Meanwhile, Patty had a close escape while out horse-riding at Bourton: 'The Lord very kindly Preserv'd her when in immanent danger by a Fall from a Horse which ran away with her, being affrighted' (13 July). Patty came back to London a few days later – accompanied by Mrs Snooke. Cue for Richard to depart home to his wife, leaving sister-in-law to try and talk sense into William. She stayed in town for a month, returning on 22 August with 'son Francis' who had not been mentioned for over a year in the diaries. He was by then twenty-five and appears to have been on a two-week holiday to visit the family. Richard and Francis travelled the county together, 'visiting Leachlade and Fairford Church', taking tea with friends, and 'dining on a haunch of venison' before Francis started his return journey to Portsmouth on 5 September. His father and stepmother accompanied him as far as Cirencester, where he left to catch the Bath stagecoach.

Richard appears to have missed the gossip and news of London – and gleefully announces 'had the General Evening Post for the first day' on 16 September. But he still appears to have suffered poor health. 'October 4th Indispos'd with a Cold that came on yesterday – head poorly, bowels indifferent and great chilliness.' He remained 'indisposed' throughout the whole of the next fortnight ('Very poorly indeed last night, being oblig'd to rise twice with a purgeing. I was very low, could not get any sleep for a great while'). But without wishing to dwell on such matters spare a thought for what it must have been like to wake up in the night, feeling nauseous and with diarrhoea. No running water in the house. No flush toilet – indeed no inside privy, simply a chamber pot under the bed. And no light. None at all – not even a street light outside. No matches. In theory, Richard could have fished around in the dark for his tinderbox and a flint, and tried to strike it before lighting a candle, but with other 'imperatives' this seems unlikely. And, having endured the 'purging', he then had to face getting up a second time and going through the whole rigmarole all over again. Not a pleasant thought, so no wonder it was mentioned in the diary. That was the reality of life in the country before modern sanitation and lighting. No doubt Betty never heard the last of it – though oddly neither she nor Anna receive much of a mention until 1783. But Richard's health improved in time, and with it his appetite, so that by mid-November he was happy to 'walk to [Upper] Slaughter' before dining with Sister Snooke 'on brill, a fine Rump of Beef and Rice Pudding'. A week later he was back for more – 'Din'd on Chine, 2 nice Fowls roasted, and a brace of Woodcocks'.

His health restored, he was also able to resume his favourite pastime – recording household expenditure that autumn on a new pair of sheets (13s. 6d.) and a featherbed with bolster (£2 8s. 5d.). Rather against the fashion of the time he also bought a dozen pewter plates for twelve shillings, a scotch carpet for two pounds and paid his half of the cost of altering the wash house ('a moiety of £11/5/0 – viz. £5/12/6d.').

What is apparent is that the winters were far colder than we experience now – as early as 1 November Richard comments that there was 'a good deal of Snow in the morning' – and four days later it had not improved: 'Snow in the morning which lay on the Hills'. Throughout the whole of November there are repeated references to the fact that the snow was lying and that there was a 'Black Frost, very Cold'.

Then the bilious attacks returned: 'December 23rd – Very ill in the Night with pains in the Stomach, violent Cholic. Took some Rhubarb Tincture.' It can hardly have made for a jolly Christmas Day (when he remarks that he was 'not quite well, with appearance that my complaint was bilious with a touch of Jaundice. Dull day. Some little small rain. Not cold.') Rhubarb seems to have been a popular remedy for 'Wind or a stomach disordered' – he took rhubarb, sugar candy, powdered liquorice, cream of tartar and caraway seeds mixed in equal quantities and these were then ground up before being added to water. Mind you, he also dealt with the stomach pains by taking four cloves of garlic, 'pricked with a needle a great many times', night and morning! Let us hope that he also remembered his own advice: 'Rosemary – helps a disagreeable breath.'

The diary for the year ends with the comment that 1782 had been 'remarkable for general sickness, for much wet at the time of Harvest, much of which received great Injury, particularly the Barley'. He concluded that 'the Lord has a Controversy with the Inhabitants of our Land, and that He had many ways to bring deserved Judgement upon us'.

The diary for 1783 starts with a catalogue of Richard's complaints about his state of health – his almost continual biliousness and 'stomach disorders'. So he notes on 3 January that his 'complexion is more yellow than it has been' and began a new medicine. He appears to become increasingly grumpy – forever complaining that if there was a windy evening he 'was oblig'd on account of the Smoak to leave our Parlour and have a fire upstairs'. However, he was luckier than his neighbour (5 March: 'alarm'd early with Mr P's. Chimney being on fire') or indeed the inhabitants of Messina ('Feb 5th – Awful Earthquake at Messina in Sicily – great damage'). Much of the historic town of Messina was devastated and widespread damage occurred in Sicily and southern Italy – some 40,000 people perished.

Travel was still a major and potentially dangerous enterprise, so when he set off for London with his wife (no mention of his daughter) in early 1783 he refers to 'many anxious fears which demand great Praise. A dull day for travelling – much Snow fell the past night, and very foggy. Cold'. The trip seems to have been prompted by the need to visit Haberdashers' Hall ('Went with Mr Clugh to make him free' i.e. to enrol him as a freeman of the city of London). Interestingly Richard makes reference to eating at one of the many takeaways which existed in London ('Din'd with Wife and Patty on beef stakes behind St Clements Church'). London was full of establishments selling cooked meat on a takeaway basis. It is as well that Richard avoided the pork – notorious for being 'off', undercooked and being a source of worms.

He returned to Bourton to note various items about the sky at night ('March 18th – a total Eclipse of the Moon'). On 27 April he saw 'much of the Northern Lights at night, very flashing'. This reference to the Aurora Borealis may seem surprising to us in the twenty-first century, but records of the time show that the aurora was seen in southern parts of the country comparatively frequently, indicating that the auroral zone has drifted northwards over the last 200 years. The Stroud apothecary Thomas Hughes, whose diaries are in the Exeter Museum, records sightings of the aurora on no fewer than seventy-one occasions between 1771 and 1813. It must have been an awe-inspiring sight to gaze at the Heavens on a starry night, just as the overwhelming darkness of a moonless night is something that few of us experience nowadays.

Richard also noted in August 1783 'a remarkable Phaenomenon seen in various parts between 9 and 10 o'clock at Night' but without giving an explanation – perhaps because he simply did not know what to make of the extraordinary storm. Heavy clouds of volcanic ash had been drifting towards the country ever since the Laki volcano exploded in Iceland on 8 June 1783. Unknown to Richard, it reached England on 23 June, when he noted 'mostly gloomy, very warm'. The next day was 'still gloomy – a sort of fog in the air'. The records he kept over the following months refer constantly to a stifling heat, a constant haze and to huge electrical storms which illuminated the ash cloud in a fearsome manner.

Richard would not have known that the volcanic ash contained millions of tons of hydrogen fluoride and sulphur dioxide. The Laki eruption is believed to have caused two million deaths worldwide, making it the most catastrophic volcanic explosion, in human terms, ever recorded. A quarter of all Icelanders perished along with half their livestock. An estimated 23,000 people died in England – mostly from lung damage and respiratory failure. Outdoor workers were particularly affected because they were exposed over a longer period of time. Harvests failed and cattle died, and at the year-end Richard was to note: 'This year has been remarkable for very hot weather and a great deal of terrible Thunder and Lightning, by which very much Damage was done ... much sickness has attended.' The whole episode does rather put into context concerns in 2010 about disruption to air travel caused by the Eyjafjallajökull volcano – a minnow in comparison to the nearby Laki volcanic fissure.

Two further visits to London occurred in 1783. The diary contains various hints that 'Cousin Frank' Kearse had been unwell and presumably was unable to make his selling forays into Sussex, Kent and Essex. Richard's son William, now in charge of the business, appears to have started making those visits himself, and it is probable that he asked his father to cover for him in the shop on those trips: 'May 29th –Arrived safe at London Bridge ... June 3rd – son set out for Kent' and 'October 24th – got to London in safety ... November 6th – son William returned from his Kent and Sussex journeys'. On the first visit he refers to going to see the Exhibition of Pictures – probably at the Royal Academy. On the later visit the highlight seems to have been a visit to see 'Sir Ashton Levers Collection of Natural Curiosities – and Curious they indeed are. Din'd at a Beefstake house. Fine day, mild.' This was on 4 November and Richard notes that his other son, Francis, had come up to London on a visit. They had a rude awakening the following morning: 'Rose early on account of a great fire in Aldersgate Street' – a reminder that all Londoners remained very 'twitchy' if there was any sort of conflagration in the vicinity. The Great Fire was clearly etched in memory...

In between visits to London there were various trips – for instance to Woodstock and Blenheim – usually 'accompanied by Mrs Snooke and my Wife' but it has to be said that a large number of the outings were with Mrs Snooke alone: 'Rode out on horseback with Mrs Snooke – fine day 'til Evening.' There is no reference to Richard following the hunt, but someone in the family would have been sufficiently aware of the scene to compile the paper cut-out showing the fox being chased.

Richard again mentions his ill-health: 'October 13th Began upon a Medicine for my Nervous Complaint.' Towards the end of the year it was his young daughter Anna who was giving cause for concern: 'December 1st – very Low on hearing my Dear Daughter was so poorly.' No specific mention of her illness appears but 'December 10th poor Anna very ill' was followed by 'Poor

Anna ill with a fever – had a blister – took some of James Powder'. She remained very ill and on 13 December was 'exceeding bad – was bled with a leach'. But time, if not the leeches, appears to have healed her and by 20 December it was noted: 'Anna better. Frost, dull day, cold.' It was nearly another year before Anna gets mentioned again – still on account of her health: '3rd October Dear Anna began to prepare for inoculation' – in other words she was put on a special diet. 'Wednesday October 13th – This day poor little Anna her Cousins Martha and Eliza were inoculated for the Smallpox.' Elsewhere he records that he paid Mr Hayward two guineas to perform the inoculation. Six days later 'poor Anna began to fail' and 'wife went to sleep at Mrs Snooke's on Account of the poor Baby'. It is not clear whether this is for the sake of Anna, or so that Richard could get an undisturbed night's sleep! By 21 October he notes 'The smallpox came out in poor Anna & Eliza' and thereafter Anna remained 'very poorly – had between two and three hundred pustules' until Friday 5 November: 'Through the goodness of God – my Wife and Anna returned from Mrs Snooke's – the Dear Baby through great mercy finally recovered from Inoculation.' The same day's entry showed that Maria came to stay – and that Preston (presumably the new servant) joined the Hall household.

The diary entries reinforce the fact that Richard seems to have had very little 'hands-on' involvement in parenting. Living in the country, and over a half-century on from what was fashionable during his own infancy, Richard may well have seen a change from employing a wet-nurse to Betty feeding Anna herself. Wet-nursing was still popular – but prevailing books on childcare were starting to express the view that 'mother's milk is best'. It was, however, still the fashion to bind babies tightly in swaddling clothes in order 'to receive and retain all the evacuations of nature' as one writer put it in 1826. Only the children of the poor went without bindings – and it is hard to imagine that young Anna would have been able to avoid the skin complaints and discomfort caused by being wrapped in soiled 'bandages' all night and day. The whole episode of the smallpox inoculation is a reminder of how 'hit and miss' the process was – after all, it was introducing a potentially fatal illness into a child in circumstances where it was impossible to predict the strength of the dose or likely reaction.

The work of Dr Edward Jenner, a country doctor from Berkeley in Gloucester, was soon to transform matters, and in 1798 he published his *Inquiry into the causes and effects of the Variolae Vaccinae*, explaining the link between cowpox and smallpox, and noting that milkmaids who caught the former rarely went on to be afflicted with the latter. History states that it was 14 May 1796 before Dr Jenner extracted the cowpox serum from a young milkmaid by the name of Sarah Nelmes. She had come to see him for treatment for cowpox, having sores on her hands. He experimented by injecting the serum into an eight-year-old boy (James Phipps, the son of his gardener). The boy developed cowpox, and, in order to complete the experiment, Jenner then waited for two months before introducing smallpox into the boy's system. He failed to catch the highly infectious and often fatal disease – because, as Jenner surmised, he had developed an immunity. Poor James – the experiment had to be repeated on many subsequent occasions before Dr Jenner was satisfied that the immunity was permanent!

AN
INQUIRY
INTO
THE CAUSES AND EFFECTS
OF
THE VARIOLÆ VACCINÆ,
A DISEASE
DISCOVERED IN SOME OF THE WESTERN COUNTIES OF ENGLAND,
PARTICULARLY
GLOUCESTERSHIRE,
AND KNOWN BY THE NAME OF
THE COW POX.
BY EDWARD JENNER, M.D. F.R.S. &c.
LUCRETIUS.
London:
PRINTED, FOR THE AUTHOR,
BY SAMPSON LOW, Nº. 7, BERWICK STREET, SOHO:
AND SOLD BY LAW, AVE-MARIA LANE; AND MURRAY AND HIGHLEY, FLEET STREET.
1798.

All this was ten or more years in the future. However, an uncorroborated diary entry from one of Richard Hall's children hints at earlier experiments – stating that Richard went to meet Dr Jenner in the 1780s, that Richard was introduced to a humble milkmaid, 'that the figure of the cross was cut upon their arms and that they were bound together until their blood did intermingle', and that a week later the good doctor counted the blisters – 'one hundred, a good reaction'. So it is quite possible that, before experimenting with syringes, Dr Jenner used a 'person to person' inoculation. It was hardly likely to be effective for widespread use as one imagines that the humble milkmaid might have been somewhat less humble if she were asked to submit herself to being 'mutilated' on more than one occasion!

Richard would have got on well with Edward Jenner – both of them were avid fossil collectors. Jenner was also a great observer of the natural world – spending years of research into the nest-raiding and egg-laying habits of cuckoos! He was the first person to establish that it was the fledgling chick (and not its parent) which ejected the other eggs from the nest – an observation which gained him admission as a Fellow of the Royal Society in 1789. He also carried out observations on angina as well as experimenting with hydrogen-filled balloons, launching one from the grounds of Berkeley Castle in September 1784 (just two years after the Mongolfier Brothers in France experimented with the first hot-air balloon). The *Gloucester Journal* of 6 September 1784 noted:

> On Thursday last at two o'clock a balloon was launched from the inner court of Berkeley Castle, which rose to a very great height, and was visible for a quarter of an hour. The same afternoon it was seen to descend in a field where some people were reaping, near the Smith's shop, in the parish of Kingscote, about ten miles from Berkeley. The reapers were so much terrified, that they could not for some time be prevailed upon to approach it.

Ballooning in the latter part of the 1780s became a craze which swept the country – the *Public Advertiser* of 13 September 1784 issuing the warning:

> The Balloon Mania, it is feared, will not subside, till some fatal calamity shall be the result of it. One of these balloons, filled with turpentine and other matter of that kind, falling last night on the leads of a house in Tottenham Court Road, the leads melted by the fire... Within these few days more than fifty have been sent off from Westminster and its vicinity.

Returning to his own journal of expenses for 1 October 1783 Richard refers to the cost of going to Evesham for the day. He listed the turnpikes (1s. 6d.), the driver (half a crown) and the actual transport (6s. 7d.). The same journey the following year (May 1784) was five times the price – largely because he appears to have had no dinner the first time around! For the second trip he shows the main expense as being the post-chaise at one guinea. He also had to pay the driver 2s. 6d., turnpikes 1s. 6d., the waiter and 'horsler' sixpence each, plus 4s. 10d. for dinner and 1s. for

Mr Roper (it is not clear what he did but he was probably the innkeeper). 'Horsler' may have been Richard's own spelling for 'ostler' (the original spelling was 'hostler'), which could either denote the owner of the hostelry or (as now) the person who tended to the horses. The total for the day's outing: £1 11s. 10d.

Richard's clothing list would appear to be a quite separate inventory of items – '2 night[shirts]; 2 necks [possibly neckerchiefs – i.e. strips of cloth worn round the neck – but in context more likely intended to mean shirts – i.e. clothing which came up to the neck]; 1 new fine plain [shirt?]; 2 Ruffles; 1 Fine Holland; 3 pairs Silk Stockings, 1 pair gauze, 3 pairs worsted; 2 night caps – linen; w. shoes [walking shoes?]; 1 linen hands. [handkerchief] – 1 blue ditto, 1 silk; cloth coat and waistcoat; silk waistcoat; a white dining waistcoat; silk breeches; 5 stocks [stiffeners worn round the neck inside the shirt collar]; and finally, muffetees [a muffler or muff worn round the wrists, often of fur. Ladies fashions were for muffetees made of swan or even peacock feathers].' Given that we know that Richard was not too fond of washing – or changing his clothes – it seems safe to assume that this list represented an inventory of wearing apparel – perhaps the items which he had bought during the year – rather than the items taken on a journey where he was not even staying overnight. Alternatively it may have been an aide-memoire ('these are the things I need to pack when I go on one of my journeys'). An interesting omission: no underpants (men went 'commando'). The list shows that clothing was still ornate, what with his ruffles and stocks, but there was an emphasis on keeping warm.

It is clear from the accounts of these journeys that travel was getting faster – and more reliable. The various Turnpike Trusts – formed to take over responsibility for the surfacing of particular stretches of road – were beginning to have a major effect on both travel and transport. For instance, the next year (1784) saw the establishment of John Palmer's mail service linking London and Bristol. Businessmen realised that faster passenger services – particularly those which could run through the night, meant lower overheads because of the saving in overnight accommodation. And the invention of bands of metal springs – in place of leather straps – meant that travel by coach

Cut-out showing a highway robber pointing his blunderbuss and (bent!) sword drawn.

was starting to be more of a pleasure and less of a serious adventure.

For Richard, the end of 1783 was a time for reflection: 'This year has been remarkable for very hot weather and a great deal of terrible Thunder and Lightning – by which very much damage was done. A fine plentiful Harvest and Peace restored – much Sickness has attended.' The reference to peace being restored is presumably to the Treaty of Versailles in 1783. A simultaneous war with both France and the American colonies had brought Britain to its knees, and the coming of peace, even where it represented a defeat of old policies, was clearly popular. The diary for 1784 gives details of a cold, snowy journey up to London ('January 15th – set out for London with Wife & Sophy in a Post-Chaise. B[reakfast] at Burford. Stopp'd at Oxford and Benson, made no regular dinner. Slept at Henley'). Poor Richard, missing his dinner! This was of course the main meal of the day. Breakfast was taken at around ten in the morning, and usually consisted of tea (or chocolate) accompanied by toast and butter. Dinner, on the other hand, was often not taken until 3 o'clock – or even later in fashionable establishments in London, thereby enabling 'afternoon tea' to be slipped in, in between mealtimes. Supper was a light meal – usually a 'cold collation'. For Richard this meant bread and cheese, but in winter months a hot gruel would sometimes be served – boiled oats to which butter and wine were added. No doubt the alcohol would have helped to ward off the chill from the draughty rooms and cold floors of the coaching inn at Henley!

* * *

For the first time the diaries suggest that neither William nor Patty were living above the shop on London Bridge – Richard 'went to Miss Stephen's at night to Son's' while 'Patty came over from her Lodgings'. The visit seems to have enabled Richard to try a new form of treatment for whatever malaise he felt he was suffering from. Hence on 30 January: 'Had a Blister plaister put on my thigh in order to make an Issue, which Mr Jones much advised to. Frost continued. Fine Day – very cold.' The following day Mr Jones took off the plaster 'and put in a Pea'. It presumably worked. because the day afterwards he notes, 'The blister was formed into an Issue' – enabling him to set off for Bourton a happy man on 3 February ('Had a safe and comfortable Journey ... Roads very fine. Very pleasant day'). But it was a cold countryside he returned to – just about every entry for the next five weeks listed snow, hard frost or 'exceeding cold'. He presumably kept some hosiery stock with him in Bourton – noting on 11 February that he 'sold two pairs of silk hose to Mr Vernon – 13/6 was paid to my son'.

Richard then made another journey to London (at the end of May) coinciding with William's absence in Northampton. The family were obviously concerned at reports of the illness of Mr Kearse (Richard's son Francis was dispatched to visit him in Town Malling). But, as luck would have it, Richard returned to Bourton on 10 June only to hear two days later that his uncle had died, and so Richard and his wife immediately turned round, and headed back to London for the funeral. It meant that there were more expenses to record: 'Boy to open gates – sixpence' seems somewhat generous. They presumably took a different route from the year before, going to Oxford via Witney before travelling to Benson where they picked up the Birmingham coach. An overnight stop at Witney cost five shillings: 'B[reakfast] at Benson two shillings and two pence, D(inner) at Colebrook 3 shillings' – in total £4 6s. 9d. one way in order to attend the funeral. 'June 15th Attended the Funeral of my Kinsman Mr Francis Kearse to the burial ground in Deadman's Place.' Francis Kearse was fifty-one when he died. There was business to attend to, so the next day sees Richard going to the Commons to prove Mr Kearse's will, and the day after 'Busy in looking over poor Mr Kearse's things'. Presumably he was sole executor and beneficiary because on 22 June he was able to go 'to the Bank. Transferr'd £100 Four per Cent into my name', before returning to Bourton two days later.

Richard's first attendance at Chapel ('to hear Mr Wilkins preach from Is[a]iah 30.15') on 4 July was not an auspicious one: 'I was so very poorly with my Nervous complaint I was oblig'd to leave the Meeting and come home.' This was followed by 'poorly in Night with a purging. Took some Tincture of Rhubarb'. He complains the next day of 'an awful Tempest of Thunder, lightning and rain, tremendous lightning. Began to lighten before 9 at night – continued more or less near 3 o'clock in the morning. Did not go to bed 'til near 3' – adding ambiguously, 'there was much wind'. But the next week he was well enough to 'Wash Feet' on 13 July, and to record a 'General Thanksgiving for Peace' on 29 July.

This was followed at the end of August by a six-day trip to Bath, accompanied by 'Mrs Snooke, Wife and Daughter'. They dined at Cheltenham, sleeping the first night at The Bear at Gloucester, taking tea at The Cross Hands (Chipping Sodbury) before staying at The Bear at Bath and dining at Mr Freeman's. Much 'drinking of coffee' took place but without any mention of any specific sights taken in during the visit. He returned to have 'the Kitchen white-washed' (7 September) and to have his 'Feet washed' (what, again?!) on 10 September. By 10 October he was able to record that he 'went out of Mourning for poor Mr Kearse who has been Departed four months this day. Dull, cold'. Richard ended that year with the observation:

> At the beginning of this year 1784 we had much Cold Weather, and Snow; a late Spring, warm summer with much Lightning and Thunder; a very fine Thanksgiving and Harvest; a remarkable plenty of Apples and fruit of almost every sort. The Year closed with a long frost and Snow upon the ground which has been from the 8th December and still continues.

With hindsight we know that this prolonged period of cold weather was a direct consequence of what became known as the Laki Haze – the cloud of toxic gas spewed out from Iceland and affecting the upper atmosphere throughout the northern hemisphere.

This marks the end of the continuous series of diaries, in which each day was recorded as it happened. Instead, from then on, Richard appears to have preferred a series of jottings, almanacs, journals, lists written out on odd bits of paper and so on.

The remaining years of the decade were significant for family 'Special Occasions'. The marriages of Richard's elder children followed in quick succession – his eldest son, William, married Miss Charlotte Glover, on 13 January 1785 and, in the same year, on the 7 April, his daughter Martha ('Patty') was married to Mr Henry Griffith of Bath. Richard appears to have made a loan to Henry on the occasion of his marriage – a loan, not a dowry payment, since it was secured by a bond and remained due to Richard until he released it under his will. Perhaps dowries were becoming less fashionable. He was later to lend Henry further sums – £300 in 1788, another £100 a year later, and the sum of £300 on a joint bond from Henry and Mrs Mary Mansford (Henry's sister) in 1793 – repayable within one year.

Son and daughter (and father!) then set about expanding their families: 'January 26th 1786. This day my son W. S. Hall had a son born to him named Richard' and 'August 20th 1786. My dear daughter Martha was confined with a son named Henry.' It seems likely that Richard went to see his daughter shortly before she gave birth – he mentions a Samuel Etheridge paying him £10 on 21 July 'on account of Mr Griffith's loan – took with me to Bath August 1st 1786 to give Mr Griffith'. '1787 – February 11th My son Francis gave in his experience to Mr Martin's Church and on the 27th was baptized.' 'September 18th Mrs W.S. Hall was again confined with a daughter whom they named Elizabeth.'

Richard's drawing – presumably intended as a bookmark, dedicated to his granddaughter 'Eliza'.

The diary for 28 November 1787 announces: 'My dear wife was

brought to bed with a son, whom we named Benjamin Snooke Hall.' Benjamin was subsequently to muse: 'The name Benjamin was probably given me from respect to the late Benjmn. Seward Esqre. and out of compliment to the Rev. Benjmn. Beddome, to whom my Father was much attached.' Richard recorded the expenses relating to his wife's lying-in.

Wifes laying in 28th Novr. 1787.
Gave Mrs. Paxford . . . . 2. 2. 0.
Nurse Davis 3. 13. 6

'May 28th 1788. Mrs Griffith presented her Husband with another son, who was named William.' 'February 27th 1789 Mrs Wm Hall was confined with a son, named William Seward.' This child died of the smallpox on 7 July 1790. On 8 July 1788 Richard's son Francis entered into the marriage state. 'This morning my Son Francis was married to Miss Mary Davies. On 10 September 1789 Mrs Francis Hall was confined with a boy named Edward who died 30 November the same year.'

It is worth remembering that by the time that Anna was born there had been an interval of twenty-four years without children and that, by the time Benjamin was born, Richard was already in his late-fifties. The changes in Richard's household, and in his lifestyle, can only be imagined! For a start the family needed another bed, and 1786 details:

Altering tent bed – a curtain, and altering Parlour Curtain (June 1786)

Irish Cloth	£1/18/00
Dimity	£0/14/00
Do.	£0/ 4/00
Tacks	£0/ 0/08
Bed Lace – fringe Thread and Tassel	£0/12/10
Bradley Taylor	£0/ 8/ 6
Cloth 2s5d, Rings & etc 1s 6½d	£0/ 3/11½
	£4/ 1/11½

Altering Tent Bed – a Curtain – & altering parlour Curtain, June &c 1786.

Irish Cloth	1.18.0
Dimity	0.14.0
Do.	0.4.0
Tacks	0.0.8
Bed lace – Fringe – Thread – Tassell	0.12.10
Bradley Taylor	0.8.6
Cloth 2s.5d – Rings &c 1s.6½d	0.3.11½
	4.1.11½

Wife's laying in 28th Novr. 1787

Gave Mrs. Paxford	2.2.0
Nurse Davis	3.13.6

And of course, as every parent knows, children do keep growing and needing new clothes: 'shoes – one shilling' is an entry appearing every three months or so. Richard also notes that he bought Anna a silver spoon (not born with one in her mouth then!) for 9s. 6d. In all he records that he spent £13 12s. 3d. on Anna in her first two years.

In 1786 there seems to have been a concerted attempt to 'smarten up' the home:

> May 6th – Whitewashed the Parlour
>
> June 29th – Whitewashed the Little Room and finished whitewashg. the New Kitchen
>
> June 20th – Whitewashed the Staircases

It was to be another two years before any more decorating was undertaken.

From time to time Richard appears to have taken an inventory of cash in the house. So he lists: 'Silver 0/5/0 Ditto 1/1/0 Ditto 0/3/6 Copper 0/0/8 Gold 6/16/6 Ditto 1/1/0 Total £9/7/8.' On another occasion a spot check revealed: 'In wife's pocket £6/6/0 In Trunk £8/8/0 In my pocket £5/15/6 Total £20/9/6.' In later years he seems to have kept more and more money about the house – by 1791 he mentions a figure of £34/6/3 and five years later he held 'in Cash about £60' – no doubt safely stashed away in the trunk!

Richard was not quite entirely absorbed with the minutiae of everyday life. In mentioning 1787 Richard notes: 'The first committee formed in London for the abolition of the slave trade.' Richard was of course writing this in the absence of any knowledge as to how the abolition movement would end – Parliament was not to approve abolition until six years after Richard's death. His diaries make no reference to the plight of slaves but he was a keen supporter of Hannah More who, besides being an education reformer, was an active abolitionist. Richard would also have heard at first hand the plight of slaves because his first wife's uncle (William Seward) raised money and went to America with George Whitfield (one of the founders of the Methodist movement) in order to buy land so that freed and escaped slaves could establish farms and be self-sufficient.

Throughout the last half of the eighteenth century there was a growing groundswell throughout the land – Parliament did not lead the change, but reacted to the continual pressure from people like Thomas Clarkson, who was the real powerhouse for abolition. He tirelessly toured the country organising petitions and rallies. He pestered and cajoled William Wilberforce into promoting the abolitionist cause in Parliament. He even managed to get 11,000 signatures opposing slavery from Manchester – roughly a fifth of the population of a city built on commerce. How? By pointing out that the business of shipping slaves was not just morally repugnant but, in business terms, hopelessly wasteful. It is estimated that 20 per cent of all slaves died in transit – of highly contagious diseases such as dysentery. But the same statistic applied to the crews who manned the slave ships, since disease affected everyone, and that sort of loss was clearly 'bad business practice'. Clarkson collected and distributed stories of the hideous squalor on board the slave ships and gave Wilberforce the facts on which to base his campaign. Two centuries later and we are all familiar with William Wilberforce, but Thomas Clarkson has been airbrushed from history.

Meanwhile slaves continued to be thought of as 'property' as seen from the contemporary newspaper cutting advertising a reward for the return of Tom, an escaped slave, in London:

RAN away from his Maſter, in St. James's Street, on Friday Morning, Aug. 26, a Black Slave; had on a full-trimmed brown Coat lined with yellow, a yellow Waiſtcoat and Leather Breeches, the Livery-Lace is yellow, black and red, intermixed; his Name is Tom, he is a ſtrong well-ſet Fellow, about five Feet ſix Inches high, and 21 Years of Age, with a Scar on his Forehead. Whoever ſecures the ſaid Slave ſhall receive Two Guineas, on applying at the Carolina Coffee-Houſe, in Birchin-Lane. Any Perſon harbouring him will be ſued.

Keep on running, Tom.

On 20 February Richard 'Bought Chambers Dictionary £10/16/0.' Ephraim Chambers had brought out the first edition of his masterpiece in 1728. He had originally trained as a mapmaker, but is regarded as the father of the encyclopaedia – heavily influencing *Encyclopædia Britannica* (1768) and other works. His was the first attempt at a truly comprehensive compendium of knowledge, bringing together the arts, sciences and humanities with a detailed system of cross-referencing. He dedicated his work to George II. A shame Richard did not buy the first edition – the two-volume set is now extremely rare … and valuable! As it was, the edition which he bought, by then in four volumes, was bequeathed specifically in Richard's will to his youngest son, Benjamin. A purchase price of £10 16s. made it an extremely expensive and valuable work of reference.

A glimpse of Richard's 'work ethic' is seen in his entry for 1786:

Early rising is a habit easily acquired, so necessary to the

> dispatch of country business, so advantageous to health, and so important to devotion, that except in cases of necessity it cannot be dispensed with by any prudent or diligent man. Let a person accustomed to sleep 'til eight in the morning rise the first week in April at a Quarter before 8, the second week at half after 7, the third at a quarter after 7 and the fourth at 7. Let him continue this method until the end of July, subtracting one quarter of an hour each week from sleep, and he will accomplish the work that at first sight appears difficult.

That would appear to mean rising at four in the morning in July. As if his moralising about slothful habits was not enough, he then sets out his advice about what not to eat: 'Avoid salted and dried meat, pork and goose, fish, cheese, much butter, rich sauces, strong beer, India Tea, Coffee, cider, raw fruit and all flatulum vegetables generative of wind (such as potatoes, carrots, moist roots and salads).' Well, that doesn't leave a lot. Instead, he recommended the use of horseradish and mustard, plus watercress, asparagus and roasted meats and poultry 'yielding more nutrition in quantity than fried and boil'd meats which are more likely to turn rancid on weak stomachs'. Listen to him, the Jamie Oliver of the eighteenth century – but he certainly does not come across as the ideal dinner guest! He also writes that it is good to breakfast on thin chocolate, cocoa or rosemary tea. And take supper on watery gruel and new-laid eggs (poached), plus oysters, finishing off with roasted apples. 'Be sure to avoid an indolent sedentary life, and use good air excessively and freely and adopt some kind of domestic labour (not attended with Fatigue) to promote circulation.' In Richard's case that seems to have meant attending church, copying out every sermon he listened to, and writing his diary, while his wife rushed around keeping the house and bringing up two children...

In August 1789 Richard embarked on a visit to Blandford in Dorset, returning via Bath, where he spent five nights. It was not actually 'the Season' for visiting Bath – generally October through to June – but he would have found a bustling vibrant city, transformed by the elegant architecture of John Wood (father and son), who between them were responsible for the Royal Crescent, The Circus, and the Assembly Rooms, which had opened in 1771. Bath stone became famous because it was capable of being cut by saw from all angles – making it ideal for intricate and ornate decoration. John Wood the elder had taken a very simple idea – the terraced house introduced to London after the Great Fire of the previous century by Nicholas Barbon – and transformed it into something aspirational. How? By combining the humble terraced house in groups of five, seven or more units, so that together from the outside they had the appearance of a single grand unit or palace, with columns and pediments and elaborate ornamentation. Today over 18 million of us live in terraced accommodation but eighteenth-century Bath pioneered terraced housing as something which wealthy tradesman and gentry could aspire to live in. Richard would have been impressed.

Bath had grown from a permanent population of some 3,000 at the turn of the century to nearly 35,000, and the city abounded with apartments to rent for the season, or hotels for short-stayers like Richard. Ever since 'Beau' Nash became the 32-year-old Master of Ceremonies for the city in 1706, Bath had developed into the main resort favoured by all of 'polite society' – not just the aristocracy, but also the growing class of gentry. Probably Richard was wise to visit it out of season – there must have been an almost unbearable throng during the winter months, and the queues for 'taking the waters' must have been immense.

Intriguingly Richard not only lists the places visited and distances travelled on his journey (Bourton to Bath, on to Blandford, Weymouth, Lulworth Castle, back to Weymouth, Blandford, Salisbury, Deptford, Warminster, Frome, Bath, and back to Bourton) but also itemises the luggage put up on the back of the coach because this would have been charged for separately. He took with him his Great Trunk, his blue box, 'wainscoat' (i.e. panelled) box, Green Bag, Great Coat, shoes, and a wig box. Seven items. No, make that eight, because as an afterthought he also packed his steam kettle. Presumably he liked to be able to brew his own cup of tea at the end of the day's journey!

Great Trunk.
blue box 20
Wainsfed box 23
Greenbag 23
great Coat & Deptford
Shoes 11 mi
Wig box.
7
Steamkettle
8.

Salisy. 23.
Warmr. 22
Bath 17
62.
Froome. 3
65

To Bath 49
To Blandford 44
To Weymouth 24
To Lulworth Castle out of the road. 8.
Weymouth to Blandford 24
149.
To Salisbury. 23.
Deptford 11
Warminster 11
Frome 7.
Bath 14.
215
To Boulton 49
264.

By this time Richard would have been familiar with his route, having acquired a copy of *Bowles Post-chaise Companion*, first published in 1782. This showed, in strip form, all the main towns and villages, places of interest, landmarks and mileages.

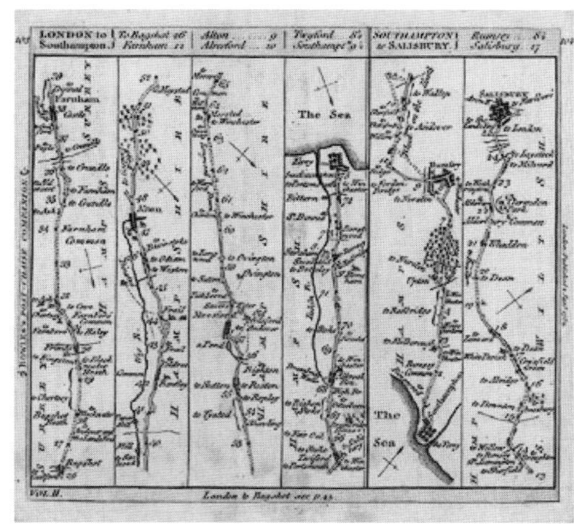

A page from *Bowles Post-chaise Companion* illustrating the journey from London to Southampton.

In the wider world the 1780s saw a quickening of the pace of the Industrial Revolution. Two giants stand out – James Watt and Matthew Boulton. Watt, the son of a Glasgow merchant, had been apprenticed as a mathematical instrument-maker and in 1751 started his own business. Twelve years later he was sent a

Newcomen steam engine to repair, and in mending it decided that improvements could be made to it – particularly by fitting a separate condensing unit in order to cool the steam and increase efficiency. In 1773 he went into partnership with Matthew Boulton, a prominent Birmingham businessman, and for the next decade sold the engines to colliery owners who found them four times more powerful than the original Newcomen designs.

Watt was to carry on with his experiments, coming up with a rotary engine in 1781. This was to have many applications because it could be used to drive a large variety of different types of machine – for instance from 1783 onwards Richard Arkwright used the Boulton & Watt machines to power all his textile factories. James Watt did not confine his brilliance to inventing the machines themselves – he also hit upon a novel way of selling them. First, he obtained an Act of Parliament (1755) giving him (and subsequently the Boulton & Watt company) a virtual monopoly over the production of steam engines. Second, he charged his customers a premium for using his machines. He did so by his calculation of 'horse power'. This was worked out on the basis that a horse could exert a pull of 180 pounds and every machine was described in relation to a horse – hence a 'twenty horse power machine' exerted a pull of 3,600 pounds. Watt then worked out what each company saved in a year by not having to keep a team of that number of horses. He charged one-third of that sum each and every year for twenty-five years. No wonder he was an extremely wealthy man when he died in 1819!

Throughout the 1780s the pace of change was quickening and would accelerate still further in the decade ahead.

A later cut-out of a crane on its wharf loading a boat – showing three of the ingredients of the Industrial Revolution: trade, transport and mechanisation.]

9

The 1790s

'March 4th 1790 died the Revd. Thos. Seward of Litchfield in his 82nd year – uncle to my first wife, to whose memory a handsome Monument is erected by his daughter Anne Seward in Litchfield Cathedral, which I have lately seen.' As mentioned previously, Cousin Anne wrote poetry. At some stage Richard had bought a volume of her poems – because later in the decade he notes: 'Lent Mrs Snooke Miss Seward's Sonnets – returned June 25th 1799.' Richard seems to have been out of contact with Anna for a number of years but now became keen to curry favour with her, so he started to include her on the list of recipients for his annual gift of oysters!

A measure of his esteem for his cousin is that she received the better oysters – that is, those from Pyfleet at 4s. 3d. a barrel. Friends of lesser importance (e.g. the local Baptist minister) had to make do with the cheaper ones from Colchester costing 3s. 4d.

Life seems to have settled down to a routine of cosy domesticity. '1790 November 10th – Mr Pratt gave us a Canary Bird.' In fact, there may well have been a whole aviary of canary birds, since another entry is for 'Mr Martin (Carpenter) – for Canary Birds.' Quantities of birdseed were then ordered from London and delivered by carrier.

'December 4th 1790 – Mrs S[nooke] moves her plants into her new green-house.' Both Richard and Mrs Snooke appeared to have been keen on plants – in June of that year Mrs Snooke had given Richard 'a Rose Jeranium, a broad leaf Murtle, a narrow ditto, and some Groundsil' – while Mrs Griffiths donated another myrtle and 'a Jeranium' in September. He refers to a 'pretty good crop of fruit – large quantities of Gooseberries and currants, many plumbs and a great many Damsons.' He also paid out eight shillings for 'Firs and Poplars', put in a 'new gate onto the street (£1/14/3d)' – and presumably wanted to make sure he could summon assistance in case of need by buying a 'Watchman's Rattle' for two shillings. (This was a metal box, engraved with Chinese ornamentation, containing a brass 'clapper' which still makes an unholy racket when shaken).

Family Tree 3 – Richard's first family

Children by Richard's first marriage to Eleanor 1733–1780

William Seward Hall
m. Charlotte Glover
on 13.1.1785

Richard	**Elizabeth**	**William**	**Henry**	**James**	**Seward**	**Charlotte**	**Francis**
born	born	born	born	born	born	born	born
26.1.1786	18.9.1787	27.2.1789	5.10.1790	8.7.1792	24.2.1794	16.10.1795	1803

Martha Hall
m. Henry Griffith
on 17.4.1785

Henry	**Elizabeth**	**William**	**Richard**	**Eleanor**	**Frances**
born	born	born	born	born	born
20.8.1786	1787	28.5.1788	21.6.1790	29.7.1792	15.5.1794

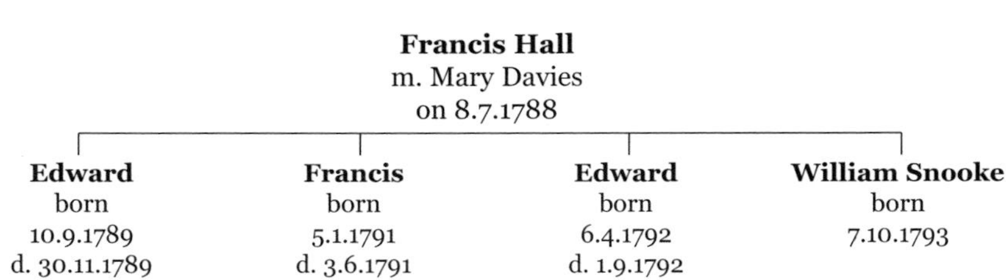

Richard's second family

Richard's children by his second marriage:

Richard
m. Elizabeth ('Betty') Snooke (1743–1818)
on 14.12.1780

Anna Snooke Hall	**Benjamin Snooke Hall**
born	born
15.3.1782	28.11.1787

There then followed a whole list of family events. On '21 June 1790 Mrs Griffith' (i.e. his daughter Patty) 'was confined with a son named Richard.' 'On 5 October 1790 Mrs W.S. Hall' (son William's wife) 'had a son named Henry. On 5 January 1791 Mrs Francis Hall had a son named after his father who died on 3 June in the same year. On 6 March 1792 Mrs Francis Hall was again confined with a son named Edward who died 1 September in the same year. On 8 July 1792 Mrs W.S. Hall had another son, named James. On 29 July 1792 Mrs Griffith gave birth to a daughter named Eleanor.' Another event took place in 1792: 'August 5th son Benjamin Hall put Into trousers.' And on the 17th of the same month: 'Daughter Anna Hall went to Boarding School at Cirencester' – where she went down with the measles on 20 August 1793.

Family events continued apace. On '7 October 1793 Mrs Francis Hall was confined with a son named William'. Benjamin, Richard's son by his second marriage, adds after this entry that William was 'the only child who lived to manhood. He was to marry his cousin Frances Griffith, who was born May 15th 1794.' On '24 February 1794 Mrs W.S. Hall was confined with a son named Seward. On 9 January 1795 Mrs Francis Hall had a stillborn child and on 16 October of the same year Mrs W.S. Hall a daughter, named Charlotte.'

Richard also found time to list local news – so we find:

> Remarkable Providence Tuesday November 12th 1793 about One o'Clock in the Afternoon Robert Betteridge – whose Father and Mother live at Bourton – was at work as a Carpenter in a Well about a mile from Stow. The wall of the Well fell in upon him and he was covered up to the Chin. It was 12 at Night before he was released so far as his arms. At last it appeared that one leg was about half way got between two stones and with every method used they could not get him out until 7 o'Clock at night on the Wednesday.

As usual domestic items caught his fancy:

1791 – plaited Coffee Pot £1/5/0
Six silver desert spoons £2/7/0
Small Turkey Carpet £3/3/
Pontipool bread basket 7 shillings
Mahogany breakfast table £1/15/0
1793 – Repairing Horse-hair bottom chairs £1/16/1d
1794 – May – a velvet waistcoat 18 shillings.

It is interesting to note that Richard never shed his love of fine waistcoats – fashion, then as now, tended to echo what was happening in France – and France after the Revolution ushered in an almost austere taste where ornamentation (being a sign of wealth) was kept to a minimum. Tastes in England in the 1790s turned towards plainer dress, and for men this meant clothes based on what they would wear when out riding. The long knee-length coat started to be turned back and buttoned behind – the forerunner of the Victorian tailcoat. But Richard, the peacock as ever, wanted to keep his velvet finery and one suspects that now into his late sixties he no longer felt constrained to follow the trends.

Drink was an important household concern and much of it was home-made. An entry for 1799 reads: 'October 23rd – Gathered our Apples, which was a much larger crop than we ever had ... much cyder made.' In general Richard and his wife seem to have been keen wine-makers rather than cider drinkers. The currant wine was bottled off the following August ('ran 44 bottles clear') and at the same time Richard bottled off twenty-one bottles of blackcurrant wine – also clear. A few days later his list shows another cask of blackcurrant wine was bottled off 'which ran 20 bottles clear'. Most years he seems to have produced between fifty and a hundred bottles of wine – in addition to both the wine he bought by the cask for home bottling, and the brewing of beer in the brew-house at the back of the kitchen. Add in the home-made cider, the occasional dozen bottles of brandy and the odd ten-gallon cask of wine brought down by carrier from London (all itemised in the account books) and we see a different side of the coin to the pious churchgoer! Now we have Richard at home relaxing with a glass or two of wine most evenings, or busy on a weekend picking redcurrants, cleaning, filling and stoppering bottles and putting them in racks in the cellar – even recording how many bottles were on each shelf ('February 6th 1800 – Upper Shelf 20 bottles, Second shelf 20 bottles, Lower shelf 18 bottles'). Getting low on stock – time to make some more!

By the 1790s Richard was spending his time going over his records, linking together events which occurred more than once, and writing these up in a series of jottings. These annual reviews extended (of course!) to the weather and so we see for 1791 a page summarising the highlights – although this appears to be composed on three different occasions as the writing appears 'normal' for the events up to February, more measured and unhurried for the spring, and decidedly rushed for the latter parts of the year! This suggests that Richard was working from a daybook (since lost) and was then summarising things at intervals during the year. Unusual weather conditions fascinated Richard. The jottings book jumps eight years from the 1791 entry and records:

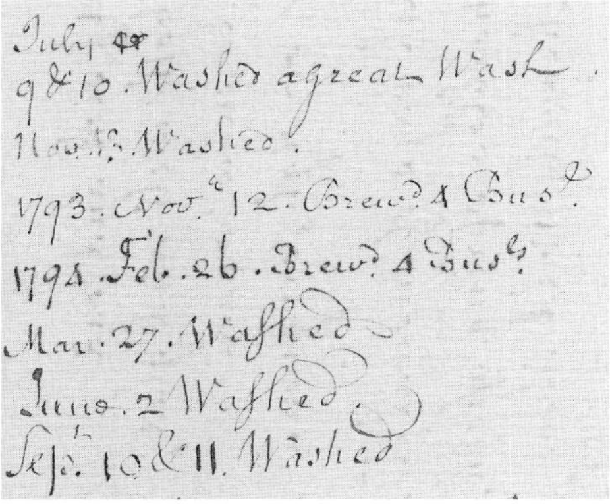
July 4
9 & 10. Washed a great Wash.
Nov. 5. Washed.
1793. Nov. 12. Brewed 4 Bush.
1794. Feb. 26. Brewed 4 Bush.
Mar. 27. Washed
June 2 Washed
Sept. 10 & 11. Washed

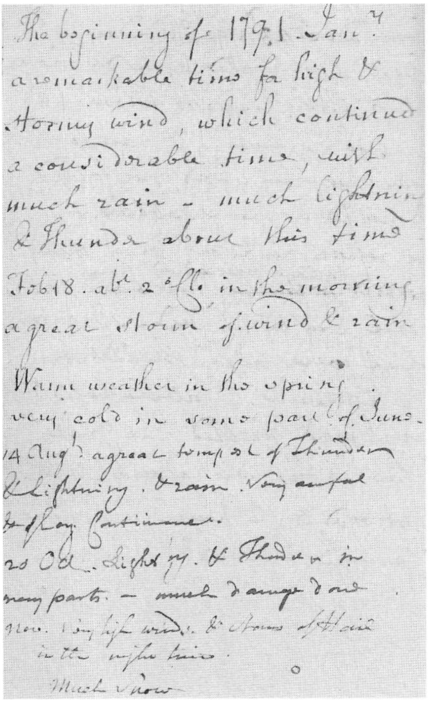
The beginning of 1791 Jan.
a remarkable time for high &
stormy wind, which continued
a considerable time, with
much rain – much lightning
& Thunder about this time
Feb 18. abt. 2 o'Clo. in the morning
a great Storm of wind & rain
Warm weather in the spring
very cold in some part of June
14 Aug. a great tempest of Thunder
& Lightning & rain. Very awful
& of long Continuance.
20 Oct. Lightning & Thunder in
many parts. – much damage done
Nov. Very high winds & storms of Hail
[illegible]
Much snow

> January 26th 1799 – Last Xmas day was one of the coldest of the present Century. The Thermometer stood at Berlin 17 degrees below the freezing point, and at Hamburgh it stood upon 18 degrees. The frost continued between the 23rd and 27th December 1798. In Vienna it was more severe than any recorded since the year 1399.

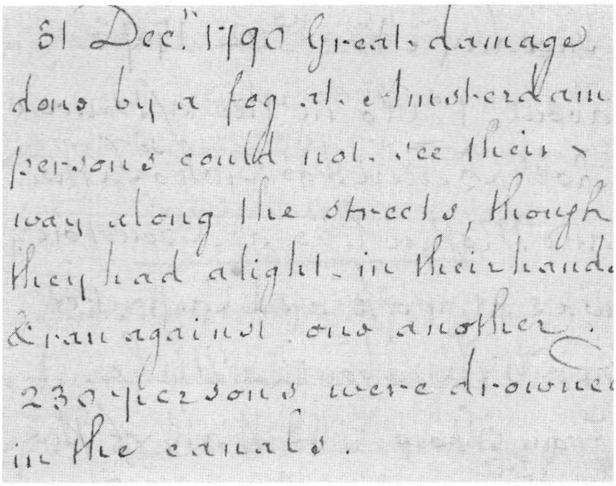
31 Decr. 1790 Great damage done by a fog at Amsterdam persons could not see their way along the streets, though they had a light in their hands & ran against one another. 230 persons were drowned in the canals.

He noted the bad fog in 1791 ('a general Fog over the Kingdom Dec. 5th & 6th – Coaches lighted from Waltham Cross to London with flambeaux' (i.e. flaming torches made of reeds soaked in animal fat).

Richard was also getting decidedly more frugal, using more and more recycled paper for his jottings. Perhaps it was difficult to buy paper locally – he writes in one letter 'please send me a quire of Cartridge Paper – not a sheet of the article is to be got at Bourton'. Envelopes were opened out, refolded and then sewn together to make jotting pads.

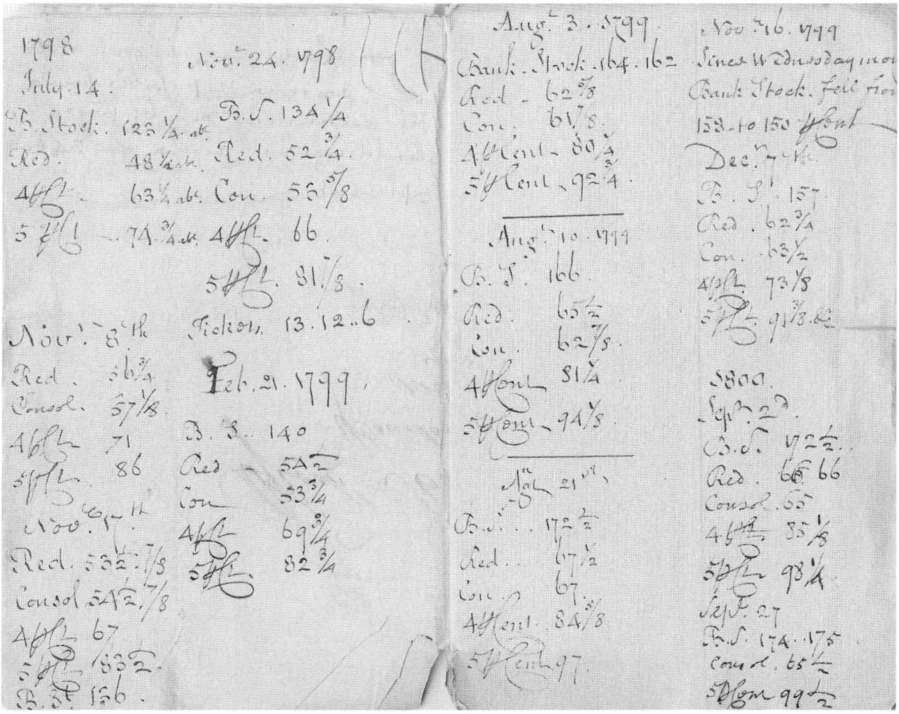
1798 July 14. B. Stock. 123¼ ab. Red. 48½ ab. 4 p Ct. 63½ ab. 5 p Ct. 74¾ ab.
Novr. 24. 798 B. S. 134¼ Red. 52¾. Con. 53⅝ 4 p Ct. 66. 5 p Ct. 81⅞. Tickets 13.12.6
Novr. 8th Red. 56¾ Consol. 57⅛ 4 p Ct. 71 5 p Ct. 86
Nov. 17th Red. 53½ ⅞ Consol. 54½ ⅞ 4 p Ct. 67 5 p Ct. 83½ B. St. 136.
Feb. 21. 1799 B. S. 140 Red. 54½ Con. 53¾ 4 p Ct. 69¾ 5 p Ct. 82¾
Aug. 3. 1799. Bank Stock 164. 162 Red. 62⅝ Con. 61⅞ 4 p Cent. 80¾ 5 p Cent. 92¾.
Aug. 10. 1799 B. S. 166. Red. 65½ Con. 62⅞. 4 p Cent 81¼ 5 p Cent. 94⅛.
Aug. 21st B. S. 172½ Red. 67½ Con. 67 4 p Cent. 84⅝ 5 p Cent 97.
Nov. 16. 1799 Since Wednesday morn Bank Stock. fell from 158 to 150 p Cent
Dec. 7th B. S. 157 Red. 62¾ Con. 63½ 4 p Ct. 73⅝ 5 p Ct. 91⅞
1800. Sept. 2d. B. S. 172½. Red. 66 66 Consol. 65 4 p Ct. 85⅛ 5 p Ct. 98¼
Sept. 27 B. S. 174. 175 Consol. 65½ 5 p Cent 99½

Richard's list of Bank Stock values

One was used entirely to remind him of items he wished to read ('Miss Hanh. More's Remarks on the present Mode of Education of Females'); books he had borrowed and returned ('Hume's History of England in 5 volumes printed in Paternoster Row 1790 and being a completely new Addition' and 'Miss Sewards Sonnets'); or those he wished to acquire ('A guide to the Lakes in Cumberland Westmoreland and Lancashire' and 'The Tenth Edition (price 3/6d) of Johnsons Dictionary of the English Language in Miniature'). Another listed pages of stock values (in this case for 1798–1800), indicating that he retained an eye on his investments – possibly coinciding with the dates of his trips to London.

Richard loved lists, and so we even have a list of the occasions when his wife 'fell down' – there is no indication as to whether she had the falling sickness (i.e. epilepsy) or was clumsy – or indeed was stoned out of her mind, either with too much of the port and currant wine, or with the opiates with which she appears to have been prescribed:

> 1791 – March 21 – Wife's bad fall at Parlour Door, fell down stairs,
> – Fall coming from the Meeting near our House.
> – Fall Mrs Snooke's coach
> – Fall Little East Cheap

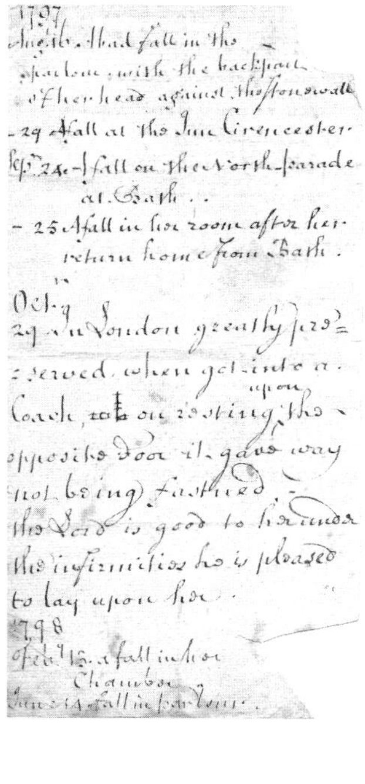
1797
Aug 16. A bad fall in the parlour, with the backpart of her head against the stone wall
– 29 A fall at the Inn Cirencester.
Sept 24 – A fall on the North Parade at Bath . .
– 25 A fall in her room after her return home from Bath.
Oct 29 In London greatly preserved when got into a Coach, on resting upon the opposite door it gave way not being fastned – the Lord is good to her under the infirmities he is pleased to lay upon her.
1798
Feb 15 a fall in her Chamber
June 14 a fall in parlour.

There were more than 20 similar entries.

There is one further possible explanation for all these falls – tapeworms. One of the risks of eating undercooked pork was the risk of ingesting worms. Tape worms could spread to the brain, causing blackouts. The risk was to rich and poor alike, and so we see Richard copying out the tale of the physician who prescribed a particular snuff to Princess Elizabeth – 'the second day she voided a worm from the Nose, since which the complaint has totally ceased.'

We have lists of expenses, including 'Carrying the Sedan Chair 1796 £3/18/6' and the same for the following year £3/9/0

– suggesting that Richard may have been having trouble walking easily because of his limp (see earlier) and therefore preferred to be carried in a Sedan.

The Sedan chair had been bought for £6/10/2d. in October 1795 – and was presumably put to good use because two years later Richard had occasion to pay for repairs of 2/6d.

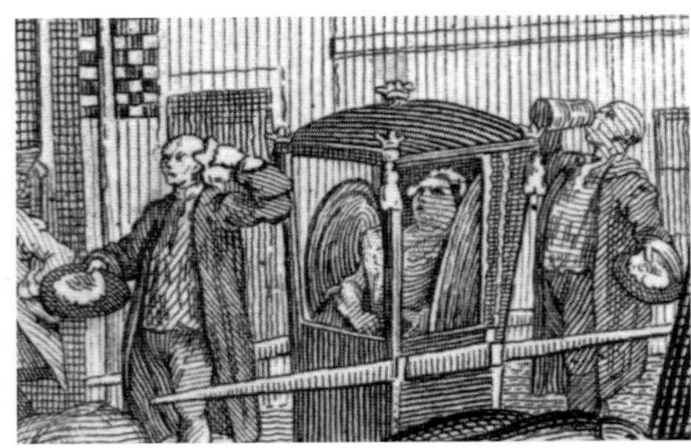

A detail from Hogarth's Beer Street showing the carriers of the sedan chair pausing to have a well-earned jug of ale. © The Trustees of the British Museum.

Richard refers to schooling for Anna – £2/12/4. From 1792 to 1796 Anna was sent to Cirencester to Miss Darke's school.

1795 Rideing-board . 0.18.0
Oct. Sedan Chair . . 6.10.2
Repair since 0.2.6.

Term appears to have started in February and ran until the end of July. The four years' tuition cost Richard £115/4/6 – plus travel of £20/16/1½d. and 'other expenses' of £29/19/0½d. to give a total over the four years of £171/14/5d. – a not inconsiderable amount. By the time she left Miss Darke's Anna was 14, and her schooling appears to have been complete. There were still diary entries relating to family events: 'February 9th 1799 Mrs Mary Hall with twins, stillborn.' Mary was the wife of Richard's son Francis. Worse was to follow – an infection set in and within a fortnight Mary had died ('March 2nd 1799 Died Mrs Mary Hall in her 29th year being born April 26th 1770.' Poor Mary – she had been married at eighteen and had a child every year for five years. She had then had several miscarriages before becoming pregnant with twins. When she died her husband Francis remarried but had no further children, and was eventually to die on 28 December 1826. For Richard, however, Mary's demise meant another list of expenses:

A Mourning for Mary March . 1799

Sundries Mr Palmer . .	1 . 16 . 6 .
Do. Wife & Anna . —	3 . 4 . 6
Sundrys —	0 . 9 . 5
Buckles . self —	0 . 1 . 0
Mantua-Maker —	0 . 3 . 0
Silk Handkerchiefs — –	
Gloves, Anna &c . .	0 . 13 . 3 .
Harris Taylor Self –	0 . 12 . 1 .
Ditto. Benjamin	0 . 6 . 11 .
A pair of black Silk stocks.	0 . 14 . 0 .
A pair of Rib'd blk & Wt. worsd.	0 . 5 . 0
	8 . 5 . 8 .

Sundries Mr Palmer	£1/16/ 6
Ditto Wife & Anna	£3/ 4/ 6
Sundry	£0/ 9/ 5
Buckles – self	£0/ 1/ 0
Mantua Maker	£0/ 3/ 0
Silk Handkerchiefs, Gloves Anna etc.	£0/13/ 3
Harris (Taylor) – self	£0/12/ 1
Ditto Benjamin	£0/ 6/11
A pair of Black Silk stocks	£0/14/ 0
A pair of Rib'd Black & W. worsted	£0/ 5/ 0
	£8/ 5/ 8

(The mantua was the name given to an often loose-fitting gown worn open at the front to reveal the stomacher (or embroidered corset). The mantua-maker was in effect a female tailor.) Richard then carried the total over to another list of expenses for 1799:

Bought oysters	£1/17/6
Gown for Mrs S(nooke).	£0/18/0
Gown Wife	£0/17/0
Wig	£1/1/0
Hat – self	£0/17/0
Horsleydown School	£1/1/0
Sheets (Brindle)	£1/1/0
Meeting	£3/3/0
Irish Cloth	£3/2/6
Mourning for Mary	£8/5/8
Total	£22/3/8
Add Anna's Journey	£4/4/0
Wife	£4/4/0
Son William	£11/0/0
Son Francis	£20/0/0
	£61/11/8

There were lists for each quarter showing household expenses and a breakdown to show, for example in March to June 1799, Butcher at £13 2s. 4d., Baker at £6 9s. 1½d. and Butter at £4 4s. 8½d. During one six-month period (January to June 1799) he paid Mrs Snooke rent of £9, unspecified taxes of £4 0s. 10d. and the new-fangled Income Tax (first instalment) of £5 5s. 0d.

Baker	1797	13.13.7½
Butcher	1797	22.4.5
Butter	1797	8.3.3½
Coal &c	1797	10.17.0
Malt &c	1797	4.12.9
Candles	1797	4.8.4
Soap	1797	1.0.6
Servts wages	1797	8.3.0
House-rent	1797	8.10.0
Taxes	1797	2.8.3
Wine &c	1797	8.3.5
Gardening & piece of Garden ground		1.4.1

He paid out wages of £3 15s. 0d and paid two guineas for currant wine, a similar amount for port, £4 5s., 8d. for Groceries, £1 5s. 0d. for Cheese, £3 6s. 0d. for coal and £1 14s. 0d. for brandy. We can deduce from this that if his figures were correct he paid out more for alcoholic beverages than he did for groceries – and certainly more than he did for coal! Richard then listed annual comparisons of expenses. Those illustrated are for 1797 and 1790. Note the figure of sixteen shillings for soap – and the comparatively high expense of £3 6s. 3d. for candles. Both items would have come from the tallow maker.

Probably because of the high cost of decent candles, Richard would often have used another somewhat cheaper source of light – rushes. An 1818 inventory of the family house shows that there were 'rushlight guards' in various rooms. Sometimes the holders were little more than spikes hammered into the wall onto which the rushes could be attached. But there were also table-mounted versions – a sort of cross between a candlestick and a pair of spring-loaded pliers. Preparing the rushes would have been a job for old and young alike. It is easy to imagine Richard taking his pony to the banks of the river running through Bourton, or down into the water meadows beyond it, carrying with him the papier-mâché case holding his pocket knife with its sharp stubby blade. He would have cut a few dozen of the tallest rushes, bundled them up and taken

1790		
Butcher	17.14.0	
Baker	14.12.1½	
Butter	6.19.7.	
	39.5.8½.	
Coal.fag.ts	15.8.0	
Candles	3.6.3	
Soap	0.16.0	24.4.5
Malt & Hops	4.14.2	
	24.4.5	
Servts Wages	7.9.6	
	70.19.7½	
Grocery	11.11.2	
Cheese	3.13.5	
	86.4.2½	

them home where they would have been soaked in water so that the green outer sheath could be easily stripped off revealing the white pithy centre. These were then cut down the whole length of the stalk into four, to produce long thin strips. They would have been left out overnight to harden off, and at some stage over the next few days the cook would have placed the strips into a pan containing any available fat (grease, suet, dripping – even beeswax if available). Once dried, the strips could then be brought back into the house, clipped into the holder, and used as desired. A rushlight made in this way, perhaps thirty inches long, would burn for an hour and at least give some light into the darker recesses of the cottage.

A table-mounted rushlight guard. Courtesy of the Ceredigion Museum, Aberystwyth.

Green grow the rushes from a paper cut-out.

Back to our lists, Richard itemises specific groceries ordered from Messrs Johnson and among the purchases was 14 pounds of moist sugar, a pound of coffee 'in lead', Churchman's Chocolate, green tea, currants, 'split pease', orange chips and, no doubt with the start of a new year approaching, 3 Almanacks. Mr Churchman may no longer be a household name for chocolate, but this was the era when the Quaker families of Cadbury and Fry, the Rowntrees and the Terrys of York were just starting their business empires, based on cocoa and chocolate. Chocolate had become a fashionable (but expensive) drink, though it was not easy to make. First it had to be stewed – for a long time, and then left to settle. The cocoa butter had to be separated and skimmed off before the concoction was reboiled with milk and, immediately before it was served, thickened with eggs. It may not have been popular with the maid who had to prepare it, but this rich, comforting concoction was believed by many to have medicinal qualities, not least as a fertility drug! The eighteenth century saw various improvements to the process of preparing the cocoa bean for use and in 1795 Joseph Storrs Fry became the first person to introduce factory mechanisation into the industry when he installed a Watts steam engine to grind the beans.

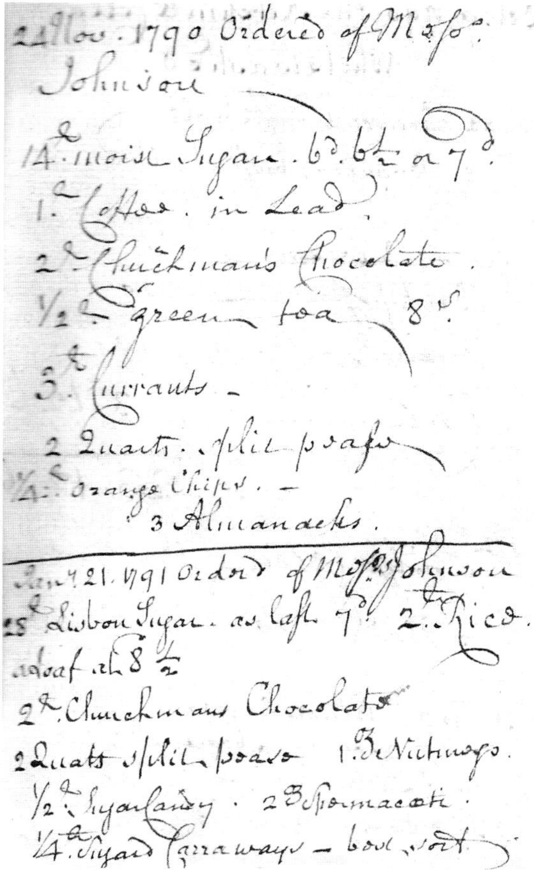
21 Nov. 1790 Ordered of Mess. Johnson
14 lb moist Sugar. 6d. 6½ or 7d.
1 lb Coffee. in Lead.
2 lb Churchman's Chocolate.
½ lb green tea 8s.
3 lb Currants –
2 Quarts. split pease
¼ lb Orange Chips. –
3 Almanacks.
Jan. 21. 1791 Order of Mess. Johnson
25 lb Lisbon Sugar. as last 7d. 2 lb Rice.
loaf at 8½
2 lb Churchmans Chocolate
2 Quarts split pease 1 oz Nutmegs.
½ lb Sugarcandy. 2 oz Spermaceti.
¼ lb Sugard Carraways – best sort

However, in many ways the business had started with Dr Walter Churchman, who was a Bristol apothecary who opened a shop in Broadmead in the year Richard was born. In 1729 he was granted Letters Patent by George II for 'the sole use of an Engine by him invented for the expeditious, fine and clean making of chocolate to greater perfection than by any other method...' Books on medicine recommended chocolate not just for its own qualities but as a mixer for other less palatable treatments. It was never sold as eating chocolate, but always in the form of lozenges or as a powder for drinking. On his death Walter Churchman's business passed to his son Charles but when he in turn died, in 1761, the business was bought by the astute Dr Joseph Fry – a fully qualified physician and apothecary. A devout Quaker, he founded what became J.S. Fry & Son, possibly the oldest surviving chocolate firm in the world. When Joseph died the business went to his wife, Anna, and an advertisement of around the time that Richard was buying his 'Churchman's Chocolate' reads:

> Patent Cocoa. Genuine and unadulterated. Made by Anna Fry & Sons, patentees of Churchman's chocolate Bristol. This Cocoa is recommended by the most eminent of Faculty, in Preference to every other kind of Breakfast, to such who have Tender Habits, decayed Health, weak Lungs, or scorbutic tendencies, being easy of Digestion, affording a fine and light nourishment, and greatly correcting the sharp Humours of the Constitution.

With qualities like that, no wonder Richard bought two pounds of it at a time – although it would have set him back around fifteen shillings – rather more than the average farm labourer earned in a week! It appears to have been enough to last for two months because the same amount was bought in both November and the following January!

There were also lists of when the clocks were cleaned ('August 27 1795 Cleaning upper Clock 1/6; March 1796 Short Clock cleaned 2/6') and lists of when the piano-forte (bought in 1792) needed tuning. The piano-forte was presumably acquired in London and intended as a Christmas present for the family – or at least, it arrived at Bourton via Mr Ward's Wagon on 15 December at a delivery charge of £1 2s. 4d. (along with a couple of barrels of oysters!). There is no mention of the make (or size) of piano – the first model to be advertised in England was a Zumpe in 1763, costing £50. So in all likelihood this was a much smaller instrument – particularly as it fitted inside a case, presumably to protect the keyboard. The instrument obviously went out of tune quite quickly – Richard seems to have been happy to pay for it to be tuned every six months or so – at five shillings a go.

And, having bought an *Introduction to Thorough Bass* in 1798, what did he play on his piano-forte? Well, in another book he lists the tunes he learned:

> Tink-a-tink
> Fair Rosell
> Leading the Troops to Battle
> Lynnon – A Welch Air

Fidellia's Grassy Tomb
Crazy Jane
The Woodsman
The Wedding Day
Softly Rise the Southern Breeze.

The 1790s were a time of war with France – and wars had to be paid for. That meant taxation. Richard seems to have been so preoccupied with the iniquities of the new Income Tax that he wrote constantly about it – and it is interesting to read some of his comments (see Appendix I). Other taxes mentioned were a 'War Tax' at half a guinea a quarter; a 'Windows and House Tax' at £1 4s. 8d. for the same period, and 'Armorial Bearings one Guinea'. The government brought in a whole raft of changes in the rate of duty – payable on paper, on printed cottons, timber, and on imported foodstuffs such as tea, pepper, sugar and raisins. There was a doubling of the rates charged by the Post Office on deliveries of over a hundred miles, and Richard noted the salient points.

Richard kept separate records of non-domestic news, so we see:

> 14th July 1791 [The anniversary of the storming of the Bastille] a large number of persons Din'd at the Crown and Anchor Tavern, Strand, to commemorate the revolution in France. A like meeting being attempted in Birmingham a large mob arose which were in opposition to the Revolutionists and committed dreadful outrages – burned 2 meeting houses, pulled down and burned about 9 houses. The Light Horse came in on the Sabbath Day and they had a quiet night. Monday 18th – the Rioting stopped.

The Birmingham Riot was obviously a huge talking point. Among Richard's papers – though not in his handwriting – is a record running to twelve pages entitled 'An account of the number of

buildings destroyed during the Riot at Birmingham 1791'. Somewhere along the line, according to our correspondent, the mob decided to pillage the home and laboratory of Dr Priestley, who 'had the good sense to retire before the arrival of the wretches who were the instruments of destruction. They began by breaking down the doors and windows and, having entered the cellars, many of them drank to an excess which deprived them of every apparent symptom of life.' The correspondent continues: 'It was hoped the laboratory and its invaluable contents would have been saved but after the effects of the liquor had subsided they broke into it and in the true spirit of the Goths and Vandals they destroyed instruments and a collection of scientific preparations . . . at length the entire building was set on fire.' Priestley and his family had in fact escaped some time earlier. The attack was no accident – earlier in 1791 Priestley had written to Burke expressing support for the principles of the French Revolution, although he was not in attendance at the dinner which so enraged the mob. The fire destroyed countless books and manuscripts and Priestley was never to return to Birmingham.

Health – and particularly the fear of a smallpox epidemic – remained a major item of concern. Hence we see:

> Saturday Nov. 30 1793: It then appear'd that a young man Clarks Son in Pigeon-house Lane, had got the Small-pox, & that it had been out about 4 days – a favourable sort. Saturday Dec. 4 – The Mother fell ill with it – another person & some children.
>
> 1798 – September 12th – Had a blister behind my Ear (for Face and Tooth ache), which rose

very Fine. [Presumably it was thought that provoking a blister to form would reduce the 'bad humours' which were causing the pain]

1799 – July 4th – Experienced God's goodness in Preserving me when in much distress from a piece of bread & butter sticking in my throat while drinking Coffee in the afternoon.

At times Richard appears rather to dwell upon his ill-health, and so it is tempting to assume that the (undated) memo bearing the heading 'How I slept last night' was written by him. The writing seems to be his – but the memo is problematic. It reads:

To bed at eleven, restless sleep until 12.30. Jumped out of bed, rubbed stomach with Belladonna and sipped a dram of Battley simultaneously until 12.45 then filled hot water bag and strapped it tightly on the chest – to bed again at 12.50 but alas only to remain there for ten minutes – pain too severe for the recumbent position. At 1.00 a.m. injected 15 m. morphia, put on dress gown and occupied easy chair, sleeping until 1.50. Awoke in pain – walked about and drank a tumbler of milk, till 2.15 – then resumed easy chair till 3.20. I then re-filled the bag with boiling water (a great and immediate relief) took a second tumbler of brandy and milk – pottered about till 4.00 then slepped on soffa till 5.00 – then up for an injection of 15 m. morphia. Re-filled bag and assumed easy chair at 5.30 and slept till 6.20, which concluded my night's rest.

Perhaps the 'soffa' upon which he reclined was the one delivered on 31 August 1799, via London, at a transport cost of half a guinea. The 'easy chair' was an eighteenth-century term for a winged chair (sometimes called a 'sick chair') and the 'belladonna' was deadly nightshade, otherwise known as 'The Devil's Cherries'. Found widely throughout Europe and the Middle East the plant was a well-known poison, but was also used for its hallucinogenic and pain-relieving qualities. Literally the name meant 'beautiful lady' – because the street ladies of Venice used to take deadly nightshade in small doses to dilate the pupils of the eye – enhancing their allure and sex appeal!

There are two problems with ascribing this note to Richard, however – the reference to injecting and the use of the word 'morphia'. This was before the days of the hypodermic needle – but Richard could have used a syringe called a clyster. This pump-like device had been the subject of experimentation by none other than Christopher Wren a century earlier. In the 1650s Wren had experimented with dogs, piercing the skin with a feather quill before injecting opium ('Come here Fido. Sit still while I stab you with this goose feather. Now I am going to pump you full of opiates and see what happens'). Presumably the dog fell asleep and there is a lovely experiment, reported on the Wellcome Institute web page, showing that Wren then moved on to try out his clyster on 'the delinquent servant of a foreign ambassador'; the experiment was apparently unsuccessful since 'the victim either really or craftily fell into a swoon and the experiment had to be discontinued.' Quite what His Excellency the Foreign Ambassador thought of his servant, delinquent or otherwise, being used as a guinea-pig in this way is not clear! Ah well, Christopher, back to the drawing board. Designing cathedrals may prove a better meal ticket... A hundred years later and solid needles were being used to pierce the skin and the balloon-like clyster could have been used to inject painkilling drugs, but there is no formal evidence of this. A similar procedure was certainly used at that time – particularly by anatomists working on cadavers and wishing to highlight certain parts of the body, that is, by pumping a solution into the organ to enlarge it. But was it sufficiently routine for a man such as Richard to have been self-administering at home? Possibly not.

The second difficulty is linguistic: opium was certainly known for its narcotic and painkilling qualities at this time – but 'morphine' (that is to say, the most common of the various narcotics found in opium) was not identified until Sertürner isolated it a few years after Richard died. The scientist named his discovery after Morpheus, the Greek god of dreams. Could 'morphia' already have been a word in circulation to describe a more general opiate? Possibly, but the *Oxford Dictionary* makes no suggestion of this and indeed shows 'morphia' as being a variant of 'morphew' – a type of skin ailment. On balance, then, it may well be that the writing was that of Richard's son Benjamin (whose handwriting was very similar to that of his father).

The year 1795 saw the death of Richard's local pastor, the Reverend Benjamin Beddome. Writing forty years later, Richard's youngest son (Benjamin) mused:

> [I recall] the death of the Revd. Benjm. Beddome M.A. for 55 years the respected pastor of the Baptist Church at Bourton on the Water aged 78 years. This occurred September 3rd. I recollect his funeral which was on Sabbathday afternoon September 6th. My father and mother attended – the Revd. Benjmn Francis of Horseley preached the sermon to a crowded congregation from Phil. 1.21.

The good pastor had suffered greatly from gout for many years, but he was a devoted and popular minister, much given to composing hymns. The night before he was to deliver a sermon he would sit down and write a hymn to go with it, introducing the congregation to both hymn and sermon the following day.

Beddome had married a seventeen-year-old girl (Elizabeth) when he was thirty-two and together they had a large family – at least ten children, but fate decreed that many of them died young. The firstborn was John, who died at the age of fifteen. Writing in 1774, William Snooke comments on the funeral of the one-year-old Joseph Beddome: 'the third of that name to die'. Benjamin (who died at the age of twenty-five) and Foskett (who died at twenty-six) had both trained as medical doctors – following in their father's footsteps since that was the pastor's original calling. Elizabeth, no doubt worn out by all the childbearing, died aged fifty-one in 1784, the same year as the sad death of Foskett (who drowned while boarding a ship at Deptford). But at least four children outlived their father, and their descendants were still living at Bourton in the 1920s. In a way the family's mortality rate was typical of the time – a third died as very young children, another third died in their teens and twenties, but the remaining third lived to a full age. Father Benjamin's death at seventy-eight was not unusual.

> 1796 – January remarkable for Mildness – very high winds and great quantities of Rain, with much Lightning and Thunder. February – the 2nd day a great fall of Snow, the flakes particularly large – 2 showers of Hail. August, this month was greatly experienced the smiles of providence in a very plentiful Harvest. The Wheat remarkably good, heavy and plentiful and all other grain fine – to which blessing was added a long time of dry fine and warm weather peculiarly suitable for getting it in. Tho' 25th August Bread sunk from 9¾d. to 7¾d. the quartern loaf.

And how would Richard have paid for his quartern loaf? Well, there had long been a shortage of copper coins in circulation and this was to continue until 1797 when the firm of Matthew Boulton in Soho, near Birmingham were authorised to produce copper coins with an intrinsic value of 2d. and 1d. This marked a significant change of venue – all official coins had been minted at the Tower Mint since the reign of Queen Anne. The Boulton coins were beautifully impractical – massive, since the twopence coin weighed two ounces and was therefore intended to contain twopence of pure copper. Richard's coin pouch, a leather purse with a metal clasp, would barely have held more than two such coins, and the weight would have ruined his pockets! The equivalent silver coins were minute in comparison. And so the 'Cartwheel coins' as they were known, were never popular – but Richard had some in his possession when he died, and they remain along with his coin pouch. Little wonder traders preferred

(Top right) The copper twopence above the tiny silver equivalent and (bottom right) 'one penn'orth' (1d.) of copper. The cartwheel coins were unique in having their inscription indented (i.e. sunk into the copper surface) rather than raised as with all previous coins.

their coinage to be in silver ... when eight of the copper twopenny pieces weighed in at one pound!

The shop continued to be a drain on Richard's expenses. Throughout the 1790s Richard kept yearly accounts detailing the expenses of repairing the shop, and then transposed these on to summaries, often repeating the information several times. High on the list of problem areas was the privy – a constant source of expense – perhaps surprising with a shop built right by the actual bridge where it might be assumed that effluent would have been discharged straight into the Thames. Not so. The tank needed constant emptying, and this would have involved the use of a 'night man' – that is, someone who would call at night, empty the tank by lowering barrels into it, and then cart it off to be spread on the ground at one of the market gardens on the outskirts of town.

Cost as at 1783	£1400.8.5

To this must be added various annual expenses

1785 Jan 15th	Bricklayer	0.15.0
	Carpenter (water tank)	1.3.6
1788 Feb 29th	Repair warehouse floor	1.9.9
1791 June 18th	Sundry repairs	10.0.0
Nov 25th	Ireland Mason	1.0.3
	Rogers Bricklayer	0.19.6
1792 August	Commissioners on presenting a petition relative to the sewer	£1/1/0
1793 February	Rogers, bricklayer at the top of the house	£3/3/0/
	Ditto for jobb at the Privy	£6/3/0–
	Mr Poynder, plumber, for Grate at the Privy	£0/10/6
1793 September –	Ditto	£4/11/0
	Ditto top of the house	£0/17/0
	Carpenter about Privy	£3/17/6
	Ditto Case to lead pipe	£1/0/8

1795 January	Cartwright, tiling	£0/17/0
	Ditto	£2/10/0
1799	Work to washhouse windows etc	£4/18/0
	Andrews, Plumbers work to sink pipe etc	£3/2/5
	Cartwright, Bricklayers work to the tyling etc	£3/8/0
	Ireland, Mason	£0/6/2
	Mr James Weeks, Smith	£0/15/0
	Westbrook, Carpenter at the Counting House	£0/12/6

[As a rough guide, multiply these figures by sixty to get a modern equivalent.]

On 14 June 1794 Richard was sent a letter from his son William, marked as being from London Bridge, in which his son mentions his great pleasure in informing Richard that 'his affairs are brought to a comfortable conclusion' and that the Dividend would be ready Monday morning. He continues:

> The Trustees have been so good to settle with Mr Richards from whom I have today had a full discharge and they have given orders to the attorney, Mr Roberts, to pay Mr Giles' debts and costs to his attorney, which they will pay Monday. They had run up costs to upwards of £12 but the bill has been taxed and reduced to between 9 & 10 pounds. Yesterday Mr Davidson delivered up the key of the house to my Brother – we are preparing to move to Peckham.

From this it appears that William had been engaged in some form of litigation with a Mr Giles, had settled the action on the basis that he had to pay the other side's costs, and had decided to dissolve the partnership with his father and leave the family business. But the fact that *Holden's London Directory* of 1811, listing professions and trades, has an entry on 'Hall Francis, hosier, 1 London Bridge' shows that the partnership was simply altered so that Francis stepped into William's shoes and was still trading from the family premises well after Richard's death.

What happened to William? Well, a clue is given in his letter when he says, 'I expect to enter into the silk trade – may God grant a blessing thereon.' It rather looks as though William lost interest in the hosiery side of things, preferred the silk trade and is perhaps the William Hall mentioned in the same directory – either as 'silk manufacturer of 4 Wood Street Spitalfields' or as 'silkman of 4 Brown's Lane Spitalfields'. The actual lease of the shop premises remained in Richard's name until he died – he left the premises to Francis in his will on condition that Francis paid the sum of £100 to each of his siblings (William and Martha).

Back at Bourton, Richard decided to expand his farming interests. He still had land at Nethercoate, Bengeworth and Sedgeberrow but wanted to acquire land closer to home. In 1796 he bought a smallholding in the nearby hamlet of Clapton. Set on a hill, a mile or so across the meadows from Bourton, it appears to have been a near-derelict farm in need of repair and modernisation. There is nothing to suggest that Richard actually intended to occupy the farmhouse himself. In his will he described the holding as 'all those my Messuages Tenements or Farm houses with the Barns Stables Gardens Orchards Lands Meadows Woods hereditaments and appurtenances whatsoever to the same Appertaining situate lying and being in Clapton' – suggesting that there were at least two 'messuages' – that is, dwellings. He bought the estate from William Fox the elder and Henry Stevens,

The charming small church at Clapton.

but the price is not recorded. In Richard's notes headed 'Of what I am possess'd' from 1796 it appears that he had to sell off his entire holding of 5 per cent bank annuities in order to pay for it.

Richard started to renovate the farmhouse in November 1796 by installing a new fire grate and then the next year 'gave Mr Harris, an Old Day Labourer, two shillings for staking out some land', building a wall and whitewashing the house. A post-and-rail fence was erected alongside a quickthorn hedge. In October he paid the carpenter John Hall (no relation) £2 7s. 4½d. for 'fresh laying down the New barn floor & putting up a partition to preserve the grain in Thrashing – including the Smith's bill'. He paid £1 9s. 0d. for fir trees and then employed Mr Palmer to plant them – presumably as a windbreak – at a cost of half a guinea, and in 1798 set about rebuilding the pigsty. Later in 1798 he decided to re-roof the house. It was previously thatched and he had to pay Mr Hall the carpenter £22 4s. 5d. for new roof timbers and Mr Brindle for slates ('slatting') £21 2s 0d. That still left him to fork out sixteen shillings for supper for the workmen.

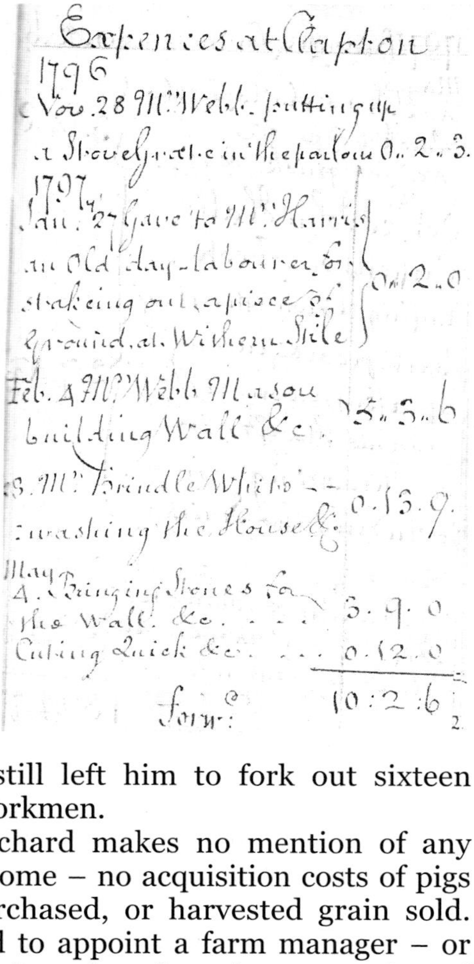
Expences at Clapton
1796
Nov. 28 Mr Webb. putting up a Stove grate in the parlour 0.. 2.. 3.
1797
Jan. 27 Gave to Mr Harris an Old day-labourer for stakeing out a piece of Ground at Withem Stile 0.. 2.. 0
Feb. 4 Mr Webb Mason building Wall &c. 5.. 5.. 6
3 Mr Brindle White-washing the House &c. 0. 15. 9.
May 4 Bringing Stones for the Wall &c. ... 3. 9. 0
Cutting Quick &c. ... 0. 12. 0
Forw.d 10:2:6

What is strange is that Richard makes no mention of any actual farming expenses or income – no acquisition costs of pigs to go in the sty, no seed purchased, or harvested grain sold. Presumably he either intended to appoint a farm manager – or put in a tenant – but it is curious that there is no mention of rent received or salary expended. A clue comes in a later diary kept by his son Benjamin – as a young man he decided to try his hand at farming (well, actually he tried his hand at most things, including being a travelling preacher, and running an ironmonger's shop in Coventry – unsuccessfully). He writes: 'In 1807 I decided on an agricultural life and arrangements were made with Mr Humphries, the tenant of the estate at Clapton, that I should go backwards and forwards to obtain some knowledge of farming. In this employment I was very comfortable, having my evenings for reading, and attending weekly exercises.' In all probability the smallholding was rented out to Mr Humphries in Richard's lifetime – with the rent being paid at a level which Richard did not think worth noting. The tenant may well have been the same person as the 'Mr Humphries – Smith' mentioned in the accounts.

Meanwhile Richard decided to take over 'the other half' of the semi-detached house which he was renting from his sister-in-law: '1798 – March 5th – Agreed with Mrs Snooke for the other part of the house paying for both the parts together £18 per Annum. Rent to commence April 5th. Mrs S. is to do the repairs with White-washing and Painting and build a rough Wall round the piece of ground by the Stable.' He presumably moved across into the new half because later that year he mentions: '1798 Sept 28th – agreed to let our tenement to Mrs S Beddome for 6 months for 3 Guineas – or at 5 Guineas a year if they continue a twelve month. If any taxes are charged to it they are to pay. Delivered the keys to Mr S Palmer Oct 3rd 1798.' Given that the pair of cottages commanded a combined rent of £18 p.a. and that the part he had previously lived in was to be sublet for around a third of that, it suggests that the 'other half' was rather larger, and that the move was occasioned by a need for more space. It meant more expenses – 'new locks and hinges 1/6d.'

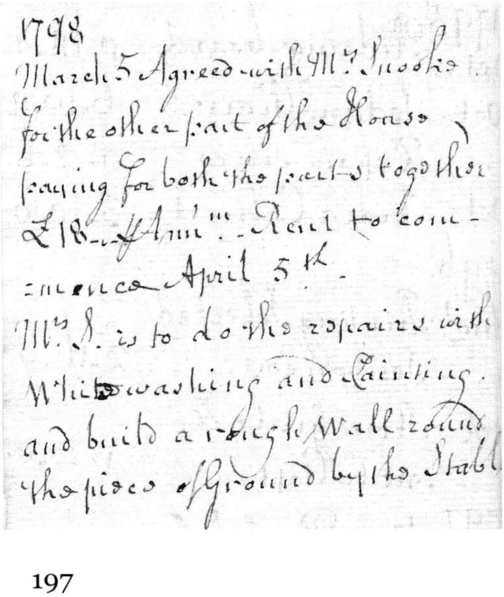
1798
March 5 Agreed with Mrs Snooke
for the other part of the House
paying for both the parts together
£18 – p Ann. – Rent to commence April 5th.
Mrs S. is to do the repairs with
White-washing and Painting.
and build a rough Wall round
the piece of Ground by the Stable

Sepr. 28. 1798. Agreed to Let our Tenement to Mr. J. Beddome &c for 6 Months for 3 Guineas – or at 5 Guineas the year if they continue a Twelve Month. If any Taxes are charged to it they are to pay them.

Delivered the Keys to Mr. J. Palmer Oct. 3. 98.

That same year Richard notes: 'Martha Hanks came to live here Oct 11th 1798 at £3.10.0 per annum as Cook.' (Note the specific reference to her duties i.e. as cook, and not just as a general servant.) Martha would have lived in, using one of the two attic rooms. The inventory prepared in 1818 (see Appendix II) shows that there was another attic room (presumably used by the children) plus two 'lodging rooms', one of which had a four-poster bed. Downstairs there was a front room, parlour, two little rooms, a kitchen, a brew-house and a cellar. We even know from Richard's jottings that the new parlour 'measured 10ft. 9in. from the fire to the window' and that the new kitchen was '13 ft. 11 in. from the fireplace and 11ft. 6in. across'. Carpets for the main rooms were needed, measuring nine feet by nine feet, ten by ten and twelve by twelve. (Carpets were, of course, squares, never fitted to the actual size of the room.)

Even though it appears to be a reasonably sized cottage, it must have been bursting at the seams – not least because Richard appears to have been carrying on a family tradition by having the 'London children' to stay. In other words Richard's eldest son, William, sent at least two of his children to stay at Bourton. Hence we see a reference in August 1796 to the carrier delivering 'a small box of Richard's things' – the 'Richard' being his ten-year-old grandson. Then in 1799 there is a reference to a visit by his eldest son, William – 'went away 28th June, took with him his daughter Betty'. She was twelve at the time, but there is no record to show how long she had been staying with her grandfather. It does rather suggest that after a period of 'detached indifference' towards children, Richard actually became far more involved with the younger members of the family – a fact borne out by comments made by others after Richard died. He even notes in his diary that when his sister-in-law, Mrs Snooke, was off on her travels, her four children would come round for meals.

Towards the end of his life Richard appears to have been more willing to relax, and to play games with his children. He bought a copy of 'Bowles Geographical Game of the World' in around 1800 – a sort of snakes and ladders, with travellers moving around the globe but being sent back if they landed at 'hostile' parts of the world. It is clear that Richard also played

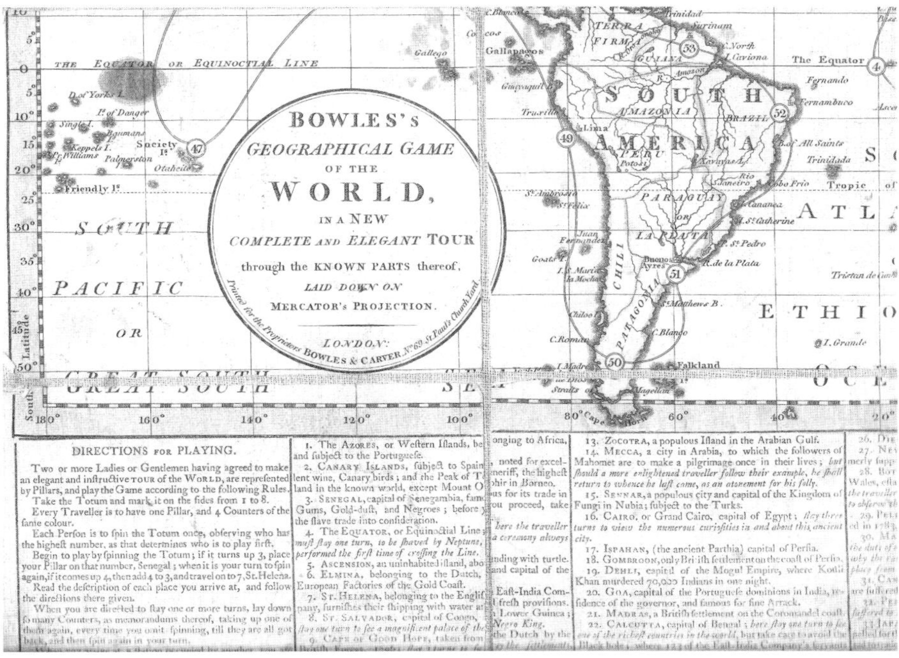

cards (Loo and Goons being examples). He also bought (but never opened) a game called 'Spellicans' – a box containing finely carved wooden sticks with hooks, being the forerunner of 'pick-a-stick' where the aim was to pick up sticks using the hooked end, without moving the neighbouring sticks.

Add to this his piano playing, and we begin to see a slightly more relaxed Richard in his old age, spending time with his younger children and grandchildren, walking his dog across the water meadows to Clapton to oversee alterations, recounting tales to the kids about going to see the King, or what it was like at the Tower of London, or how there used to be highwaymen and robbers lurking by the roadside. Slowly a rather more avuncular figure emerges – kind to children and four-legged friends, even if he remained a grumpy pious old prig to the rest of the world! It is to be hoped that he found an inner peace surrounded by his family, despite his worries about the economy, the war with France and so on.

Richard continued to list many of his own household purchases – but strangely there is no reference to the half-dozen salts he bought, presumably shortly after 1799 when they were made. Salts were sold in pairs and six survive. Later generations were to add another six, of a similar style but with Victorian markings. Presumably each diner had his or her own salt, so that no one was considered 'below the salt' – an expression used to denote

One of the set of six surviving Georgian salts.

inferior status. The interiors are gilt, to prevent corrosion, and this was used in place of the more common glass lining. Instead Richard mentions 'an India Cabinet' (i.e. a cabinet made in India) costing £3/10/0 in October 1795; 'a new Brussels carpet' in 1797, and 'a dozen dessert knives and forks (black handles)' costing 13s. 6d. in July 1799.

By now the war with France was beginning to create serious hardship among the rural poor, and Richard notes tellingly:

> 1800 – Memorable for the highness of corn – some wheat sold for £40 and £46 the load – bread very dear. In London the quartern loaf at 1s.6½d. The poor in the Country were obliged to eat very bad bread – distressing to behold. 1800 – September 17th – General Riots on account of the dearness of Corn and Bread. 1801 – A Melloncholly time for the dearness of Grain and all sorts of provisions. Wheat about £55 and £60 the load. Malt 15 shillings a bushel. Mutton nine pence p. lb., Veal nine pence p. lb., Beef eight pence p. lb., Bacon 16 pence p. lb., Cheese ten pence (Cheshire twelve). Eggs have been as high as 2½d. each – in April was at four for 2d. Butter 1s.6d. p. lb. in London, at Bourton 1s.2d. Bread (March 5th) was at 1s.10½d. the Quartern Loaf. The Quartern Loaf on April 1st was 1s.9¼d.

The price of bread had for many years been fixed by the Court of Assize and from time to time Parliament extended the court's powers – for instance it regulated apprenticeships as well as laying down rules for the size, weight and price of loaves – varying according to the price of wheat. It was an offence to sell underweight loaves – and bakers were easily caught out if they broke the law, because the law required them to put their own mark on their loaves. It was to avoid prosecution that bakers took to selling bread in batches of thirteen rather than twelve – hence the expression 'a baker's dozen'. Bakers could also be punished for selling adulterated bread – but it was not uncommon for alum to be added to the mixture – either by the baker or by the unscrupulous miller who sold the flour. Alum was used because it was a bulking agent – it helped the bread expand in size, as well as whitening it. It also stiffened the mix and therefore was used to disguise poor wheat. The fact that it was a mineral salt produced via a process which involved the use of large quantities of stale urine, and which would have done the consumer no good at all, was not the issue! Worse still, alum manufacture necessitated the use of what was called 'pure'. Another name for 'pure' is dog faeces! People were paid to pick up the 'pure' from streets throughout London... Another slice of bread anyone?

Meanwhile Richard was busy noting with concern the spiralling National Debt. As a prudent businessman he would have been horrified at the idea of the country piling up debts which could not be met out of present taxation income. 'February 1800 – the National Debt stands at between Four and Five Hundred Millions.' This contrasts with an entry in 1783: 'National Debt Funded and Unfunded exceeds 245 Millions.' Running totals were kept. He notes in December 1798 'one thing we are certain of is that the expenses of the ensuing year will exceed those of any preceeding year, and that Mr Pitt will in the course of 7 years have doubled our National Debt and more than have doubled our Taxes!' Richard was also vexed by the Irish question, and in particular with the proposed Union between the two countries, noting that in a speech in 1800 Mr Fox had stated: 'To pretend that the measure is taken with the consent of the Irish people is adding mockery to injury. While Martial Law is proclaimed in Ireland and the people restrained from meeting to express their sentiments it is insulting them to say that the union is made with their free good will.'

It had been Richard's practice to go up to London every six months – but by now it was such a routine and uneventful journey that it did not merit an entry in the diaries – unless of course he arrived in a thunderstorm. So his record for the journey to London in 1795 simply stated: 'Got to London August 13th about One o'Clock. About ten at Night came on a great Thunder and very awful Lightning which lasted some hours. Some rain was with it. The storm was very general and did much damage.' In other words, the actual journey was no longer worth a mention – better roads and the (English) invention of elliptical springs to provide proper suspension for carriages saw to that. Also, for the first time, wheels were fitted with hoop tyres (as opposed to a number of separate metal strips). Having a single hoop of metal, put on to the rim of the wheel while hot and then nailed into position, meant that it drew the rim in tight when the iron band cooled and shrank, making for a far more even, smoother ride. When in London Richard found time to write home to his children – addressing the envelope to himself (as householder) but adding the words 'Master Benjamin Hall'. In one particular letter, dated 1799, he asks Benjamin to thank his sister for her letter – while complaining that he wishes that it had been written 'with more perspicuity'. He explains to his son that he is 'considerably engaged' (presumably with business) and lists where he is due to take breakfast that day ('with Mrs Hainsworth in Hackney'),who is coming to take tea, and where they would be dining ('with Mr Reynolds at Broken Wharf, who has been so obliging as to give us a pressing invitation'). He ends it with the words 'Dear Benjamin from your Affectionate Father Richard Hall, London Bridge July 27th.'

Another letter, intended for his son Francis, was considered sufficiently important to be prepared in draft. Perhaps he was anxious to avoid offence and wanted to appear grateful! The draft remains:

> Son Francis, July 25 1800
> Your kindness dear Son claims an early and grateful acknowledgment and we thank you for the brace of Turbot but sorry I am to add that there was some alloy attending your desire to please us by the neglect of not sending them in time for the North Coach. The coach I suppose arrives there by 5 or 6 o'clock in the morning and your fish did not come to hand til between 7 and 8 o'clock last night. The weather was very warm indeed – I think the hottest day we have had this summer. You did not recollect that shrimps spoil the soonest of any fish and therefore are particularly bad travellers in this season – but notwithstanding the unpleasant deficiency we are much obliged to you. I am glad to hear you had a safe and pleasant journey to Bath and left William well – it is a great Mercy to be preserved.

One rather suspects that Francis would have received the letter and concluded that his best was never good enough for father – while father would have remained convinced that his son was too stupid even to know that fish go off in the heat!

Ever the supporter of the King (he rarely mentioned the words 'George III' without the preface 'Good King'), Richard notes 'His Majesty compleated his 63rd year June 4. 1801.' As it turned

His Majesty. compleated his 63d year. June 4. 1801.

out, this was to be Richard's final entry in his diary. On 17 June 1801 the 72-year-old Richard set out for London with his wife and Mrs Snooke. They got as far as Witney when Richard was taken ill, and the party was forced to return. His son Benjamin takes up the story:

> My father continuing to get worse, Dr Cheston, a Physician from Gloucester, was sent for who came on the 23rd. Dr Cox also came on 26th and Mr and Mrs Griffith from Bath. My brothers in law [in modern parlance his stepbrothers] William and Francis with my cousin Eliza came on the 30th. July 2nd, a little before 6 o'clock in the morning my dear father departed. Mr Davidson an esteemed friend of my father and one of his executors came on Monday 6th. On Sunday 7th my father's remains were interred in the Meeting Yard at Bourton – the Revd. Thos Smith of Shipton-on-Stour officiated. On the following day Mr Davidson and Mr Francis Hall left for London and Mr Griffith & Mr William Hall for Bath. The following brief Memoir of my father was inserted in Dr Rippon's register: 'July 2nd 1801 Died Mr Rd Hall of Bourton on the Water Gloucestershire in the seventy third year of his age. He was for many years a minister of the church of Christ in Carter Lane Southwark in the time of Dr Gill. His illness was sudden and he was in great pain for several days, but it pleased the Lord to afford him consolation. His mind was much occupied by the Holy Scriptures and with great patience and resignation he bore the afflicting hand of God, acknowledging that the ways of the Lord were just and equal. He expressed warm emotions of tenderness to his family, especially the younger branches of it whose concerns appeared very much to interest his heart. He spoke of the importance of early instruction in Divine things and the benefit of having the mind stored

> with the treasure of God's word, the advantage of which he had experienced, and hoped his youngest son would be a follower of those who walk in the ways of the Lord.'

As already mentioned, Dr Rippon ended with the words 'Mr Hall was certainly not distinguished among his religious connections for the felicity of his disposition but we are given to understand that he has left behind him the testimony of an affectionate husband a kind father and a sincere friend.' The family were outraged and, according to son Benjamin, they wrote to tell Dr Rippon what they thought of him. Unfortunately no trace of the letter remains!

And what then? Richard's widow went back to the house and remained there as a widow until her death seventeen years later. The house may have been somewhat cluttered with Richard's belongings based on the description of it in the 1818 inventory (Appendix II). Meanwhile Benjamin continued as a day scholar at Dr Collett's school. He recalls:

> Mr Collett was an unusually fat man – the most extraordinary I have ever seen outside of a show. On one occasion he was in London when he was taken in one of the streets for Lambert, a celebrated giant, and so followed by the crowd out of curiosity as to be obliged for a time to take refuge in a shop. To a naturally timid boy, rather more pitied than he ought to have been, such a master was somewhat formidable, especially when he flourished the cane in dignified style and made little and big feel the weight of his hand.

Thereafter Benjamin went to Mr Huntley's school at Burford which was the largest and most respectable school in the neighbourhood. Benjamin did indeed follow his father's wishes, being baptised as a young man in 1806. He then spent many years, as we have already learned, as an itinerant preacher, travelling on his pony to local Baptist meeting halls which were without a minister. He married and had children, and over the ensuing centuries they have in turn produced clergymen, accountants, engineers, teachers, silversmiths – and even the odd lawyer!

Anna went on to marry the son of her half-brother William

Seward Hall – in other words she married her nephew. If Richard had survived to see the wedding he would have been in the unusual position of being both father to the bride and grandfather to the groom! Meanwhile sons William and Francis returned to London Bridge and carried on with their respective businesses. They all had children. And they in turn had children. And so the world revolves...

Richard's widow clearly found it painful to throw out any of Richard's things – so his papers, his collections, his odds and ends remained. After her death Benjamin presumably felt reluctant to dispose of items, which were his last link to his father – so this 'rubbish' was placed in tea chests and stored. And each generation for the next two centuries has taken one look at the tea chests and left them well alone! Occasionally a commemorative newspaper was added to the pile of eighteenth-century periodicals and papers – Victoria's accession, Dr Livingstone's explorations, the outbreak of the First World War. But nothing has been taken out and it remains as a sort of time capsule, a commemoration of the life and times of a man who lived through a most extraordinary period of change.

There is an interesting postscript to the friendship of Richard and William Snooke, both of them married to Seward daughters. There exists a letter, written in 1912 by a Caroline Mary Griffith, to her distant family in Australia. She was a direct descendant of the marriage between Richard's daughter Martha and Henry Griffith. The letter appears on the site hosted by Rootsweb.com as part of the Griffith family history. The letter was headed: 'Chiefly impressions or traditions handed down to us by those who have gone before'. After describing the history of Richard and William, Caroline Mary goes on to say:

> The two friends, Richard Hall and William Snook, were 'gentlemen', and rather eccentric ones, of Bourton-on-the-Water. My aunt used to tell a story of some extraordinary arrangement they made between themselves (based on the expectation that one sister, who was delicate, would die first), in order to keep the Seward property to which their wives were heiresses, from going out of the family. But the

> wrong sister died, with the result that the usual fate of the Griffiths in money matters happened, i.e., not much of the property came to that side of the family in which our great-grandmother Martha Hall belonged.

It would appear from his will that Richard did try and keep his side of the bargain – his assets were scrupulously divided so that Bengeworth and the assets acquired from the Seward inheritance passed only to the children of his first marriage. Maybe this was part of a plan not to dilute the inheritance (as opposed to a deliberate attempt to bar the earlier children from sharing in Richard's later fortune). Perhaps Eleanor was the sickly frail one – perhaps Frances, the jovial wife of farmer William, was the one everyone expected to survive. But she died childless, and so the Seward inheritance was absorbed into the Snooke fortunes. But eccentric? Wherever did Caroline Mary get that from!

Appendix I

Lists, Recipes and Miscellanea

Richard kept lists of anything and everything – he adored facts and jotted down snippets of pseudo-scientific information as if it had all the authority of absolute fact. These 'factoids' pepper his journals. Sometimes he pasted in newspaper cuttings, or copied out passages from favourite books to create a sort of 'running miscellany'. He also kept collections of things which took his interest – shells, fossils, old coins. There follows a small taster of some of the things which took his fancy...

Miscellany

Pit coal – so far from doing any harm, that they are rather beneficial, by drying up the too great humidity of the blood, and preserving the body from putrifaction, for it has been observed by Galon that all bitumens, being kindred, mend the disorders of the air by dispersing their too great humidity. Where the atmosphere is very moist and full of watery vapours, so hurtful to human bodies, the burning of Coal is certainly very proper. In former times when the plague and other infectious diseases were common they used to burn bitumen to purify the air; and this is certain, that in London since the burning of Pit Coal has been almost universal no plague has ever affected that city, nor any disease of that kind. There are mines of coals dug in various parts of England. Those brought from Newcastle, improperly called Sea Coal, are remarkable for their being generally small and caking on the fire.

The Bat: a little Bird that flies in the night; Kimshi describes it as a mouse with wings. We sometimes call it the flittermous. It is a creature between fowl and beast. It is the only fowl, as Pliny observes, that has teeth and teats, that brings forth animals and nourishes them with milk.

Camels milk is the thinnest of all others.

Greyhounds – said to out-live all other dogs.

The Polypus, whose method of producing its young is very singular – the young one issues from the side of its Parent in the form of a small pimple which becomes, in the space of a few days, a perfect animal and drops from its parent to shift for itself.

The Flounder, the Plaice, the Sole, and almost all the flat fish swim with their white side downwards – both their eyes are placed on one side (the upper side).

Monday January 10th 1763 – heard the unfortunate story of two young men, well acquainted, who went shooting near Polesworth. They were in adjoining fields separated by a hedge when some birds arose, upon which one of them fired and unfortunately killed his companion.

Ants – there are five sorts – the hill ant, Jet Ant, the Red Ant, the Common or yellow Ant, the small black Ant

The wings of a fly are supposed to have the quickest motion of any natural substance which lives.

The Cockatrice is called the king of serpents because of his majestic pace, for he does not creep upon the ground like other serpents but goes half upright. Writers differ as to the Production of this animal – some say it is bought forth of a Cock's Egg, which is generated by the putrified seed of an old Cock, and sat upon by a snake or toad and so becomes a cockatrice. It is said to be about half a foot in length, the hinder part like a Serpent, the fore part like a cock. The eyes of the cockatrice are red. Its poison is so strong there is no cure for it and it kills not only by touch but by sight and hissing. [Curiously this seems to be a description of a cobra – the clue is that Richard then goes on to say that its only predator is 'a small weasel which eats rue' – in other words a mongoose – presumably believed to live on a diet of rue in order to counteract the venom!]

October 1788 Counterfeit Half Guineas look well – of Inferior Gold – of a deep cast, the O in Georgius look more like a G.

Oxford paper: A woman paid a two-penny piece for a Glass of Spirits – which was afterwards observed to be made to unscrew – in which was found a Bank Note for £50.

Publish'd in an American paper by order of the College of Physicians of Philadelphia: Half an Ounce of strong Oil of Vitriol, poured upon an equal quantity of powder'd salt-petre in china or glass vessels, produces a vapour which has been found very beneficial in destroying the infection of Sick-rooms.

Coffee: the medical effects; assists digestion, promotes the natural sensations and prevents a disposition to sleepiness.

A violent Hiccough which had resisted a great number of medicines was at last cured by sucking Womens' Milk' [first find yourself a woman…].

1800: The clear produce of the Post Office this Year was Six hundred and Ninety Nine Thousand pounds.

The method of the Americans proving their Powder is to spread a small quantity on a Sheet of writing paper and set fire to it: if the powder be good the smoak rises perpendicularly and the paper is not bruised nor even spotted.

The first legal Interest was fixed at ten per cent by Henry 8th on January 31st 1545 – Repealed by Edward 6th in 1549 and revived by Queen Elizabeth June 15th 1571. Interest was reduced to 8% by James 1st on January 24th 1625 – Reduced to 6% by Charles 2nd in 1660. In Queen Anne's reign September 29th 1714 it was reduced to its present Standard of 5%.

To Blacken Picture Frames: Ivory Black Size Glow [i.e. glue] – a little boil'd up together.

Mr Clay says this of the Sovereign 'He has more personal and social virtue than any Prince in Europe'. I feel great curiosity to know how you get the scales by which to ascertain the exact quantum of virtue in every European Prince.

It is not wholesome to Fan yourself during Perspiration.

Avoid salted meats – those who eat them have pale complexions, a slow pulse, and are full of corrupted humours.

Walk not too long at a time, stand not for hours together in one posture, nor lie longer than necessary; be sure to avoid sitting up late;

immediately after you awake rub your breast where your heart lies with the palm of your hand.

Upon a Stone on Broadway Hill: To London 89 Moreton 7 Worcester 22 Evesham 7.

Whitchurch Shropshire was 3 Weddings, the Brides all Sisters. One after a Courtship of 14 years, another 14 months, another 14 days.

1790 December 12th – Mrs Snooke's Parrot died which she had had full 19 Years. Epitaph On Mrs Snooke's Parrot buried 22 Dec 1790 Drop a tear, poor Poll is dead Her friends surround her funeral bed. No more can hear her pretty prattle, For she is gone, no more to rattle. Her Mistress has her coffin neatly made, With true affection, and without parade. With weeping eye, she took her last Adieu. And said 'Alas my dearest Bird, I weep for you'.

24th March 1736 – 'the tide so high at Westminster that the lawyers had to be fetched out of the Hall in boats' – 1801 Almanack.

For Breakfast, a little is enough. For Dinner too much is too little. For Supper, too little is too much.

Liquorice: almost the only sweet that quenches thirst.

From the time of Henry 8th to the Accession of his present Majesty there were only thirty Bills of Divorce – and from that time to the present there have been no less than 93.

Remedy for the Kings Fever: several opiates have been tried without the desired effect. Mr Addington suggested a prescription which had been tried by his father. A pillow, filled with hops, was placed under His Majesty's head, which acted as a soporific, and produced the most compleat success.

Salisbury Cathedral has as many doors as months, as many windows as days and as many pillars as hours in the whole year.

In walking over ice or frozen snow take short steps and lean forward and you will rarely if ever meet with a dangerous fall.

To remove fruit stains from Lace Muslin, Callico, Linen etc soak it in water and expose the place to the vapour of burning brimstone. The vapour will remove the blemish in less than a minute.

To take out oil or greasy spots in silk, or grease out of woollen cloth; dab the spot with a piece of wet brown paper rolled up with a red hot coal in it. When one piece of paper and coal fails, let the stain be dabbed with another 'til it disappears and can then be brushed.

A shark has 144 teeth, notched like a saw on its edge, dispos'd in six rows and arranged in various directions. These teeth when he sleeps lie flat in his mouth, but when he seizes his prey, he has the power of erecting them by a set of muscles which join them in the jaw.

It is reported of the Leopard that it is of a sweet smell and by its odour it draws the fawns, does etc near it and then makes a prey of them.

Hippopotamus – supposed by some to be the Behemoth mentioned in Job.

Hackney Coach New Act 1800 1 s the first mile, 6 d for every additional halfmile. Coaches engaged by time to be paid one shilling for the first forty minutes and sixpence for every twenty minutes after. The hire of a coach for the day to be 18 s instead of 14 s 6 d the day to consist of 12 hours – the distance to be limited to twenty miles from the metropolis.

The expense of collecting the income tax amounts to one hundred and fifty two thousand pounds per annum, something less than 6½d. in the pound.

Cambridge Intelligencer: Eight millions sterling are the estimated expenses of France for the present year. The estimated expenses of Great Britain for the same period are upwards of forty millions.

Hand-bill September 17th 1800 (on account of the Riots about the dearness of Bread): Well disposed inhabitants of this City, upon the appearance of the Military, are requested to keep all the individuals of their families and servants within doors, and where such opportunities can be taken, to remain at the back rooms of their houses.

French troops in Paris – during the present Excessive heat, an additional allowance of Vinegar is to be given to them – stricter attention is given to the cleanliness of their barracks, and they are forbidden to bathe but under an observation from Officers, that they may do it when cool, and not after meals.

Books in the Old Testament	39	In the New	27	Total	66
Chapters	929		260		1,189
Verses	23,214		7,959		31,173
Words	592,430		181,253		773,692
Letters	2,728,100		838,380		3,566,480

To take Rust off Steel – Powder of Putty, mixed with water – rub it on with a piece of smooth wood.

It is an actual fact that one shop only, in the Strand, cleans weekly Fiveteen hundred dozen pairs of Silk Hose.

1547 silk stockings first worn by the French King. 1561 Queen Elizabeth wore the first pair of silk stockings in England.

A Swedish natural Philosopher remarks –land turtles find their appetite diminished in September and lose it entirely in October. They pass 4 months in the year without absolutely eating anything. The same naturalist has Observed that a leech is perhaps the most prolific of all worm-kind. One of them preserved in an Outhouse pot has produced 150 leeches.

Asia – the Second Grand Quarter in the World containing 1 Siberia 2 Turkey in Asia 3 Tartary 4 Persia 5 Arabia 6 India 7 China

Africa is the Third Grand Quarter in the World. Territories: Egypt, Barbary, Bildulgerid, Zaara, Nigritia, Guinea, Nubia, Abysinia & Ethiopia

America – the Fourth Grand Quarter in the World – is divided into North America and South America.

Canada: the finest place in the world, and the vilest spot on the earth; one time an uncultivated forest of wild beasts; and another a mine of wealth. Ceded by the French for Martinico, who love rum and sugar, and kept by the English, who love hunting and felling trees.

Norway – near Sweden – a Kingdom of Europe bounded by the Atlantic Ocean, produces oak and fir timber, pitch and tar, copper and iron.

Russia – furs, red leather, linen & thread, iron copper sail-cloth, hemp & flax, pitch & tar, wax, honey Isinglass, linseed oil, potash soap, feathers, hogs bristles, musk, rhubarb and other drugs, timber.

London & Westminster – one Million forty five thousand & seventy five people.

Nuremburg – a city of Germany. It is very populous and has the best inland trade of any town in Europe – their clock work and manufactures in iron, steel, ivory, wood and alabaster are much admired, and afforded exceeding cheap, and from hence come most of those toys we call Dutch toys.

In Egypt, part of Africa, the musketos or gnats will not suffer people to sleep in the Night.

Peru – in South America – the Andes are the highest mountains in the world. The most valuable tree they have is that which furnishes them with Quinquina, or Peruvian bark, and this grows chiefly in the Province of Quitto on the mountains and near the city of Quitto, and is the size of a cherry tree, bearing a long reddish flower from whence arises a pod with a kernel like an almond but the fruit does not seem to have the same virtues as the bark. Many excellent balms, gums and drugs are also found here – particularly that called the Balsam of Peru.

Rosemary – helps a dis-agreeable breath. Rue leaves, eaten, sweetens the breath after eating Onions etc.

Spirit of Turpentine – for a prick with a fork or needle, nail or thorn.

Wash childblains with warm Brandy, if not broke.

An immediate relief for Appoplexies or Palsies – put salt into the mouth of the person afflicted.

For Purgeing – one ounce of Hartshorn shavings, one ounce burnt Hartshorn, a drahm Cinamon boil'd in a quart of Water 'til it comes to a pint – sweeten it as you like it, and add a drahm of Gum Arabic.

Ague – advice given in a Newspaper – a spoonful of powdered Snake root in a glass of Brandy & Water a little before the fit is expected, and endeavour by keeping himself warm, to bring on a perspiration.

Putrid sore throats – take candid Narbonne honey and mix with a tumbler of boiling water, a gill of Hollands, and the thin rind of a lemon, being first well sweetened with the honey. This will make a rich balsamic drink for the evening; in the morning for breakfast take a toast and spread some of the same honey on it. This, in 2 or 3 days will effectually remove the disorder.

In the Isles of Scotland they cure the Scurvy & the Jaundice, to which they are subject, with the powder of snail shells and scurvy grass.

Dr Adams – years are from one in four to one in six or seven to the healthy. December January and April are from observation found to be the most sickly months and June the most healthy in the year. January is to June as 11 is to 1.

For the Dropsy – shortness of breath, warming the blood – 2 oz Mustard seed, 2 oz Horseradish sliced, steeped in wine – a glass or two taken in a day.

Or another for Dropsy: Parsnips boiled in water. Drink the water.

For the Itch – Brimstone Posset. One ounce flour of brimstone put into an old saucepan – mix it with about three quarters of a pint of Milk, put it to boil, keep it stirring – it will turn to Curd and Whey. Strain it, drink near half a pint warm, morning and evening. May rub your hands with the curd.

For heaviness in Head – ½ oz Salvolatile Drops, 6½ oz Lavender Drops, mixt together. Take a large teaspoonful 3 times a day in a small tea cup of water with a nob of sugar.

Dr Cadogan – the Original of all Chronic Diseases are Indolence, Intemperence and Vexaton. We must never loose Sight of the three great principles of Health – Activity, Temperence, and peace of Mind.

Sprains, bruises & such like complaints. A strong brine of salt and Water to be used as Hot as you can bare it to be fomented with a piece of new scarlet cloth. Keep the cloth on and do it often. [Another] bran boil'd in urine, make a poultice, put it onto a cloth and apply it hot, while one is cooling to get another ready.

For pain in Stomach – 4 cloves of Garlick pricked with a Needle a great many times – take them Night & Morning.

A Salve – for burns, Cuts, and sores. Hogs Lard half a pound, Beeswax 2 oz – cut pretty small. Put them to melt over a slow fire – pour it into a porringer, or large gallipot – when cold cut it as you want it.

For a Bruise, swell'd and black – spread a Poultice of Vinegar, Oil & Oatmeal, to be pretty wet with the Oil.

Salt, Spirit, & Oil of Amber, called the Powers of Amber; to be rubbed on the Head to revive a person when near dead in an Appoplexy. Except in extream cases it would be too powerful to use, one of them may be tried.

An Emetick – Camomile flower-seed with a good deal of salt put into it.

Dr Clarke, of Edinburgh, has discovered that eating two or three boiled herrings at bedtime, and tasting no other food that night, will remove the gout, if not totally cure it. If thirst ensues, chewing hay or straw will excite an exudation, from the Salival glands, and afford relief.

Salt Prunella – an Excellent thing for a Sore Throat – taken night and morning. (Very disagreeable).

If the Bowels out of order or opress'd with Wind – one ounce of Cardimum drops – take a Teaspoonful in a Teacup full of Camomile Tea, twice a day. Or as an alternative: 2 oz of mutton suit (i.e. suet) near the kidney, cut it very small and let it simmer in a pint of milk 'til it comes to half a pint then strain it off and take a coffee-cup full warm, frequently if the stomach will bare it. Richard obviously favoured this recipe because he repeats it as 'For a Dysentry – Half a pound of Mutton suet from the inside of a loin of Mutton – pricked and pounded – boil in a pint of milk – taken in the Quantity of a Coffee-cupful every three hours and continued even if the patient should throw it up again.]

VIPER DROPS So prepared as to contain all the sanative Qualities of that Creature, heightened. They tho given in a very small quantity, excel in Power and Efficacy almost all other Medicines given in any Quantities, for the relief and cure of those afflicted with the following and many other Disorders: Viz. Natural Weakness, Weakness from Venereal Injuries, Inability, Sterility from those or other causes, Wastings of Flesh, Lowness of Spirit, immoderate Fluxes, Fluor Albus, &c. Hysterical or Hypocondrical Disorders, Pains in the Back or Kidneys, Injuries of the Ureters or Urethra from Stone or Gravel; with a multitude of other Disorders. It chears enlivens and restores, strengthens and invigorates to a Miracle: creates appetite and helps Digestion. It is pleasant to take even to the weakest and nicest Persons. This

VIPER DROPS,

SO prepared as to contain all the ſanative Qualities of that Creature, heightened. They, tho' given in a very ſmall Quantity, excel in Power and Efficacy almoſt all other Medicines given in any Quantities, for the Relief and Cure of thoſe afflicted with the following, and many other Diſorders, viz. Natural Weakneſs; Weakneſs from Venereal Injuries; Inability, Sterility, from thoſe or other Cauſes; Waſtings of Fleſh; Lowneſs of Spirit; immoderate Fluxes, Fluor Albus, &c. Hyſterical or Hypocondriacal Diſorders; Pains in the Back or Kidneys; Injuries of the Ureters, or Urethra from Stone or Gravel; with a Multitude of other Diſorders. It chears, enlivens, reſtores, ſtrengthens and invigorates to a Miracle; creates Appetite, and helps Digeſtion. It is pleaſant to take, even to the weakeſt and niceſt Perſons. This Medicine is highly ſerviceable in many Complaints, outwardly applied; to Wounds, Bruiſes, Aches, Pains, Burns &c.

Advertisement in the *London Evening Penny Post* (Monday, 9 September 1751).

medicine is highly serviceable in many Complaints, outwardly applied, to Wounds, Bruises, Aches, Pains, Burns &c. It is sold only by the Proprietor, Richard Rock on Ludgate Hill in phials sealed up ... for 1/6d each.

Dr Ratcliff's Receipt for Gout 5 oz Raisons, stoned. 1 of Rhubarb, Sliced 2 Drams Coriander seed 1 Dram Saffron 1 oz Sena Leaves Quarter oz. Cochineal 2 drams Fennel Seed 1 oz Liquorish Root sliced Infuse these ingredients in one Quart of French Brandy ten days in a stone bottle, shaking it often, be sure to keep it close-stopp'd. Then decant off the clear, and add to the Ingredients one pint and a quarter more of brandy. Let it stand a Months time shaking it often until within 5 or 6 days of decanting. This you may mix with what you poured off first – take a Wine Glass when the pain is violent and if not relieved in two hours, take another. [Perhaps because of his diet Richard was all too familiar with gout and would have sympathised with the drawing entitled *The Gout* published

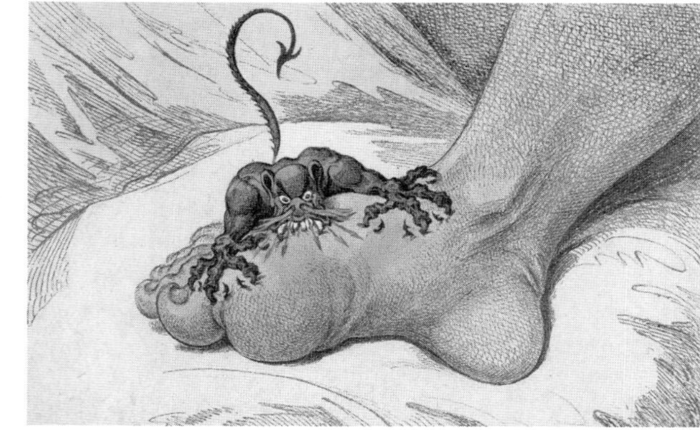

in 1799 by James Gillray. Cartoonists tended to portray gout sufferers as figures of fun, but anyone who has suffered from gout will identify with the evil creature whose sharp fangs are about to bite into a foot already gouged into by sharp claws...]

For Oppression in the Stomach – mostly Wind About 5 grains of Rhubarb, or, as much as will lay upon a silver 2d with an equal quantity of Nutmeg, every other Night.

Marseilles Vinegar – an antidote to a putrid Fever. Take rue, sage, mint, rosemary & wormwood of each an handful. Infuse them over the fire in two quarts of strong vinegar – strain the liquor through a flannel and add to it half an ounce of camphire dissolved in 3 ounces of rectified spirit of wine. With this wash the loins, face and mouth on approaching affected persons or places. Smell a sponge dipped in this decoction, wear also camphire in a bag near the stomach.

Mr Stead – for purging and uneasiness of bowels – with wind: Take regularly a large Tea Cup of strong Camomile Tea, twice or three times a day. Chew a bit of rhubarb every night for six nights going to bed

The moſt violent TOOTH-ACH cured in a few Minutes, without drawing, by a Tincture which gives immediate Eaſe in the Tooth-Ach, and cures all Diſorders whatſoever, in the Mouth or Gums; in a few Days will faſten the Teeth if ever ſo looſe; and with a little continuance, will ſpeedily cure the Scurvy in the Gums. It alſo prevents the Teeth from rotting, keeping thoſe that are decayed from becoming worſe, and takes off all diſagreeable Smells in the Breath, and cauſes a Diſcharge of all Scorbutic Humours lodged in the Gums, which deſtroy the Teeth. By applying this Tincture outwardly, it will remove all Kinds of Swellings in the Cheek, or Pain in the Ear, and is an abſolute Cure for the Head-ach, if ever ſo violent.

☞ The above valuable Tincture, is likewiſe Sold by T. Wood, Shrewſbury, D. Salmon, Pool, and T. Hilditch, Oſweſtry.

It is ſold by Mr. Hamilton's Appointment, Wholeſale and Retail, at the Golden Head, oppoſite Somerſet-houſe in the Strand; and at the Golden Head, in the Minories, in Bottles, 2s. 6d each, ſealed and ſigned with his Name, to prevent Counterfeits.

– as big as an Horse Bean, or in powder as much as will lay upon a silver penny.

Wearing a wig, day in and day out, without washing regularly had a common result afflicting Kings and Commoners alike – head lice!

11. THE LOUSE is a Creature ſo officious, that it will be known to every one at one Time or other; ſo buſy and ſo impudent, that it will be intruding itſelf in every one's Company; and ſo proud and aſpiring withal, that it fears not to trample on the beſt, and affects nothing ſo much as a Crown, feeds and lives very high, and that makes it ſo ſaucy, as to pull any one by the Ears, that comes in its Way, and will never be quiet till it has drawn Blood; it is troubled at nothing ſo much as at a Man that ſcratches his Head, as knowing that Man is plotting

Recipes

A cheap family Dinner without Bread: Beat up boiled potatoes fine with a little butter and some pepper & salt and having added some steaks of any kind of meat send the dish to the oven. The juices of the meat will give a great richness to the potatoes which will rise and leave a fine crust like a batter pudding.

Knuckle Broth – Take the pieces of knuckles cut off from the Legs and Shoulders of Mutton – about 18. Put them into a Gallon of Water with the bottom of a Penny Loaf, or a large crust of bread & 2oz Hartshorn shavings – boiled very slowly it comes to two quarts. Take a Tea-cupful as often as you like.

Marmalade – Sevil oranges. Grate or pare the first rind very thin, boil it in water until soft, shifting the water when boiled very tender. Pound it in a marble mortar. To a pound of pulp put a pound of sugar, squeeze the juices of each orange, let it simmer about ten minutes.

To make Lady Dorset Cakes: Take a pound of sugar, beaten and sifted. A pound of butter – work them together with your hands then put in 6 eggs – leave out two whites, put in two-pennyworth of Mace then put in a pound of fine flower. Work it in by degrees. Put in 4 or 5 spoonfuls of Rosewater, a grain of Amber Greece, then take half a pound of Currance. Put them into the pans and put them into a quick oven. Let them not be done Brown. (Three quarters of a pound of sugar is enough).

To make Ripe Gooseberry Vinegar: 10 quarts boiling water – let it stand 'til cold. 4 quarts of full ripe chrystal gooseberries, mash them well and put them to the water. With 5lb of coarse brown sugar, let the mixture stand (stirring the matter some times) 24 hours then strain it through a Flannel bag, and put it into a Cask in a warm place, covering the bung hole with a thin cloth or perforated bung, to keep out dust and flies. At the end of nine months it will be fit for use.

To make Currant Wine: To every Quart of Juice put 3 Quarts of Water. To every Gallon of liquor 3 pounds and a half of moist sugar. Keep stirring it with a stick 'til the Sugar is dissolved. And put it into the barrel; let it stand a few days then put a Quart of English brandy to every twenty gallons. It must not be stopp'd down 'til it has done hissing. To prevent flies getting in, put a tea-cup over the bung-hole. After the juice is squeez'd out, put the water that is to make the wine upon currants and squeeze the whole dry.

Substitute for Coffee: Wash and scrape two or three parsnips, cut them into pieces the size of a small bean place them in an Oven until scorched of a brown colour, after which grind them in a coffee mill or crush them in a mortar. They will then furnish an excellent substitute for Coffee if prepared in the same way.

To make a spice drink – take Mace, cloves and cinnamon of each a Quarter of an Ounce, a whole Nutmeg Grossly Bruis'd, boyl altogether in a Quart of Water near half an hour, let it cool then strain a Quarter of a Pint at a time and put a little Claret in it and drink it several times a day. Sweeten it with loose sugar. It is good for looseness or bloody fluxes.

The Following Receipt for the Bite of a Mad Dog was taken out of Cathorp Church in Lincolnshire, the whole town being bitten by a mad dog; all that took this Medicine did well, and the rest died Mad. And it has since been found effectual in every instance, not only to humankind but to Dogs, Cattle, and other animals. Take the leaves of Rue, pick'd from the stalks, bruised, six ounces. Garlick, Venice Treacle and Mithridate, and the scrapings of Pewter of each 4 ounces, boil all these over a slow fire, in 2 Quarts of Strong Ale, til one pint be consumed, then keep it in a bottle close stopp'd, and give of it nine spoonfuls to a man or a woman, warm, seven mornings together, fasting, & six to a dog, this the Author believes will not (by God's Blessing) fail, if it be given within 9 days after the bite of the Dog. Apply some of the ingredients from which the Liquor was strained to the bitten place.

To make Irish or Orange Bitter. Isinglass – one ounce, a bit of Cinnamon, Spring Water half a pint. Stir it over a slow fire until it is dissolved. Strain off the liquor, and add to it a half pint of white wine and half a glass of brandy and the juice of a lemon. Smother it with sugar to your taste. Let it boil a little then pour it into a basin. The lemon peel, when cold, cut into what shape you please – it does not require to be cleared like other Jellys.

Fossils, stones and shells

Fossils from London 28 Feb 1790: A piece of marble A pearl shell A piece very neat polish's like a brain stone 3 large shells 2 small do. 4 pieces with Coriamoides on one side and polished on the other A piece of marble 5 small chalk fossils 3 pieces copper ore 2 pieces Bath stone 1 piece Cornish diamond 11 small pieces – etc sundry.

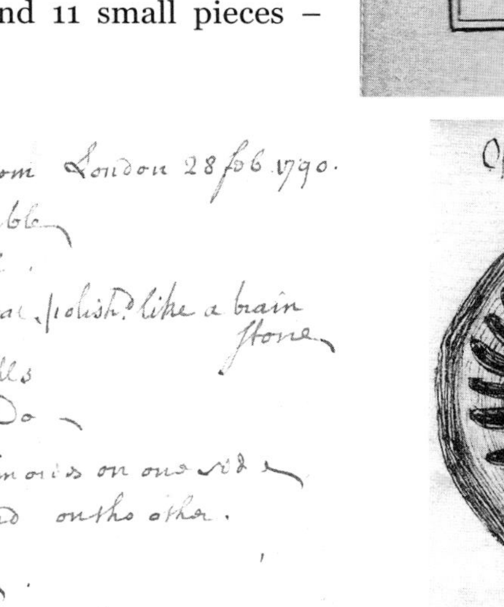

Fossils from London 28 feb 1790.
a piece of Marble
a pearl shell.
a piece very neat polish'd like a brain stone
3 large shells
2 small Do
4 pcs with Coriamoides on one side and polished on the other.
a pc. Marble.
5 small pcs. Chalk fossils.
3 pcs. Copper Ore
2 pcs. Bath stone
1 pc. Cornish Diamond.
11 Smalls pieces &c Sundry.

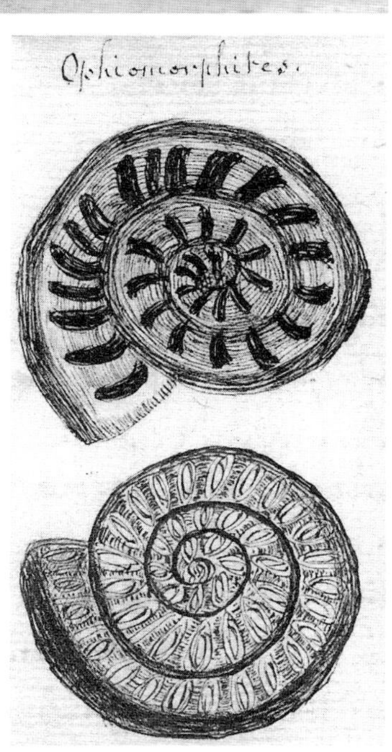

The Cornu Ammonis or Ammon's Horn, so called because it is like the horn of a ram which was consecrated in the temple of Jupiter Ammon. They were formerly taken for petrified serpents and several authors have compared them to the nautilus, or have confounded them with each other. There are plenty of the fossil kind in the county of Oxford, of different colours and shapes and sizes but always are so curled up that the place of the head is in the circumference and the tail is in the centre of the stone.

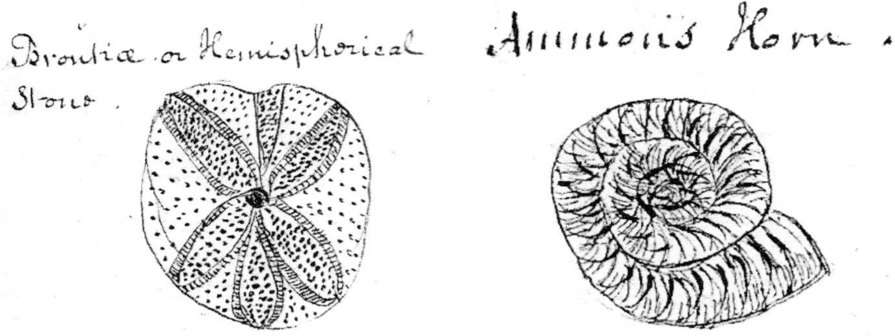

Amber is a hard bituminous substance – brittle, somewhat transparent. It is found in large quantities in Prussia which is the country where it is chiefly got, particularly in the Baltick Sea where it is found swimming upon the water, and is taken in nets.

The Beril is a gem blueish-green like sea water for which reason it is called by the Italians Aqua Marina.

The Emerald is a green shining transparent gem and has a very agreeable appearance.

Appendix II

Wills, Probates and Inventories

The will of Richard's father is short and simple – a life interest in the matrimonial home to his widow, and everything else passing to Richard:

I Francis Hall of Saint Saviour Southwark in the County of Surry Hosier make this my last Will and Testament as followeth I give to my beloved Wife Mary Hall all my ffreehold Estate in the parish of Newington Butts in the County of Surry for her own Life and after her decease to my Son Richard Hall forever I also give to my said Wife all my Plate and household ffurniture that is in my dwelling house at Newington and after all my debts are paid I give to my Son Richard Hall my ffreehold Estate at Easington also my ffreehold Estate at Kelmscote both in the County of Oxford also all the rest and Residue of my Estate what kind soever I give to my said Son whom I do appoint my sole Executor but my Mind and Will is that my Wife may order my Burial where she pleases and how she pleases in a plain way Witness my hand this Twenty fourth day of April 1754

Fra Hall

6th April 1759

Which Day appeared personally John Crouch of the parish of Saint George Southwark in the County of Surry Grocer and Jonathan Bond of the parish of Christ Church in the same County Gentleman and being sworn on the Holy Evangelists to depose the truth made Oath that they well knew and were acquainted with ffrancis Hall late of the parish of Saint Mary Newington Butts and formerly of Saint Saviours Southwark in the County of Surry deceased for several years next before his death and with his Manner and Character of hand Writing having often seen him write and Write and Subscribe his Name to Writings and

I Francis Hall of Saint Saviour Southwark in the County of Surrey hosier make this my last will and testament as followeth: I give to my beloved wife Martha Hall all my freehold estate in the Parish of Newington Butts in the County of Surrey for her own life and after her decease to my son Richard Hall forever. I also give to my said wife all my plate and household furniture that is in my dwellinghouse at Newington and after all my debts are paid give to my son my freehold estate at Casington also my freehold estate at Rolinstote both in the County of Oxford also all the rest and residue of my estate of what kind so ever I give to my said son whom I do appoint my sole executor but my Mind and Will is that my Wife may order my Burial where she pleases and how she pleases in a plain way. Witness my hand this 24th day of April 1754 [signed] Fra Hall

6th April 1759 Which day appeared personally John Crouch of the Parish of St George Southwark in the County of Surrey and Jonathan Bond in the Parish of Christ Church in the same County, Gentleman and being sworn on the Holy Evangelists to depose the truth make Oath that they well knew and were acquainted with Francis Hall late of the Parish of Saint Mary Newington Butts and formerly Saint Saviours Southwark in the County of Surrey deceased for several years next before his death and with his manner and character of handwriting often seen him write and subscribe his name and writings and having now seen and diligently perused the last will and testament of the said deceased hereunto affixed beginning thus I Francis Hall of Saint Saviours Southwark in the County of Surrey hosier and ending thus Witness my hand this 24th day of April 1754 and thus subscribed Francis Hall those deponents jointly and severally depose that they do verily in their consciences believe the said will to be totally wrote subscribed and dated by and with the proper hand of the said Francis Hall the deceased. [Signed] John Crouch Jonan. Bond. The same day John Crouch and Jonathan Bond were sworn to the truth of the premises before me Arthur Collier surrogate present Nathan Bishop Notary Publick.

The Grant of Probate continued: This Will was proved at London the Ninth day of April in the year of our Lord One thousand seven hundred and fifty nine before the Worshipful Arthur Collier Doctor of Laws Surrogate of the Right Worshipful Edward Simpson Doctor of Laws Master Keeper or Commissary of the Prerogative Court of Canterbury lawfully constituted by the Oath of Richard Hall the son of the deceased and the sole executor named in the said Will to whom administration was granted of all and singular the Goods Chattels and credits of the Deceased having first sworn duly to administer.

Richard's estate was altogether more complicated. He wrote out the contents of his wainscoat boxes, and his red trunk, as follows:

These Writings etc with other papers are Contain'd in my Wainscoat Box: The Probate of Mr Edwd. Baxter's Will. Assignment of Sundry Bonds etc from Wm. Snooke and his Wife Frances to Richard Hall dated 8 Nov. 1754. The Admeasurement of Bengeworth Estate. Extract from the Award of Inclosures. The Purchase of the Kings Rent which used to be paid for Bengeworth Estate – dated 6th Feb. 1787. Release from Miss Elizab. Robarts to Wm. Snooke and Richd. Hall dated 26 May 1773. My late Wife Eleanor Hall Administration to her Father Mr Benj'n. Seward. Probate of Mr Francis Kearse's Will. Mr Henry Griffith's Marriage Bond. Mr Henry Griffith's Bond to Richd. Hall for £300 dated April 7 1788. Mr Henry Griffith's Note to Richd. Hall for £100 dated March 17 1791. Mr Henry Griffith & Mrs Mary Mansford their Joint Bond to Richd. Hall for £300 – Dated 23 April 1793 (Paid Oct 16 1794 & Bond Deliver'd).

Writings etc in my Old Wainscot Box. Probate of my Father's Will. Mr James Poultney's Receipt in full for Finishing my House held by Lease at London Bridge dated 4 July 1767. Rect. etc for Div'ds. paid on Edward Baxter's Will before the Death of his last Sister. A book and papers relating to Cousin Fran. Kearse's Affairs. A Small Ledger 1754. The Writings belonging to Sedgeberrow Estate. A letter from Mr Snooke & Mrs Joseph Robarts respecting the Note due from Mr Robarts to his Marriage Settlement. A Deed of Trust – relating to Mr Robarts Settlement.

In the Red Trunk The Title Deeds to Bengeworth Estate. Deed of Partition of the Real Estate of Mr Benj'n Seward dated 1754 – some papers relating thereto. Lease for a Year from Wm. Snooke & R. Hall to Mr Jonathan Bond 1754. Deed to lead the Uses of a Fine Wm. Snooke, Richd. Hall and their Wives to Mr John Crouch. 1754 Deed of Partition of the Personal Estate of Mr Benj'n Seward and the Residue of the Personal Estate of Mrs Elizab. Seward between Wm. Snooke & R. Hall 1754. Probate of Mr Seward's Will June 2 1753. Deed of the Trusts of Mrs Seward's Charity. £4.15.0 part of Ground Rent for House at London Bridge – Jas. Poultney & Richd. Hall dated 6 June 1767 – afterwards purchased by R.H. Lease from the City for a House at London Bridge dated Dec 10 1765. Lease of Avon Close to Mr Michael Cartwright 12

Sept 1787. Executorship Accounts of Mrs Elizab. Seward. Probate Mr Edward Bliss's Will dated 18 May 1739. Two receipt Books. A Ledger 1753. A Green Ledger 1756. The Act of Parliam't for the Inclosure of Bengeworth Fields 1775. Agreement with Mr Price, & Instructions for a Lease – which was drawn but not signed.

These Writings &c, with other papers are Contain.d in my Wainscot Box.

The Probate of Mr. Edwd Baxter's Will.
Assignment of Sundry Bonds &c from Wm Snooke and his Wife Frances to Richd Hall. datd 8 Nov. 1754.
The Admeasurement of Bengworth Estate.
Extract from the Award of Inclosure.
The purchase of the Kings Rent, which used to be paid for Bengworth Estate – datd 6 Feb. 1787.
Release from Miss Eliz. Robarts to Wm Snooke and Richd Hall – dated 26 May 1770.
My late Wife Eleanor Hall Administratx to her Father – Mr Benjn Seward.
Probate of Mr Francis's Kearses Will.
Mr Henry Griffith's Marriage Bond.
Mr Henry Griffith's Bond to Richd Hall for £300 – dated April 7. 1788.
Mr Henry Griffith's Note to Richd Hall for £100. – dated March 17. 1791.
Paid Oct. 16. 1794 Mr Henry Griffith and Mrs Mary Mansford their Joint Bond to Richd Hall – for £300. – Datd 23 April 1793.

Writings &c in my Old Wainscot Box.

Probate of my Fathers Will.
Mr James Poultneys Receipt in full for Finishing my
House held by lease at London Bridge – dat.d 4 July 1767.
Rec.t &c for Div.ds paid on Edw.d Baxters Will, before
the death of his last Sister
A book & papers relat.g to Cous.n Fra.s Kearses Affairs.
A Small Leidger 1754.
The Writings belonging to Sedgeberrow Estate.
a Letter of Mr Snooke & Mr Jos.h Robarts respecting
the Note due from Mr Robarts to his Marriage Settlem.t
a Deed of Trust Relating to Mr Robarts Settlement.

In the red Trunk

1 The Title Deeds to Bengworth Estate
2 Deed of partition of the real Estate of Mr Benj.m Seward
dated 1754 – some papers relating thereto.
3 Lease for a Year from Wm Snooke & R.d Hall to Mr
Jonathan Bond – dated 1754.
4 Deed to lead the Uses of a fine Wm Snooke Rich.d Hall
and their Wives to Mr [illegible] 1754.
5 Deed of Partition of the personal Estate of
Mr Ben: Seward and the Residue of the personal
Estate of Mrs Eliz: Seward – between Wm Snooke & R.d Hall
1754.
6 Probate of Mrs Sewards Will. June 2.d 1758.
7 Deed of the Trusts of Mrs Sewards Charity.
£14.15.2 & 1/2 part of Ground Rent for [illegible] at London Bridge – Ja.s Poultney

Red Trunk

9. Lease from the City. For House at London Bridge dated Decr 10. 1765.

10. Lease of Avon Close to Mr Michl Cartwright 12 Sept. 1787

~~11 Executrs Acct of Mrs Eliz. Seward~~

12. Probate Mr Edwd Bliss's Will dated 18 May. 1739.

13. Two Receipt books

14. A Leidger 1753.

15 A Green Leidger 1756

16. The Act of Parliamt for the Inclosure of Bengworth Fields. 1775.

17. Agreemt with Mr Price, and Instructions For a Lease, – which was drawn but not signed.

Presumably, in order to explain his wishes fully and to make life easier for his executors, Richard then wrote down his instructions:

> In the event of my Death … My last Will and Testament is in my Mahogany Box, and a duplicate thereof in the care of my sister Ann Snooke. My Executrixes and Executor, are my Wife, my Sister Ann Snooke, and Mr James Davidson, Fish Street Hill. I desire my Wife, whom I have made my Residuary Legatee, to take all my keys into her hand. I desire to be Interred in the Meeting Yard at Bourton with little ceremony and that no funeral Sermon may be preached. A Bond given from me to my Wife before our Intermarriage is in the hand of Mr William Palmer of Bourton. I desire my Will may not at any time be in possession of either my Son William Seward Hall or my Son Francis Hall. Likewise in said Mahogany–box is a Deed of Appointment of my Estate at Bengeworth dated 15 April 1796.There is One Hundred Pounds New South Sea Annuities standing in my name which

My last Will and Testament is in my Mahogony Box, and a duplicate thereof in the care of my Sister Ann Snooke

My Executrixes and Executor are, my Wife my Sister Ann Snooke, and Mr. James Davidson Fish Street Hill

I desire my Wife to take all my keys into her hand. whom I have made my Residuary Legatee.

I desire to be Interred in the Meeting Yard at Bourton, with little ceremony, and that no funeral Sermon may be preached.

A Bond Given from me to my Wife before our ~~Intermarriage is in the hand of Mr. Willm. Palmer of~~ Bourton.

I desire my Will may not at any time be in the possession of either my Son William Seward Hall. or my Son Francis Hall.

Likewise in said Mahogony box, is a Deed of Appointment of my Estate at Bengworth dated 15th. April 1796.

belongs to the estate of Scipio Guy, a Bankrupt, for which I am accountable if legally called for – it is a concern of so long standing as to originate with Mr William Seward and came into my hand from Mr Benjamin Seward's Estate. There is also accumulated Interest thereto belonging, a moiety of which is in my hand and the other moiety in the hand of my Sister in Law Ann Snooke, which we are equally accountable for (see a Memorandum signed by each of us). I request my Executrixes and Executor to be careful in delivering to my Sons William and Francis Hall and my Daughter Martha Griffith the writings belonging to the Bengeworth Estate that they do not therewith deliver any other, with which they have no concern, and that they take a sufficient acknowledgement of the Receipt thereof. Information to my Executrixes and Executor: My Personal Estate is Debtor to my Wife for £500 by virtue of a Bond I gave to her at the time of our Marriage – which Bond is in the hand of Mr William Palmer Senior. The Gold Watch with a chased Case, which was my late Wife's I gave to my Daughter Griffith at the time of her Marriage, as I also did the piece of Embroidery worked by my Daughter. There is £1650 Old South Sea Annuities standing in my name which belongs to the Estate of Mr Edward Baxter decd. to whom Mr William Seward was Executor. Mr Benjamin Seward was Executor to his Brother William. Mr Benjamin Seward died 30th March 1753. After Benjamin Seward's Decease Letters of Administration were granted to his Daughter Mrs Frances Snooke, then Wife of Mr William Snooke (my Wife being not quite of Age). A Letter of Attorney was granted to me by the said Mrs Frances Snooke to receive the Dividends on the said Annuities which I began to do about December 1753 and continued the same regularly paying them every Half Year to the Sisters of the said Mr Edward Baxter til the time of the Death of Mrs Sarah Baxter (who was the last surviving unmarried Sister) which took place in 1781, when there was half a year Dividend due 5th April 1781 which I paid to Mr Richard Harvey her Executor October 13 1781. At the time of Mr Benjamin Seward's death the Stock stood in his name and continued to do so, 'til the Death of Mrs Frances Snooke (who died 25th May 1766) when it was judged proper my late Wife Eleanor Hall should Administer to her Father Mr Benjamin Seward, which she did December 31st 1766. March 23rd 1767 she Transferred the said Annuities from her said Father's Name into mine, in which it now stands. See the Probate of Mr Edward Baxter's will dated 19th December 1732. N.B. the last Dividend I received was due 5th April 1781. I have received none since Mr Baxter's Death 'til Dec 3rd 1792. I have received 11 and a half Year's Dividends on My Baxter's old Annuities and therewith made up the £1650 to £2000 and disposed of the other part of the Dividend for the discharge of Debtors etc. There is likewise One Hundred Pounds New South Seas Annuities standing in my Name which belongs to the Estate of Scipio Guy Deceased, a Bankrupt, particulars of which are as follows: Mr William Seward decd. was an Assignee to Scipio Guy – the late Mr Benj. Seward was Executor to his Brother Mr Wm. Seward. At the time of Mr Benj. Seward's Decease there was one hundred pounds New South Sea Anns. standing in his name which belong'd to the Estate of the said Scipio Guy, and has since been Transferr'd into my Name, in which the said One Hundred Pounds now stands. And also there was in Mr Benj. Seward's hand at the time of his Decease a Balance of Cash of £66.16.11 belonging to the Estate of the said Scipio Guy which was at Mr Seward's Death divided between Mr

What I am possess'd of this Fifteenth day of June 1796.

A Freehold Estate at Bengworth Worcest.
A Copyhold Estate at Sedgeberrow Worcestr.
A Leasehold House at London Bridge which Lease Expires Xmas 1826.
A Freehold Estate at Clapton Gloucester.

£600.. New South Sea – Annuities.
£1000.. South Sea – Stock.
NB. April 22 1796 I sold all my 5 p Cent Bank Annuities and with the produce & an Addition purchased the above Estate at Clapton.
£1100.. Lent On Mortgage Octr 15 1795 on Lady Selina Skipwith's Estate.
£300.. Oweing me on Bond by my Son in Law Mr Henry Griffith.
£100.. Oweing me on Note of hand by my Son in Law Mr Henry Griffith.
In Cash about .... £60.. –

1796 List of possessions

> Snooke and myself, his Sons in Law, to account for. Since which the dividends on the £100 New South Sea Ann's. have been from time to time received and divided between Mr Snooke and myself during the life of Mr Snooke and since his Decease (which took place Dec 9th 1779) the Dividend on the said £100 has been from time to time received and divided between Ann Snooke Widow and Administratrix of the said Mr Wm. Snooke and myself and we are each accountable to the Estate of the said Scipio Guy for a moiety of the said £66.16.11, when legally demanded, which together amount to £178.11.11 this 9th day of August 1791 (see the Account in my Ledger) and which Dividends are Annualy increasing.

The 1796 list presumably needed updating and so in 1801, just months before his death, Richard prepared a revised inventory of assets:

An account of what I am possessed, Jany 29th 1801.
A Freehold Estate at Bengworth.
A Freehold Estate at Clapton
A Copyhold Estate at Sedgeberrow
A Leasehold House London Bridge

Personal.

1000 £ South-sea Stock
600 £. New South-sea Ann's.
a Moiety of 100 £ New S. Sea Ann's.
Lady Skipwith on Mortgage £1100.
Palmer & Wilkins On their Notes. 300.
Cash about .... 115.
Son in law Griffith on Bond & Note 400,,

An account of what I am possess'd, January 29th 1801
A freehold estate at Bengeworth
A freehold estate at Clapton
A Copyhold estate at Sedgeberrow
A leasehold house London Bridge
Personal
1000£ South Sea Stock
600£ New South Sea Ann.'s
A moiety of 100£ New S. Sea Ann.'s
Lady Skipworth on Mortgage £1100
Palmer & Wilkins on their Notes £300
Cash about £115
Son in Law Griffith on Bond and Note £400.

Richard's actual will was made on 28 May 1800 – presumably not in London since it was witnessed locally in Bourton. It is a complicated document dealing with the conflicting demands on his estate from his adult children by his first marriage, by his widow, and by his (infant) children by his second marriage. Broadly speaking, the 'Seward inheritance' (i.e. the Bengeworth Estate) had already been taken out of the equation by a Deed of Appointment made in 1796. Interestingly the London Bridge premises went wholly to Francis, the younger son. Richard appears to have been particularly keen to ensure that neither of his elder sons (William and Francis) could have any guardianship rights over young Anna and Benjamin. Richard refers specifically to 'mourning rings costing not more than One Guinea' to be distributed to his nieces. His widow was bequeathed his shells and fossils – presumably at that stage all catalogued and marked with their correct Latin tags. Unfortunately, subsequent family members were less fastidious and consigned the collection to an ancient bread-bin, whereupon all the name tags became detached. But there are some lovely patterned cowrie shells – presumably from the Pacific Ocean, which still remain from the original collection.

Last Will & Testament of Richard Hall

This is the Last Will and Testament of me Richard Hall late of the Parish of Saint Magnus the Martyr in the City of London and now of Bourton on the Water in the County of Gloucester. I give and bequeath unto my Dear wife Betty Hall six hundred pounds which I direct to be paid to or retained by her within one month most after my decease over and besides what she will be entitled unto by virtue of the Bond by me given and entered into for her benefit provided to our intermarriage and I give and devise unto my said wife all those my two messuages and lands situate in Sedgeberrow in the County of Worcester with their appurtenances being Copyhold and in hold of the Manor of Sedgeberrow by virtue of two grants thereof by Copy of Court Roll of the said Manor for the lives of certain persons therein named. To hold the same unto and to the use of my said wife for and during the joint lives of her and such person or persons on whose life or lives the same shall be held at the time of my decease and from and after the decease of my said wife I give and devise the said Copyhold Messuages and Lands with their appurtenances unto my son William Seward Hall his Executors Administrators and Assigns for and during the life or lives of such person or persons on whose life or lives the same shall be held at the decease of my said wife and I do hereby direct that all expenses which may be incurred in the removal of my life or of any life or lives which may happen to die during the life time of my said wife shall be paid and defrayed by my said Son William Seward Hall his Executors Administrators and Assigns. And I give and devise unto Ann Snooke of Bourton on the Water aforesaid widow and unto James Davidson of Fish Street Hill London Shirt Maker and their heirs all those my Messuages Tenements or Farm houses with the Barns Stables Gardens Orchards Lands Meadows Woods hereditaments and appurtenances whatsoever to the same Appertaining situate lying and being in Clapton otherwise Clopton on the hill in the County of Gloucester and which I lately purchased to me and my heirs of and from William Fox the elder and Henry Stevens with their and every of their appurtenances. To have and to hold the said Messuages or Tenements Buildings Gardens Orchards hereditaments and premises with the appurtenances unto the said Ann Snooke and James Davidson their heirs and assigns to the uses upon the trusts and to and for the intents and purposes hereinafter mentioned expressed and situated of and remaining the same (that is to say) to the use intent and purpose that my said wife Betty Hall and her assigns shall and may have take and enjoy yearly and every year during her natural life. One annual rent or yearly sum of sixty pounds of lawful money of Great Britain to be issuing and giving out of our charges and chargeable upon in all my said Messuages Lands and Tenements free from all restrictions whatsoever and to be payable at Michaelmas Christmas Lady Day and Midsummer in every year by four equal portions the first payment to begin and to be made upon that of the said four feasts or days of payment which shall first happen next after my decease and I do hereby give unto my said Dear wife and her assigns the usual powers by sistuss and action to recover the said annual rent or own when the same shall be behind and in arrear and to my said Messuages Lands Tenements and hereditaments charged and chargeable with the said annual rent or sum of sixty pounds and the powers for the same to the use of the said Ann Snooke and James Davidson their heirs and assigns for ever upon Trust that they the said Ann Snooke and James Davidson and the survivor of them and the heirs and assigns of such survivor do and shall pay and apply the rents issues and profits of my said Messuages Lands and Hereditaments for and towards the maintenance and education of my Son Benjamin Snooke Hall and my daughter Anna Hall in equal shares and proportions until they shall respectively attain their age of twenty one years or until they shall die under that age without having any issue of their bodies lawfully begotten which shall first happen and if either of them my said Son Benjamin Snooke Hall or my daughter Anna Hall shall die under the age of twenty one years then that they the said Ann Snooke and James Davidson and the survivor of them his or her heirs or assigns do and shall pay and apply such rent issues and profits for and towards the maintenance and education of the survivor of them my said Son and daughter until he or she shall attain his or her age of twenty one years or shall die under that age without leaving any issue of his or her body lawfully begotten which shall first happen. And in case my said son Benjamin Snooke Hall and daughter Anna Hall shall live to attain their respective ages of twenty one years upon trust that they the said Ann Snooke and James Davidson or the survivor of them or the heirs and assigns of such survivor do and shall convey and assign the same Messuages Lands and Hereditaments unto and to the use of my said son Benjamin Snooke Hall and my said daughter Anna Hall share and share alike as tenants in Common and not as joint tenants and of their respective heirs and assigns for ever but if either of them my said son and daughter shall happen to die under the age of twenty one years without having any issue of his or her body lawfully begotten then upon trust that my said trustees or the survivor of them or the heirs or assigns of such survivor so and shall convey and assure the same Messuages Lands and Hereditaments unto and to the use of the survivor of them my said son and daughter and his or her heirs and assigns for ever. And in case my said son Benjamin Snooke Hall and my daughter Anna Hall shall both happen to die under the age of twenty one years and there shall be any child or children of the body or bodies of either of them lawfully begotten living at the time of the death of the survivor of them then that my said Trustees and the survivor of them and the heirs and assigns of such survivor do and shall after the decease of them my said son and daughter stand seized of and interested in my said Messuages Lands and Hereditaments in trust for all and every the child and children of the bodies of my said son and daughter lawfully to be begotten equally to be divided between them (if more than one) share and share alike and they to take as tenants in common and not as joint tenants and for them and their respective heirs and assigns for ever such shares to be conveyed to them respectively at their respective ages of twenty one years. But if my said Son Benjamin Snooke Hall and daughter Anna Hall shall both die under the age of twenty one years and without having any child or children of either of their bodies lawfully begotten living at the death of the survivor of them and in such case I direct that my said Trustees and the survivor of them and the heirs and assigns of such survivor shall stand seized of any interest in the same Messuages Lands Tenements and Hereditaments To the use of or in the trust of my said Dear wife Betty Hall and her assigns during the time of her natural life without impairment of waste. And from and immediately after her decease I give and devise the same Messuages Lands Tenements and Hereditaments unto my daughter Martha Griffith (wife of Mr Henry Griffith) and her heirs and assigns to hold the same unto the use of my said daughter Martha Griffith her heirs and assigns for ever. I give and bequeath unto my said son Benjamin Snook Hall the sum of four hundred pounds and unto my said daughter Anna Hall the sum of four hundred pounds both which legacies I direct my Executors within one month next after my decease to pay and apply to their advancement in life in such manner as my said wife and the said Ann Snooke shall think most proper. And I do hereby nominate and appoint Guardians of the persons and estates of my said children Benjamin Snook Hall and Anna Hall during their respective minorities. And I give and devise unto my son Francis Hall his Executors Administrators and assigns all that my Leasehold Messuages or Tenements situate in the parish of Saint Magnus the Martyr London Bridge which I hold by virtue of a lease from the city of London during the remaining term of the said Lease and which expires at Xmas 1826 provided always nevertheless subject to an annual ground rent of twenty one pounds fifteen shillings payable quarterly to the said City of London and likewise subject to all other Covenants and agreements made and maintained in the said lease which are to be paid and fulfilled by my said son to the expiration and of the said lease his Executors Administrators and assigns and further with this special obligation that my said son shall pay to his brother William Seward Hall the sum one hundred pounds and to his sister Martha Griffith the like sum of one hundred pounds both which sums I direct to be paid within twelve calendar months most after my decease. And I will and direct that all debts which may be due to me from my said son Francis Hall at the time of my decease be fully paid and discharged by my said son to my executrix and executor in three months most after my decease. I give and bequeath unto my said son William Seward Hall twenty pounds my pair of large Sauce boats and my silver tumbler which was my grandfathers'. And I give and bequeath unto my said son Francis Hall my pair of silver candlesticks my two gold arobus and my tortoiseshell snuff box with silver hinges and finished with silver which was my fathers and which I request he will not part with. I give and bequeath unto my said daughter Martha Griffith my work cabinet my charming Ring with a purple stone set round with Brilliants my silver tea kettle and lamp and my mother of pearl snuff box which was my own mothers and I request she will not part with it and I give and bequeath unto my said daughter three hundred pounds which is owing to me on Bond from her husband Mr Henry Griffith with all interest that may be due thereof at the time of my decease and also one hundred pounds which is owing to me on a Note of Bond from her said husband with all interest that may be due thereon at the time of my decease. I give and bequeath unto my daughter Anna Hall my Gold piece value five guineas and two gold pieces value two guineas each my silver pint mug and all my Mourning Rings except that set with brilliants before given to my daughter Martha Griffith. And I likewise give and bequeath unto my said daughter Anna Hall my following Books viz. my Octavo Bible with the Common Prayer therein the Book of Martyrs Mr Henrys Dialogues and Invitations and the Nonconformists Memorial. And I give and bequeath unto my said son Benjamin Snooke Hall my gold watch two gold pieces value two guineas each and all my silver coins or pocket pieces my green velvet purse with a silver top and a silver boot my snuff box with a pebble set in silver and likewise my silver coffee pot and a ring with a small purple stone and diamonds on the sides. And I give and bequeath unto my said son Benjamin Snooke Hall my following books viz. my Quarto Bible in Red Moroco with the Chambers Universal Dictionary of Arts and Sciences in four volumes folio the Universal Bunyan's Pilgrims Progress. And I give and bequeath unto my said Dear Wife Betty Hall for her own proper use and benefit all my china and linen and also all my Household Goods Pictures and furniture of household whatsoever which I shall be possessed of or entitled unto at the time of my decease. And I also give and bequeath unto my said wife my Morro Ring set with diamonds my plain agate ring and all the rest of my plate not hereinbefore otherwise disposed of. And I also give and bequeath unto my said wife all my shells and fossils and my Pocket Bible printed by Pasham and all the rest of my books not hereinbefore otherwise disposed of and likewise all my manuscripts of every kind and it is my particular request to my wife that she will not at any time lend any own or show of money to any person or persons whoever that may want to borrow and it is farther my earnest request and desire that should my wife again marry she will take special care that my daughter Anna Hall and my son Benjamin Snook Hall shall not thereby suffer any loss or diminution in their natural expectances from her substance should both or either of them survive her. I give and bequeath unto my Sister in Law Ann Snooke Ten Guineas and to each of my nieces the daughters of my said Sister in Law a Mourning Ring of a guinea value. And I give and bequeath unto my esteemed friend Mr James Davidson of Fish Street Hill London ten guineas and all the rest and residue of my personal estate of what nature or quality not hereinbefore otherwise disposed of and which shall remain after satisfaction of all my just debts legacies and funeral expenses and the charges of my Executrices and Executor (hereinafter named) in or about the proving of this will or otherwise relating to my estate. I give and bequeath unto my said Dear wife Betty Hall provided always nevertheless that in regard two thousand pounds Old South Sea Annuities are standing in my name in the books kept by the South Sea Company which belong to the estate and are subject to the will of Mr Edward Baxter deceased together with any balance of cash that may be in my hands at the time of my decease by Dividends received on the said two thousand pounds Old South Sea Annuities. Now I do hereby will and direct that the said Old South Sea Annuities with any balance of cash in my hands relating thereto as aforesaid be respectively retained in the hands of my said wife for the purposes only of the will of the said Mr Edward Baxter anything hereinbefore contained to the contrary in any wise notwithstanding. And I will and devise that my said wife so transfer the aforesaid two thousand pounds Old South Sea Annuities into her name which are always subject to the will of the aforesaid Mr Baxter (to whose estate they only belong) and apply the interest or dividends thereof in the most convenient manner and way corresponding with the design of the said Testator. And further it is my will that if it shall please God to remove by death either my said wife or my said Sister in Law Ann Snooke before my said daughter Anna Hall or my said son Benjamin Snooke Hall shall have attained their ages of twenty one years that a fit person and one of property be appointed to join the survivor as guardian to my said children to be made by that survivor and my daughter Anna Hall and my son Benjamin Snooke Hall. But it is my will that neither my son William Seward Hall nor my son Francis Hall shall at any time be chosen Guardians or Guardian or Trustees to my said daughter Anna Hall or my said son Benjamin Snooke Hall. And I nominate constitute and appoint my said wife Betty Hall my said Sister in law Ann Snooke and the said Mr James Davidson Executrixes and Executor of this my last will and Testament and do hereby revoke all former wills and other Testamentary Dispositions by me at any time heretofore made and declare this to be my last will and testament on witness whereof I have to each sheet of this my will (containing with this seven sheets of paper) subscribed my name and to the top of the first and to the last sheet have put my seal this twenty eighth day of May in the year of our Lord One thousand eight hundred.

Richd. Hall

Signed Sealed Published and Declared by the said Richard Hall the Testator as and for his last will and Testament in the presence of us who at his request and in his presence and in the presence of each other have subscribed our names as witnesses thereto (all erasements and conditions being first made).

Willm. Palmer, Saml. Palmer, Bourton on the Water, James Goodman servt. to Mr S. Palmer.

This Will was proved at London this fifth day of September in the year of our Lord One thousand eight hundred and one before the Right Honorable Sir William Wynne Knight Doctor of Laws Master Keeper or Commissary of the Prerogative Court of Canterbury lawfully constituted by the Oath of Betty Hall widow the relict of the deceased Ann Snooke widow and James Davidson the Executors named in the will to whom Administration was granted of all and singular the Goods Chattels and Credits of the said deceased they having been first sworn (to wit) the said Betty Hall by Commission and the said Ann Snook and James Davidson before the worshipful Samuel Pearce Parson Doctor of Laws and Surrogate duly to Administer.

Inventories

Two inventories cast light upon the family possessions. The first was made in respect of the household goods at 1 London Bridge and was prepared on 15 May 1794. The list describes the furniture and effects – other than trade and shop fittings – and reveals thirteen separate rooms. No mention is made of a privy – presumably because it was outside. Even the shop had a featherbed – no doubt because an apprentice slept there overnight. Indeed, it is the sheer number of beds which catches the eye. Assuming that a bolster would not have been appropriate to a single bed, it looks as though there were seven double beds, one single, plus a 'straw pallice' (i.e. palliasse). In theory, sixteen people could be in occupation. From the description of the

Hall household it is assumed that there were only two domestic servants 'living in' – presumably in 'No. 3 – Left hand' with its 'Stump bedstead ... a wainscoat chest of drawers, round table, square dressing glass' (i.e. mirror) and stove with 'tin fender'. The other rooms contain rather more furniture and benefit from 'window curtains' (as distinct from 'bed curtains'). In the main bedroom there is a half tester bed (i.e. with a canopy) with what is described as 'Harrateen furniture' ('Harrateen' being a type of woollen fabric, used here for the drapes, canopy and curtains). The main bed had a goose feather mattress and pillows – other mattresses appear to have been mostly 'feather' (of unspecified origin) or 'flock' or straw. 'Scotch carpet' appears to have been laid in strips – presumably around the sides and bottom of the bed – in most rooms. Only the dining room had a Wilton carpet.

As the Hall family would only have justified half the beds, the rest were either an indication that rooms were let out (a common way of generating an income, then as now) or shows rather more than one apprentice or shop assistant living in. There is no mention of any spinning or knitting machines, suggesting that by 1794 the Hall business had moved entirely away from manufacturing silk stockings, and was now wholly involved in the sale of general haberdashery.

There appears to have been a kitchen (Room 10), a dining room (9), and a backroom where tea was taken, with its 'fretwork mahogany tea table, a Japan Ditto ... a draft board, sundry stones shells and Fossils and a painting of fruit'. Books were described separately and the list suggests mostly religious tracts, pamphlets and Bibles together with a dictionary and '4 Maps, of Europe, Asia Africa and America'. *Buchan's Domestic Medicine* is singled out and was presumably returned to Richard because it remains with his papers to this day. The family interest in astronomy was reflected in the orrery – a clockwork mechanism used to show the movement of the planets around the sun, and named after the Earl of Orrery. Some years earlier the Earl had commissioned the instrument-maker J. Rowley to make just such an instrument copying the invention of George Graham.

The list of linen is interesting with its reference to 'Diaper Table Cloths' – diaper meaning 'diamond patterned'; Huckerback towels – which the *Oxford English Dictionary* defines as being 'made of stout linen or cotton fabric', and 'Jack Towels', meaning roller towels. The family appear to have been musical, with a 'harpsichord in a Walnut Tree case' along with a violin and a flute. Ornaments seem to have been dominated by shells and fossils, along with miniature portraits and 'sundry Moths and Insects framed and glazed'. Even the canary in its cage was listed in the inventory (in the dining room, next to the mahogany knife case). The parrot cage in the backroom was presumably without an inmate (since none was mentioned) but indicates the popularity of keeping caged birds as pets. The cellar, containing ‘a beer stand, 2 wash tubs, 2 pails and sundry garden pots’, counted as the thirteenth room in the house.

The total value (£125 15s. 6d.) seems somewhat low – roughly ten pounds per room, but perhaps reflects that this was a ‘family valuation’.

The exact reason for obtaining the inventory is not clear, but it certainly looks as though Richard was wishing to identify those items which belonged to him and which he had left in London when he re-married. Almost certainly it was part of a financial settlement reached between father and son when William decided to quit the business

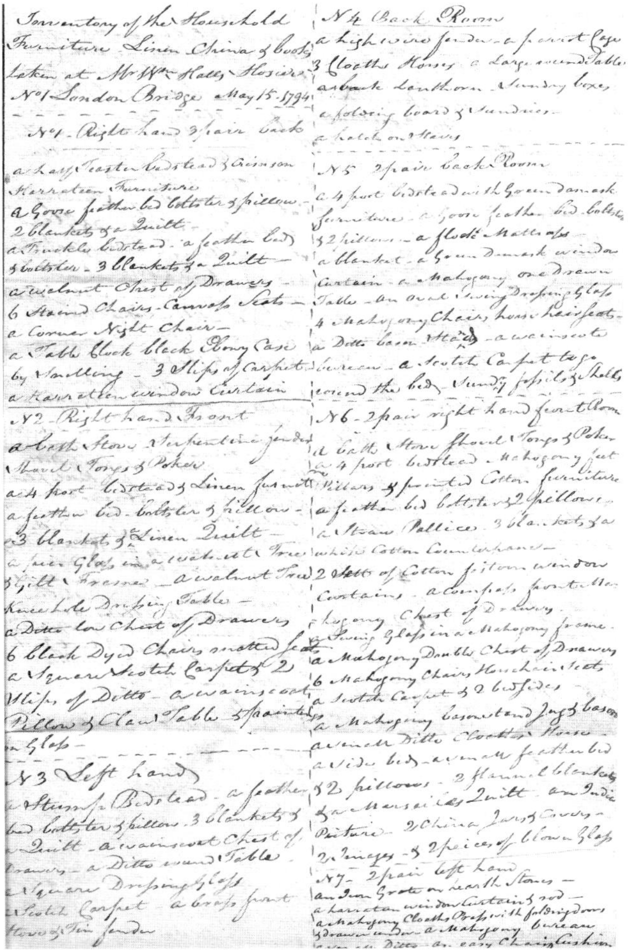

Inventory of the Household Furniture Linen China & Books taken at Mr Wm. Hall, hosier No. 1 London Bridge May 15, 1794.

and become a 'silk man' (see Chapter IX). William's letter announcing his move to Peckham, quitting the partnership with Richard, was dated within a month of the inventory having been prepared.

No. 1 Right hand and spair back A half-tester bedstead and crimson Harrateen Furniture A goose-feather bed, bolster and pillow. 2 blankets and a quilt A truckle bedstead – a feather bed Bolster, three blankets and a quilt A walnut chest of drawers 6 stained chairs – canvas seats A corner night chair A table clock – black Ebony Case by Smolling [?]. 3 slips of carpets A Harrateen window curtain

No. 2 Right hand front A bath stove, serpentine fender Shovel tongs and fender A 4-part bedstead, Linen furniture A feather bed, bolster & pillow 3 blankets. A linen quilt A pair glass in a walnut tree Gilt frame. A walnut tree kneehole dressing table. A ditto low chest of drawers. 6 black dyed chairs – matted seat A square Scotch carpet 2 slips of Ditto. A wainscoat. Pillow, Chair, Table 5 paintings on Glass.

No. 3 Left hand A Stump bedstead. A feather bed bolster & pillow. 3 blankets a wainscoat chest of drawers a ditto round table. A square dressing glass A Scotch carpet A brass front stove, tin fender.

No. 4 Back room A high wire fender. A parrot cage 3 Cloaths horses. A large round table A Lanthorn [lantern]. Sundry boxes A folding board and sundries A hatch and stairs

No. 5 Spair back room A 4 part bedstead with Green Damask furniture – a goose feather bed bolster, 2 pillows, a flock mattress A blanket, a green damask window curtain. A Mahogany one drawer table. An oval swing Dressing Glass. 4 Mahogany Chairs – horse hair seats A ditto basin stand, a wainscoat bureau. A Scotch carpet to go around the bed. Sundry fossils and shells.

No. 6 Spair right hand front room A bath stove. Shovel tongs and poker. A 4 part bedstead, mahogany feet. Pillows. Printed cotton furniture. A feather bed, bolster, 2 pillows. A straw pallice, 3 blankets, a white cotton counterpane 2 sets of cotton festoon window curtains. A compress front mahogany Chest of drawers. A swing glass in a Mahogany frame. A Mahogany double chest of drawers. 6 Mahogany chairs, horsehair seats. A Scotch carpet and 2 bedsides [i.e. slips] A Mahogany basin stand Jug and Basin A small ditto Cloaths Horse Side bed. A small feather bed. 2 pillows, 2 flannel blankets a Marseilles quilt, an India picture. 2 China jars & Covers. 2 ... & 2 pieces blown glass.

No. 7 Spair left hand An iron grate on hearth stones A harrateen window curtain & rod. A Mahogany cloaths press with folding doors & drawer under. A Mahogany bureau. A small ditto. An easy chair.

Linen
4 Diaper Table Cloths, 2 Small Do -
4 Damask breakfast Ditto -
4 Diaper Table Cloths -
1 pair Home & 1 pair Sheets
4 pair Russia Ditto - 3 pair Ditto
2 pair Lancashire Ditto - 2 odd Sheets
8 pr Pillow Cases - 6 Diaper hand Towels
9 huckaback Towels - 2 Jack Ditto
2 old Ditto - 20 hand Towels -
a breakfast Cloth - 2 pudding Ditto
a Cotton Counterpane -
a sett of blue Check bed Curtains
- - - - - - - -
Books
one vol folio in boards - 1 Do unbound
5 Do 4to & the plates to Do of a Miscellaneous Tracks relating to antiquity
Baileys Dictionary - Buchans Domestic
Medicine - Thompsons Travels - Non-
conformists Memorial 2 Vol -
Winchesters Tracks - Philadelphian Magazine - a Dictionary -
Henrys Meditations - Herberts
Poems Janes [illegible] -
36 bound books - Sundry Pamphlets
4 vr bound - [illegible] bibles Hymns
& Psalms - a family bible -
Crudens Concordance - Clarke
on the Testament - 4 Maps
of Europe Asia Africa & America - an orrery - 3 Portraits
framed & Glazd -
No 8 - 2 pair back Room
a fast oak Mahogany Tea Table -
a Japan Ditto - a small one Draw Table
a draft board - a Slip of Floor Cloth -
Sundry Stones Shells & fossils - a painting
of Fruit - Sundry Shells in a Drawer -
- - - - - - - -
No 9 - Dining Room
a Steel Stove - fender Shovel Tongs & Poker
3 Sett of blue Damask feston window
Curtains - 2 Oval Pier Glasses in Carved &
Gilt Frames - 2 Square Mahogany
Dining Tables with 2 Flaps - a Square
Pillar & Claw Table - a round Ditto
Mahogany Dumb waiter - 6 Ditto

No 9 Contd
a Marble Slab on a Mahogany
Stand - a Mahogany book Case
glazd Doors - a Harpsichord in
a walnut Tree Case by Kirk-
koffo - walters Stops - a Violin
& flute - a high Mahogany Chair
a Ditto Stool - a Japand Urn
& Mahogany Stand - 2 waiters
Cat & Knife Tray - Sundry
Moths & Insects framed & Glazd -
Sundry Stones Shells & Fossils
a Canary bird & Cage - a Mahogany Knife Case - a Sett of Cruets with Silver Tops - 2 Small
Miniature Portraits -
No 10 - Kitchen
1 Trivet - 2 Crane Hooks - fortune & 2 Spits
Cookholds - Dripping Pan Stand - 2 gridirons -
a Copper Boiler - a Tea Kettle - 2 porrage
Pots & Covers - 3 Saucepans & Chocolate Pot
a pair of Princes Metal Candlesticks
1 pr Short Ditto - 3 light brass Ditto -
a brass Ladle - a Tin fish Kettle plate
Stove - 5 Saucepans & Covers - 6 Candle
sticks - 10 patties & Coarse tin ware -
bread basket Japan Sugar Ditto &
3 Tin Canisters - 14 Oval & Round Dishes
12 Large Plates - 6 Small Ditto -
Sundry Queens ware - 4 water plates
a Meat Screen lined with Tin
a Deal Table with 2 Flaps - 6 wood Chairs
a pair of bellows - Salt box - Spice box
& 2 Sieves - a Japan Patent Jack
a Deal Cupboard under Dresser -
a Hatch on Stairs
- - - - - - - -
No 11 Store Room
an Eight Day Clock in a walnut Tree
Case by wright - a Square Mahogany
2 flaps Dining Table - a 2 flap Deal
Table - a Small Cloaths Horse -
a plate warmer - 2 frying Pans -
a fortune - a Tin fish Kettle
a Copper warming Pan - a brass Do
a small Lanthorn - a Japan
Tea Tray - 3 flat Irons & 2
Stands - a pewter water Dish
4 round Dishes - 10 plates a

Cushion. Linen case. A Scotch carpet 2 setts of window curtains... [?] A purple ditto.

Linen 4 Diaper Table cloths, 2 small ditto 4 Damask Breakfast Ditto 4 Diaper Table Cloths 1 pair Lancashire Sheets 4 pairs Russia Ditto, 3 pair Ditto 2 pair Lancashire Ditto, 2 odd sheets 8 pr Pillowcases, 6 Diaper Hand Towels 9 Huckerback towels – 2 Jack Ditto 2 old Ditto. 20 hand towels A breakfast cloth – 2 Pudding Ditto A cotton counterpane A sett of blue check bed Curtains

Books One vol. Folio 1/2 bound. 1 Ditto unbound. 5 Ditto 4to [quarto]. Plates to ditto. Miscellaneous Tracks (tracts) relating to Antiquity. Baileys Dictionary. Buchans Domestic Medicine. Thompsons Travels. Non-conformists Memorial, 2 volumes, Winchesters Tracks. Philadelphian Magazine. A Dictionary. Harveys Meditations. Herberts Poems. James Beauties [?]. 36 bound books. Sundry pamphlets – 4 bound. Pashams Bible. Hymns & Psalms. A family bible. Crudens Concordances. Clark on the Testament. 4 maps of Europe Asia Africa & America.

An orrery. 3 Portraits framed & Glazed.

No. 8 Spair back room A fretwork Mahogany Tea Table. A Japan Ditto. A variable [?] one-draw Table. A Draft Board. A slip of floor cloth. Sundry stones shells & fossils. A painting of fruit, sundry shells in a drawer. No. 9 Dining Room A steel stove. Fender shovel Tongs & Poker. 3 sett of blue Damask festoon window curtains. 2 oval pier glasses in carved gilt frames. 2 square mahogany Dining Tables with 2 flaps. A square pillar & claw Table. A round Ditto. A Mahogany Dumb Waiter. 6 Ditto Chairs Sattin hair seats brass nailed. 2 Elbow Ditto. A Wilton carpet.

No. 9 Dining Room A steel stove. Fender shovel Tongs & Poker. 3 sett of blue Damask festoon window curtains. 2 oval pier glasses in carved gilt frames. 2 square mahogany Dining Tables with 2 flaps. A square pillar & claw Table. A round Ditto. A Mahogany Dumb Waiter. 6 Ditto Chairs Sattin hair seats brass nailed. 2 Elbow Ditto. A Wilton carpet. A marble slab on a Mahogany stand – a Mahogany book Case, Glass Doors. A Harpsichord in a walnut tree case by Kirkhoffe... [?], a violin, a flute, a high Mahogany Chair, a Ditto stool, a Japan'd Urn, a Mahogany stand, 2 waiters. Cut(lery) and knife tray. Sundry Moths & insects framed & Glazed. Sundry Stones Shells & Fossils. A Canary Bird & Cage. A Mahogany Knife case. A set of cruets with Silver Tops – 2 small miniature portraits.

No. 10 Kitchen 1 Trivet, 2 Crane Hooks. Footman [i.e. kettle stand] 2 Spits... [?] Dripping Pan Stand. 2 Gridirons. A copper Boiler. A Tea Kettle. 2 Porrage pots & covers. 3 Saucepans. A chocolate pot. A pair of Princes metal candlesticks. 1 pr shorter Ditto.3 high brass Ditto. A brass ladle. A tin fish kettle plate & cover. 5 Saucepans & covers. 6 candlesticks. 10 patties. Loose tea ware [?]. Bread basket. Japan Sugar Ditto. 3 Tin Cannisters. 14 Oval & round dishes.12 large plates. 6 small Ditto. Sundry Queens Ware. 4 water [?] plates. A meat steamer (?) lined with Tin. A Deal table with 2 flaps.6 wood chairs. A pair of bellows. Salt box. Spice Box. 2 sieves. A Japan Patent Jack. A Deal cupboard under Dresser. A Hatch on stairs.

No. 11 Store Room An eight day clock in a walnut tree case by Wright. A Square Mahogany 2-flap Dining Table. A 2-flap Deal Table. A small cloaths horse. A plate warmer. 2 Frying pans. A footman (i.e. kettle stand). A tin Fish Kettle. A copper warming pan. A brass Ditto. A small Lanthorn [lantern]. A Japan Tea Tray. 3 Flat irons & 2 stands. A pewter [?] water dish. 4 round dishes. 10 plates. A tureen. A copper stew pan. A bell metal Saucepan. 1 brass 1 copper Urn. Part of a set of China containing 35 pieces. A tea-pot Cover. 6 cups & saucers. 6 blue and white cups & saucers. Basin. 6 candle Basins & Saucers. 27 china plates. 3 Ditto bowls. A dragon basin. 2 mugs. A tureen cover. 14 soup plates. 4 Dishes. 9 Patties. 4 basons. 2 jugs. 4 Round dishes. 15 pieces of Queens

Store Room Continued
1 brass - 1 Copper Urn - Part of a set of China containing
35 Pieces - a Teapot & cover - 6 Cups & Saucers - 6 blue & white Cups & Saucers & bason,
6 Candle basons & Saucers - 27 China Plates 3 Do bowls - a Dragon bason & 2 Mugs
a Tureen & Cover - 14 Soup Plates - 4 Dishes - 9 patties - 4 basons - 2 Jugs - 4
round Dishes & fifteen Pieces of Queens ware - 4 Red Dishes & Sundry Jars
2 Glass Decanters - 20 wine & Jelly Glasses - a Tumbler - a Mahogany
Knife Tray 2 waiters & 1 Japan Do - Candle box & Lamp - 2 pair of
Plated Candlesticks - a Dish Cross - 2 pair of Snuffers & Plated Stand -
a plated Cruet with 5 Glasses - 12 brown handle Knives & forks 12 small
Ditto & 10 forks} Shop No 12 - a feather bed bolster & pillow - 2 blankets & a Rug
NB Cellar - a beer Stand - 2 wash tubs 2 pails & Sundry Garden Pots

All the Effects in the Foregoing Inventory is valued at One Hundred & Twenty five Pounds fifteen Shillings & 6d by
John Fletcher
for Saml Barton
Houndsditch

Ware. 4 Red dishes & sundry Jars. 2 Glass Decanters. 20 wine & jelly Glasses. A Tumbler. A Mahogany knife tray. 2 Waiters. 1 Japan Ditto. Candle box, lamp, 2 pairs of plated Candlesticks. A dish cross [?]. 2 pairs of snuffers. A plated stand. A plated Cruet [?] with 5 glasses. 12 brown-handled knives & forks. 12 small Ditto. 10 forks.

No. 12 Shop A feather bed, bolster & pillows. 2 blankets & a rug.

No. 13 Cellar A beer stand. 2 wash tubs. 2 pails. Sundry Garden Pots

All the Effects in the Foregoing Inventory is valued at One Hundred & Twenty Five pounds fifteen shillings & 6d by John Fletcher for Samuel Burton, Houndsditch.

* * *

Quite separate from this, there is the inventory prepared when Richard's widow, Betty, died in 1818. This shows all her possessions, room by room, in Bourton and would appear to have been prepared for probate purposes:

An Inventory and Appraisement of the household goods and furniture, plate linen, china, glass, pictures, books, wearing apparel, trinkets and other effects, late the property of Mrs Betty Hall, deceased, of Bourton-on-the-Water in the County of Gloucester.

An Inventory and Appraisement of the Household Goods and Furniture, Plate Linen China Glass Pictures Books, Wearing Apparel, Trinkets and other Effects late the property of Mrs Betty Hall Deceased at Bourton on the Water in the County of Glocester

In the Brewhouse

Cast Iron furnace Grate & Lid — Brewing Copper Grate & Lid
Six brewing tubs — one small tub Iron bound — Tram & 2 Stools
Ladle pail, Steps & Sundries — Two Coal boxes & buckets
Quantity of Earthenware, Skimmer & Ladle, Tin Saucepan
Brass Kettle, Frying pan & Plate Rack

In the Brewhouse Cast iron furnace grate and lid – Brewing Copper Grate and Lid – six Brewing tubs, one small tub iron-barred – tram and two stools – ladle, pail, steps and sundries – two coal boxes and buckets – quantity of earthenware – skimmer and ladle, tin saucepan, brass kettle, frying pan and plate rack. **In the Cellar** 4 iron barrels – ironing stove and pipes, meat safe, 3 shelves – deal side-table, 2 Copper boilers, Tea kettle and chaffing dish – 2 barrel trams – Sundries. Pail and earthenware. **Kitchen** Kitchen grate and fire irons, iron-back, sway and pinks, ironing stove, smoke-Jack, 3 Flat-irons and stands – one Box Iron – fender – 3 chopping knives and one pair sugar nippers – copper tea kettle, 2 spits and holdfast, 6 Brass candlesticks – 4 tin candlesticks and snuffers, warming pan – dust pan, bellows and sundries – coal box and stool – Old Deal table and stool – a lead cistern – oak dining table – Meat hastener – Deal side table with brackets – clothes horse – ironing board and trestles – 3 chairs, small dining table, dryer and shelves – tin oven – tin tea kettle and tin articles – copper saucepan – 3 tin cans – 18 pewter plates and one dish – quantity of earthenware – Deal cupboard – 2 pewter water plates and dish – china dishes and plates – earthenware, knife-tray, knives and forks – mahogany tray and bread basket – casks, knife tray and cheese board – Tea tray and Earthenware. **Little Room** A sedan, mahogany table, pair glass, sundry prints – china dish – glass stand and sundry glasses – Bird cage and brass trivet – cabinet – 2 chairs – Tea Urn – 2 wine decanters & 4 stands – 2 trays – plate warmer – china, glass, and earthenware – 2 wine bins and barrel tram. **Parlour** One set of fine old tea china – 2 tin canisters – copper coal scuttle – mahogany dining table – mahogany bookcase with glass doors – large china jar – parlour clock – small mahogany stand – eight mahogany chairs – mahogany sofa – horse hair chest with brass nails – small mahogany table – tea chest – mahogany Pembroke table – tea caddie and work box – piano – pier glass – draught board and stool – walking stool – pair bellows – a carpet and hearth rug – parlour grate and set of fire irons and fender, large cotton (printed) window curtain complete. Passage Light day clock and case **Little Room** Brussells carpet – nest of shelves – Deal chest of drawers – Deal chest – oak cabinet **Front Lodging Room** 5 Armed chairs – mahogany wardrobe and mahogany chest of drawers – 3 bowls and three cups – 3 chimney ornaments and earthenware. Small bedstead – 3 boxes – pasteboard – Rushlight guard – brass fender – 2 boxes – trunk – old newspapers. **Lodging Room No. 2** Mahogany 4 post bedstead and furniture – featherbed, bolster and pillow, mattress – quantity of books – chest of drawers – dressing Glass – Dressing table (Deal) – mahogany bookcase – 3 carpets– 2 boxes and stool – tea tray – 3 pictures – 1 cabinet – glass case and bell – 3 old blankets. **Attic No. 1** Tent bedstead – feather bed bolster and pillow – 3 blankets – carpet – chest of drawers – dressing glass – mahogany table – Deal table – two grates, fender and fire irons – 4 chairs – a spring board with seat and trestles – 2 oak boxes – fire screen – 2 clothes horses and stool – 2 chairs and looking glass. **Attic No. 2** Dressing table – feather bed and bolster – 3 blankets – spinning wheel – tray – 3 garden stools – smoke-jack – 4 clothes baskets – Deal box and sundries – flop sieve – quantity of books, prints and fossils. Plate, plated goods etc, 134 ounces silver plate – pair plated candlesticks – coffee pot and bread rack – quantity of old china etc. **Store Room** Large iron chest – work box – quantity of books – Deal packing case – 2 boxes – quantity of fossils – sundry books and old china – small mahogany table – hair trunk – old newspapers – easy chair – mahogany wardrobe – night table – pier glass – sundry books – mahogany dining table – Turkey carpet – writing desk – linen chest – Rushlight guard – trunk – bedstead and sacking – Watchman's rattle – mahogany bureau and bookcase – barometer and thermometer – 4 post bedstead – white dimity furniture – mattress – swing glass – 4 bedside carpets – mahogany chest of drawers – oak cupboard – small mahogany bookcase – mahogany box and stand – Deal cupboard – nest of 4 small oak drawers – old telescope – mahogany chest of drawers – 2 chairs – 2 stools and covers – 2 glass cases – Map of Europe – quantity of bed linen and wearing apparel.

The goods chattels and effects enumerated in the above catalogue or Inventory are appraised and valued at the sum of Two hundred and ninety six pounds sixteen shillings. In writing my hand this 6th day of May 1818 Joseph Rensford Appraiser and Auctioneer.

And what became of 1 London Bridge and its contents? We know that the lease was not due to expire until Christmas Day 1826 – a quarter of a century after Richard died. The leasehold interest in the premises passed to Francis under Richard's will – and Francis himself expired on 28 December 1826 – just three days after the lease was due to have reverted to the City of London. Francis would have known that when the lease came to an end, the house was set to be demolished in connection with the construction of the new London Bridge. The 700-year-old bridge was unable to cope with the demands made on it, and was costing a fortune to repair and maintain. Greenwood's *Map of London* drawn in 1827 shows the two bridges side-by-side – that is, before the demolition of the old structure took place. Numbers 2 and 3 London Bridge have already disappeared, along with the waterworks, leaving Number 1 London Bridge in splendid isolation,

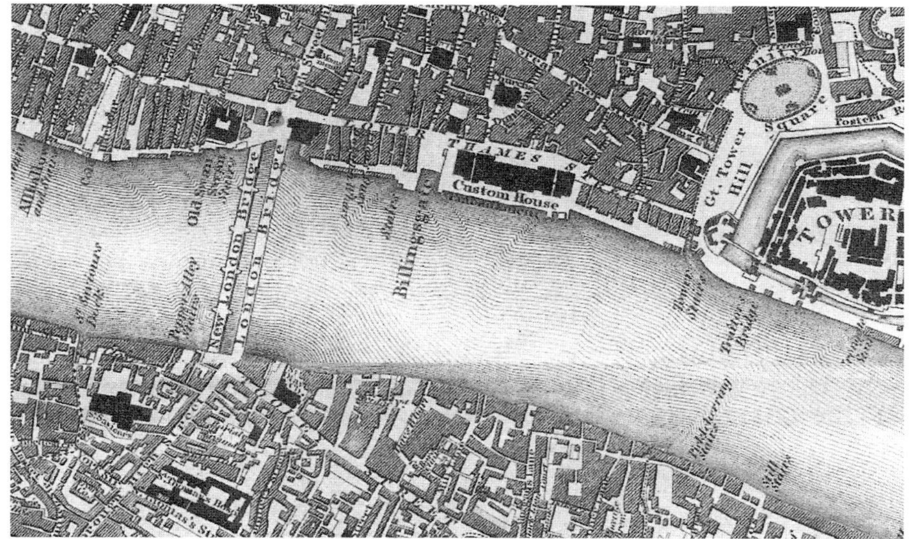

Extract from Greenwood's *Map of London*. © Mark Annand, Bath Spa University, http://users.bathspa.ac.uk/greenwood/

smack in the middle of the route onto the new bridge. No doubt it too was pulled down within a year or so of the map being prepared. Meanwhile, at the other end of London Bridge, on the Southwark side of the river, similar road works were being set in motion and within a short period of time Red Lion Street, too, had been pulled down. And so the Hall 'empire', started in the 1720s, and expanded in the 1760s, disappeared entirely from the London scene within a century of its creation, a victim of the very bridge which had caused it to be started in the first place.

Bibliography & Acknowledgements

For background historical information I am indebted to the Oxford History of England series – and in particular to *The Whig Supremacy, 1714–1760* by Basil Williams and *The Reign of George III, 1760–1815* by J Steven Watson, both published by the Clarendon Press. For social history I found the evergreen *Illustrated English Social History* by G.M. Trevelyan first published by Longmans Green in 1942 a great help, along with *England in the Age of Hogarth* by Derek Jarrett (first published by Hart-Davis, MacGibbon Ltd in 1974). For specific information about London I recommend *London: The Wicked City* by Fergus Linnane (Robson Books, 2003), the fascinating *1700: Scenes from London Life* by Maureen Waller (Holder & Stoughton, 2000) and the excellent *Dr Johnson's London* by Liza Picard (Weidenfeld & Nicolson, 2000). Other helpful background information is found in Duncan Sprott's *1784* – a collection of newspaper extracts from that year (George Allen & Unwin, 1984). Patricia Pearce's book *Old London Bridge* (Headline Book Publishing, 2001) gives a fascinating story of the old bridge from its construction in 1209 up until it was demolished in 1831. More general information is contained in the invaluable *Chambers Biographical Dictionary* (W. & R. Chambers Ltd) and (my most prized item) the full *Oxford English Dictionary*, which not only gives the meaning of words throughout history, but also their usage, first appearance, etc. It is a work without parallel.

On the family front I am of course indebted to Richard Hall and his son Benjamin for their extraordinary fondness for writing down matters which must have appeared as absolute trivia at the time – and for their descendants for having the wisdom to keep them safe until they acquired historical interest. In the case of the diaries of William Snooke I am particularly indebted to the family of Sue Garrett-Cox for allowing me to quote extracts and for the use of the portraits of William and his wife. And then there are the many other members of the family, some close some distant, who have offered help, advice and background information – my niece Michelle, cousin Allison

Blundell and the family of Charles Hall. I am also grateful to my aunt Joyce Balestra in Canada for her generosity towards a stranger (Rosemary Homfray) who turned out to be a descendant of William Snooke, and who was able to put me in touch with all the Snooke memorabilia.

Then there are the great number of 'invisible' helpers who have posted information on the Internet which has proved so rewarding and interesting. In no particular order:www.oldbaileyonline.org for its history of policing and punishment; www.footguards.tripod.com for information about sickness and medicine and for details about the Bills of Mortality; www.jennermuseum.com for information about Jenner and the history of the treatment of smallpox; www.georgianindex.net for general information about Georgian England; www.badsey.net for Peter Braby's helpful comments on Benjamin Seward;www.reformedreader.org for background details about Rippon; and www.baptistpage.org for information about Dr Gill; www.tate.org.uk for Hogarth prints; www.historyhouse.com for the story of the South Sea Bubble; www.sappho.com for background and poems of Anna Seward; www.londonancestor.com (Kent's Directory); www.cichw.net (history of London Bridge); www.umich.edu (eighteenth-century foods); www.british-history.ac.uk (information about Southwark); www.oldlondonmaps.com (for the excellent maps by Horwood); www.exchangesupplies.org (for the history of drug injection); http//users.bathspa.ac.uk (maps by Greenwood); http//collage.cityoflondon.gov.uk (picture of Red Lion Street).

I am particularly pleased to record my thanks to my favourite Baptist minister, Gary Brady – not only for sharing his passion for information about the life and times of Revd Beddome but also for putting me right about some of my howlers about the Baptist movement (I now know the difference between an Arminian and an Armenian) and for explaining Baptist beliefs and practices. He volunteered to check through the 'Baptist' elements of the text and for that I am most grateful.

A special thanks too is due to the many friends and neighbours who offered encouragement as well as snippets of information – Maggie Hodge for technical aspects about writing a book; Stephen Lombard for background information about Guinness in the early years; Eibhlin Roche, archivist for Guinness; Mike and Jean Barr for their input as pharmacists and for their comments on dispensing medicine; Allan Frey for explaining the origins of English porcelain ware and the importance of Josiah Wedgwood; Wil Gerrits for translating eighteenth-century Dutch text for me; David Pledger for putting me in touch with the site where I could find Greenwood's *Map of London* showing the old and new London Bridges side-by-side. Everyone helped in their own way to make this a shared experience.

A huge, enormous 'thank you' to Valerie Frey – not just for reading through the text and offering advice and help (you cannot pull the wool over the eyes of a former history teacher) but also for proofing the manuscript and giving encouragement. But not surprisingly the biggest thanks goes to Philippa, my ever-patient wife. Time and again I hear the cry 'Where are you?' and time and time again she gets the answer 'In the eighteenth century!' She has had to put up with my excuses to get out of the washing up ('Must just go and write a few more pages') as well as offering 100-per-cent support and encouragement, reading my drafts, correcting, making suggestions and so on. I have enjoyed immensely finding out about Richard Hall and the age in which he lived. For all those who helped me, I give a heartfelt thanks.

I dedicate the book to my lovely daughters, Emma and Jo – I have shown you where you have come from, now I leave it to you to show me the way forward.